Heaven in Transition

Heaven in Transition

Non-Muslim Religious Innovation and Ethnic Identity in Malaysia

Susan E. Ackerman

Raymond L. M. Lee

University of Hawaii Press
Honolulu

© 1988 UNIVERSITY OF HAWAII PRESS
ALL RIGHTS RESERVED
MANUFACTURED IN THE UNITED STATES OF AMERICA
93 92 91 90 89 88   5 4 3 2 1

Library of Congress Cataloging-in-Publication Data
Ackerman, Susan Ellen, 1949–
  Heaven in transition: non-Muslim religious innovation and ethnic identity in Malaysia / Susan E. Ackerman, Raymond L. M. Lee.
    p.   cm.
  Bibliography: p.
  Includes index.
  ISBN 0-8248-1121-6
  1. Malaysia—Religion. 2. Religion and sociology—Malaysia. 3. Ethnicity—Malaysia. 4. Malaysia—Population. I. Lee, Raymond (Raymond L. M.) II. Title.
BL2080.A25   1987   87-27100
306'.6'09595—dc19   CIP

*For our parents
and Tara*

Contents

ix
Preface

1
Introduction

10
CHAPTER ONE
At the Religious Crossroads:
Migrants, Merchants, and Missionaries
on the Golden Peninsula

34
CHAPTER TWO
The Cauldron of Change:
Politics and Religious Organization
in Contemporary Malaysia

61
CHAPTER THREE
The New Pentecost:
Crisis and Renewal in
the Charismatic Movement

90
CHAPTER FOUR
Ashes and Avatar:
Miracles and Identity in
the Satya Sai Baba Movement

120
CHAPTER FIVE
The Path of Mystical Dissent:
The Baitiangong Alternative
in Chinese Religion

154
CHAPTER SIX
Searching for New Heavens:
Secularization and Ethnic Identity
in the New Movements

163
Conclusion

167
Notes

189
Bibliography

199
Index

Preface

This study is a result of serendipity. Originally, we intended to research trance and spirit possession, only to discover that some of our informants did not draw a sharp distinction between our definition of trance and their involvement in various religious movements. Our initial conception of trance as a privately experienced altered state of consciousness took on a different perspective when some informants introduced us to their religious movements. Having heard that we were interested in trance—which they took to mean events related to the occult—they eagerly invited us to their meetings and to listen to their experiences. Our association with these religious seekers opened up a whole new vista of thinking about trance and possession behavior. Trance did not only function as a source of power for healing, but also as a means of identity expression. Our experiences led us to explore other new religious groups that did not necessarily focus on trance as a central activity, but emphasized the inculcation of syncretic ideologies as alternative vehicles of ethnic identity. This exploration led to six years of research with three religious movements, each representing an innovative aspect of an established religious tradition in Malaysia. Our contacts with these movements heightened our awareness of other groups and organizations that comprise the Malaysian religious mosaic. Some of these groups were short-lived while others had been around a long time. But they shared with the three movements a quest for spiritual renewal, the expression of which was irrevocably determined by events in the larger sociopolitical environment.

The non-Muslim seeker in Malaysia today can choose from a wide range of religious and quasireligious alternatives, each with its own variable set of ideologies, so that the heaven that the faithful seek is never permanent but always in transition.

During our sojourn in the Malaysian religious arena, we received guidance and hospitality from many colleagues, friends, and other individuals. We would like to acknowledge our gratitude to them: Father Paul Tan and Brother Damien Oliver of the Catholic Research Center, Kuala Lumpur; Rev. Dennis Dutton, Mr. C. R. Daniel, and Ms. Janet Lee of the Methodist Church of Malaysia; Bishop Tan Sri J. G. Savarimuthu of the Anglican Church of Malaysia; the late Father P. DeCroocq of Jesus Caritas Church, Kuala Lumpur; Rev. Johnny Yeoh of the Bible Institute of Malaysia; Dr. S. M. Ponniah and Mr. S. Vythalingam of the Malaysian Hindu Sangam; Mr. T. C. Teh of the Buddhist Missionary Society, Kuala Lumpur; Encik Tahir of the Pusat Penyelidikan Islam, Kuala Lumpur; A. M. M. Mackeen, Stephen Leong, Amarjit Kaur, R. Rajoo, and R. Dorall of the University of Malaya; and Paul Markandan, Albert Alvisse, J. Hariram, P. P. Narayanan, Joy Seevaratnam, C. M. Chew, M. Sathiavany, Pat Cox, Soanne Ong, and M. H. Loke. We are also grateful to the University of Malaya, which provided a small grant for our survey. Last, but not least, we owe a great debt of gratitude to Damaris Kirchhofer of the University of Hawaii Press for her advice and guidance.

Some of the material in chapters 3, 4, and 5 appeared earlier in a different form in the following journals: *Sociological Review* (1980), *Journal of Anthropological Research* (1981), *Contributions to Indian Sociology* (1982), *NUMEN* (1982), *Contributions to Southeast Asian Ethnography* (1983), and *Southeast Asian Journal of Social Science* (1984). We would like to thank the editors for their permission to let us reuse the published data. This book is the product of a joint effort: the order of authorship was determined at random and does not suggest differences in contributions.

Heaven in Transition

Introduction

The current increase in the number of new religions in the West and in other parts of the world has raised many questions concerning the role of religion in contemporary society. For many social scientists studying new religious movements, this phenomenon is now expressed as a problem related to the secularization process. Broadly speaking, this process entails the diminishing influence of religious institutions and symbols on various aspects of social life. It also implies the replacement of religious motivations by increasingly rational worldviews dominated by bureaucratic and technological considerations. Yet how can the decline of traditional religions account meaningfully for the rise of new religious forms? According to the secularization thesis, the loosening of religious controls tends to free individuals from ascriptive religious commitments and at the same time relegate religion to a sphere of private choice (Berger 1969:133). Traditional religious institutions no longer have a monopoly over the sacralization of personal identities. Without traditional constraints, religious institutions are compelled to compete with each other to ensure the continuation of their respective beliefs and practices. The burgeoning of new religious cults and movements, especially in the West, reflects an expanding religious market in alternatives catering to uncoerced clienteles that is concomitant with the secularization process.

The new religions in the West have been described somewhat facetiously by Bryan Wilson (1976:96) as the "religions of your choice," where the religion bears no serious consequences for other social insti-

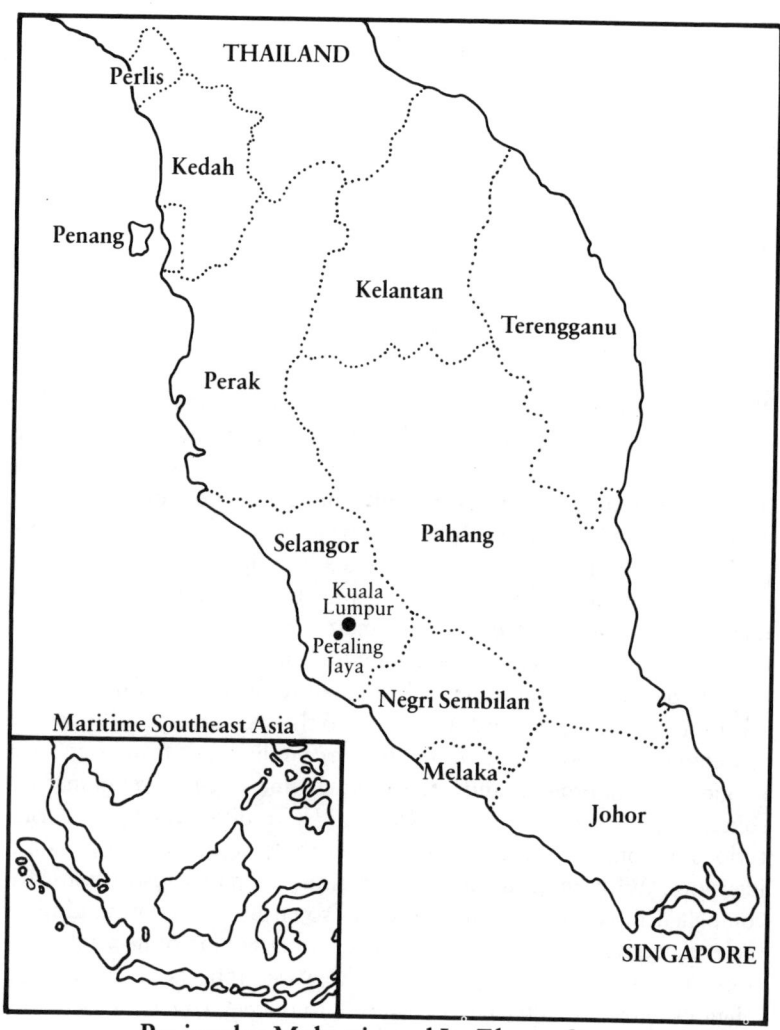

Peninsular Malaysia and Its Eleven States

Introduction

tutions and power structures. Instead, these new religions promote an individualistic mysticism that contributes to the integration of personal identities in a society characterized by highly impersonal patterns of interaction. On the other hand, Wilson (1976:97) argues that new religious movements in developing nations offer more than personal salvation, because they organize "men into stable communities and elicit from them high levels of personal commitment." The impact of these movements on the rest of society is more significant than that of the new cults in the West. This difference can be attributed to the less advanced stages of secularization in developing nations where the sense of community and personal involvement are still strong. These movements not only bring together diverse individuals who share certain motivations, but also provide a medium from which new definitions of self and society are forged and activated. Unlike the individualistically oriented cults in the West, the new identities promoted by religious movements in developing nations transcend the individual to effect the total transformation of a community.

Wilson's broad distinction between the new religious movements in the West and those in the Third World contains an evolutionary assumption that glosses over the complexity of the secularization process in many developing nations. First, secularization is not a uniform process in many developing societies. Some segments of a developing society may be more urbanized, and therefore more secularized, than other segments. Religious movements in the more urbanized segments may resemble to some extent those in the West. Other movements may be more group-oriented in purpose. These differences suggest that secularization does not necessarily progress in a unilinear fashion. Rather, uneven secularization has important consequences for organizational differences in religious movements, as we will attempt to illustrate in chapters 2 and 6.

Second, the secularization thesis implies a paradox: on one hand, individuals are able to exercise greater choice in religious preferences without having to submit to an ecclesiastical authority; on the other hand, individual liberty is circumscribed by the increased authority of the secular state. The state may impose its will, explicitly or implicitly, on the direction of religious developments. In other words, individual choice in religious matters may be an illusion. In some developing nations, the government may define the limits of religious pursuits so that the individualistic appeal of some movements is confined to a particular religious field. Religious choices are determined by the political context in which secularization is occurring, as we will show in the following chapters.

The three religious movements discussed in this book emerged in Kuala Lumpur, the capital city of Malaysia.[1] Secularization in Malaysia has occurred at a rapid rate, especially in the more urban parts of the country. Within this context we can argue that the three movements are somewhat comparable to their Western counterparts in terms of their voluntaristic and individualistic characteristics. But on a broader sociopolitical level, these movements do not correspond to those in the West. The reasons for this difference become clear when we examine the complex relationship between ethnicity and religion in Malaysia.

Ethnicity and religion are the central components of social identities in contemporary Malaysia. The meaningfulness of social relationships is determined to a large extent by *bangsa* or *kaum* (race, ethnicity), of which Malay, Chinese, and Indian are the main official categories.[2] Ethnicity in Malaysia is not only the property of individuals (regarding how they define themselves vis-à-vis others), but also a tool of the state for resource allocation and political control. The state comprises an alliance of several political parties, each of which is ethnically based with appeals to specific ethnic constituencies. The Malays dominate this alliance, controlling the main channels of political negotiation. Like ethnicity, religion in Malaysia is deeply intertwined with the individual's sense of self and power, thereby complicating the picture with the increase in the potential for political mobilization. The conjunction of ethnicity and religion in Malaysia dichotomizes the religious arena into a Muslim and non-Muslim field. The former is principally a Malay domain, since all Malays are Muslims by birth. Malays who voluntarily venture into the non-Muslim field are liable to lose their social and political privileges (in the areas of employment, education, and business), implying that Malay-Muslim identity is materially reinforced.[3] On the other hand, Chinese, Indians, and other non-Malays who are Muslims do not necessarily enjoy the same ethnic status as Malays, although they can occasionally use their religious position to advance their interests (see Nagata 1978; Lee 1986b). In the non-Muslim field, the connection between ethnic identity and religious affiliation is less rigid and, more importantly, it is not undergirded by any material privileges. Typically, a Chinese is a Buddhist-

Taoist and an Indian a Hindu; but Christianity, Baha'i, and various new non-Muslim movements attract members from all non-Malay ethnic groups. Despite the relative looseness of the association between ethnicity and religion in the non-Muslim field, there is an undefined sense of solidarity among non-Malays that they are *not Muslims*.

In the present period, ethnic relations between Malays and non-Malays have assumed greater religious significance as the non-Malays confront the Malays on the question of Christian, Hindu, and Buddhist rights. In order to understand the religious conflict of the 1980s, we will examine about two millennia of history so as to trace the process in which religions imported into the Malay Peninsula were gradually particularized as specific ethnic identifiers. The history of Malaysian religions, as summarized in chapter 1, is not only a history of intercultural contacts but also an account of religious change in association with shifting political forms on the peninsula. Religious change in the postwar period is related unequivocally to increased urbanization on the peninsula. Unlike the scattered urban centers of the early twentieth century characterized by transient communities, the fast-growing cities of modern Malaysia are populated by diverse ethnic groups competing for limited resources. In chapter 2, we trace the manipulation of religious ideologies and symbols in ethnic conflicts, particularly in postindependence Malaysia, as heightened consciousness of Malay, Chinese, and Indian identities are organized in urban confrontations.

Our study will focus mainly on religious activities in Kuala Lumpur. Beginning as a nineteenth-century Chinese mining camp, Kuala Lumpur was later transformed into a colonial center of administration, commerce, and transport. Since the end of World War II, the city has become a modern industrial center ringed by six-lane highways, factories, and sprawling suburbs. It is within the greater metropolitan area of Kuala Lumpur that the ferment of religious developments is most visible and the social impact most widely ramifying. Kuala Lumpur exemplifies the basic features of urbanization in Malaysia. Formed during British colonial rule, the pronounced Chinese character of Kuala Lumpur and other west coast cities persisted even after independence in 1957. Only since the late 1960s has the Chinese disposition of Kuala Lumpur been gradually diluted by an influx of rural Malay migrants. The movement of Malays into the city has accentuated ethnic awareness among both the urban Chinese majority and the Indian minority.

Beginning in the mid-1970s, several forms of Islamic fundamentalism began to spread among Malay youth, particularly in the urban areas. This may partly be attributed to the rising consciousness of Islam around the world. Alternatively, this phenomenon may be interpreted as a Malay strategy of reinforcing ethnic identity in the face of a large, urban non-Malay population. In this century, as in previous centuries, Islam has provided a vehicle for political expression among the Malays. Relatively speaking, the Malays—despite their factions and conflicts—are more united politically under the banner of Islam than the non-Malays. The emergence of Islamic fundamentalism in the 1970s has revitalized Malay ethnicity.[4]

In contrast to Malay-Muslim unity, the non-Malay population is religiously and politically fragmented. The Chinese and Indians of Malaysia adhere to Christianity, Hinduism, Islam, Buddhism, Taoism, and other religions. None of these religions, with the exception of Islam, are politically organized. Because only a small minority of Chinese and Indians are Muslims, most follow non-Muslim religions that are not explicitly politicized. Yet some of these religious traditions have become cradles of new urban-based movements, which to varying degrees reflect dissatisfaction with established religions on one hand and political conditions on the other. Within the Christian tradition, neo-Pentecostalism—or the Charismatic Renewal—has emerged as a popular movement among many Chinese, Indians, and Eurasians. Another new religious group that has gained a large following among urban dwellers is the Satya Sai Baba movement, whose leader is a widely acclaimed Hindu saint resident in South India. He has become the focus of worship among many Hindu Indians and non-Hindu Chinese. The Charismatic Renewal and the Satya Sai Baba movement are both instances of cultural diffusion from outside the social system that have been particularized in relation to the ethnic and political situation in urban Malaysia. Meanwhile, Baitiangong, an indigenous syncretic Chinese movement in the Kuala Lumpur area, has captured the attention of many Chinese of all religious persuasions, as well as a small number of Indians. Although Baitiangong is an indigenous Malaysian movement, it derives its focal symbols and themes from the imported Chinese folk and Christian traditions. Nevertheless, each of

Introduction

these three movements is concerned to varying degrees with the problem of ethnic identity.

Despite their independent development, Charismatic Renewal, Satya Sai Baba, and Baitiangong all became popular among non-Muslim urbanites during the mid-1970s. It was at this time that the implications of the changing ethnic composition of Kuala Lumpur were becoming more definite and concrete. Urbanization has sharpened the division between Malay and non-Malay, while avenues for effective non-Malay political participation have narrowed. The multiethnic membership in these new religious movements suggests new forms of non-Malay alliance that are explicitly apolitical. In chapters 3, 4, and 5, the history and activities of each movement are described and discussed. The significance of the three non-Muslim religious movements as interfaces between individual actions and social change is examined in chapter 6. At the individual level, each of these movements offers direct access to supernatural power for thaumaturgical purposes and ecstatic experiences. Members of these movements do not express political issues directly, since their predominant concern is in propagating new religious ideologies and forms of worship. Yet at the group level, these religious experiences seem to provide an idiom for consolidating ethnic identity. Historically, the particularization of all universal religions that have reached Malaysian shores involves a complex, syncretic process of cultural transformation and redefinition of ethnic identity. We argue from this premise that the tradition of religious syncretism in Malaysia provides a crucible for constructing new bases of ethnic awareness in response to various social and political changes.

The data reported in this study were collected between August 1977 and April 1984. During these six and a half years of research, we interviewed leaders and members of the Charismatic Renewal, Satya Sai Baba, and Baitiangong movements. We also observed and participated in a wide range of their activities. Intensive fieldwork was conducted between 1977 and 1979, thereafter we kept abreast of developments in the movements through newspaper reports and intermittent follow-up interviews. Later in our fieldwork, we interviewed several representatives of various traditional religions in Malaysia in order to place the three movements in their proper perspectives. Our exposure to the three movements was somewhat uneven. We had access to more information on two movements than on the third. In this regard, we had wider experiences with the Charismatic Renewal and Baitiangong movements than with the Satya Sai Baba movement. The variations in the level of contact can be attributed to our entry point in the development of the movements. When we began our investigations in 1977, Charismatic Renewal and Baitiangong had just begun to gain momentum—both movements were relatively new compared to Satya Sai Baba which had already been established for more than five years. We were in a better position to observe firsthand the developmental processes in the former two movements than in the latter. Members in Charismatic Renewal and Baitiangong were eager to share their experiences with anyone who showed the least interest in them. For this reason, we were able to learn much about the two movements from members who had perceived us as sympathizers or potential followers. We faced greater difficulties, however, in penetrating the more established networks in the Satya Sai Baba movement. We relied largely on the accounts provided by a central figure in the movement who, during our period of acquaintance with him, abruptly became a firm opponent of Satya Sai Baba.

After four years of studying these movements, we felt somewhat confident in approaching our contacts for help in conducting a survey. In early 1982, we prepared a short, open-ended questionnaire in English and Chinese to tap information on members' backgrounds and their religious experiences. We distributed our questionnaires to Baitiangong members through their leader and to Satya Sai Baba devotees through an Indian assistant with wide connections in the movement. We had less success with the members of Charismatic Renewal, because most of the groups we had observed between 1977 and 1982 had disintegrated by the time the questionnaire was ready. Among our remaining Charismatic contacts, we only managed to distribute questionnaires to ten individuals. This sample is too small to warrant meaningful statistical analysis and therefore no tabulated data appear in chapter 3. Even with the cooperation of Baitiangong members and Satya Sai Baba devotees, we were unable to plan a systematic random survey for two reasons. First, the turnover rate in both movements was high, making it difficult to determine their population sizes at any point in time. Second, with shifting populations it is impractical to compile a membership list for random sampling. The feasibility of producing such a list was further reduced by the incomplete records of both movements. These methodological problems suggest that refinements are required in survey techniques applied to religious movements.

During our research, some respondents attempted to convert us but we subtly resisted their efforts. Nevertheless, they were willing to relate to us their religious experiences and life histories. One reason for this high level of cooperation was their perception of us as researchers of psychic phenomena. This obsession with the supernatural comprised the vital link in our relationship with them. This field experience suggests that the informants' understanding (or misunderstanding) of the research role is shaped more often by their needs than by the researchers' self-presentations.

The eagerness of our informants for "scientific" validation of their experiences motivated them to communicate to us the personal meanings of their involvement in the three religious movements. Their personal accounts form the basis of our descriptions of the Charismatic Renewal, Satya Sai Baba, and Baitiangong movements. In addition to these descriptions, which reflect our informants' understandings and interpretations of events, we also propose middle-range generalizations for relating these movements to the secularization process in Malaysia. It is through these generalizations that we attempt to reach an interface between personal religious experiences and broader changes in Malaysian society.

CHAPTER ONE

At the Religious Crossroads: Migrants, Merchants, and Missionaries on the Golden Peninsula

THE legendary Golden Khersonese, more mundanely known as the Malay Peninsula, has drawn a multiplicity of ethnic groups to its shores during the course of the past two millennia. The population movements along the coasts and through the forests of the Malay Peninsula each left their distinct cultural residues. A series of encounters among the ethnic groups that reached the peninsula—including nomadic hunting and gathering peoples of the forested interior, as well as seafaring Indonesians, Indians, Arabs, Chinese, and Europeans in search of trade and wealth in the coastal entrepôts—produced a religious tradition remarkable in its complex diversity.

The strands comprising the Malay Peninsula's religious tradition—animism, Buddhism, Hinduism, Islam, Christianity, and various forms of Chinese folk religion that are not easily classified—can be viewed in relation to changes in the scale of political establishments through time. Animism was the religion of the decentralized, dispersed tribal societies that preceded and continued to coexist at the peripheries of the Indianized trading states that flourished from the first until the mid-fourteenth century A.D. Imported religions, such as Buddhism and Hinduism, provided ideologies and symbols that enhanced centralization of political authority during the early period of state formation on the peninsula (Wheatley 1975). By the fifteenth century another imported religion, Islam, was ascendant in the royal courts of northern Sumatra and the Malay Peninsula, the rulers of which were active participants in the lucrative Muslim-dominated maritime trade. European colonial domination beginning in the sixteenth century gradually created the economic and infrastructural basis for a larger scale, more complex political entity, tightly integrated into world markets. Christianity, although introduced to the peninsula within the framework of the colonial state, did not serve as an ideology that legitimated colonial rule. The relationship of Christianity to the state differed fundamentally from that of the earlier imported religions. The British policy of indirect rule over the Malay states of the peninsula conferred official recognition on both Islam and the position of the Malay rulers as special provisions within the legal system underpinning the secular colonial state.[1]

Ethnic diversity accompanied the increasing scale and complexity of the peninsula's political establishments. With the Islamization of the peninsula's coastal trading states, religion became a fundamental component of ethnic identity. The Malay community's adoption of Islam as both state ideology and a marker of ethnic identity defined the social boundary between the Malays and non-Malays. As a consequence of the strong association among Islam, the indigenous polity, and Malay identity, Christianity's influence on the peninsula was limited to the non-Malay ethnic groups which lacked ties of allegiance to the traditional Malay states. The colonial authorities officially discouraged Christian missionaries from proselytizing the Islamized indigenous community which, in any event, was highly resistant to the propaganda of other religions. Christian missionary efforts were therefore directed mainly toward the massive population of Chinese and Indian immigrants who provided most of the labor required by the tin and rubber industries, the foundation of the colonial economy. To a lesser degree, Christian missionaries also sought converts among the aboriginal tribal peoples inhabiting the forest areas. Unlike Buddhism, Hinduism, and Islam, Christianity has, except during the period of Portuguese rule in Melaka, been peripheral to the state.

Animism in an Evolving Tradition

Animism, the oldest strand of the Malay Peninsula's religious tradition, was predominant during the period preceding the formation of the earliest states. The Paleolithic and Neolithic animists who migrated from the mainland of Asia to the Malay Peninsula included the ancestors of the Negritos and Veddas, those of the Australoids and the Papuan-Melanesians, and also those of the Indonesians (Coedès 1968). The descendants of these migrants, regarded as the aboriginal peoples of the peninsula (or the *orang asli*), remain steeped in animistic beliefs and practices,[2] having been influenced only to a limited degree by the imported religions. The ancestors of the present-day *orang asli* and Malays organized themselves into small groupings of hunters and gatherers in the jungles of the interior and into clusters of wet-padi-cultivating villages along the coasts before the era of intensive Indian cultural influence that began in the first centuries A.D. The culture of the Neolithic coastal communities of farmers, fishermen, and traders—given the name Dong-So'n after the archeological type site first identified in northern Vietnam—was based on a relatively advanced technology. The Dong-So'n peoples had knowledge of irrigation techniques, domestication of the ox and buffalo, production of bronze artifacts, and navigation. The technically accomplished Dong-So'n peoples comprised a small, exceptional group of coastal maritime societies in a densely forested land whose largely nomadic population was predominantly Paleolithic in culture (Wheatley 1964:25–28).

In the absence of written records, the animistic religions of the Dong-So'n peoples and forest nomads remain a matter of speculation. The general features, however, can be cautiously inferred from comparisons of Southeast Asian hill tribes outside the spheres of Hindu or Islamic influence (Winstedt 1961; Wales 1957). The animistic cosmos is permeated with an undifferentiated vital essence *(semangat)* out of which emerges hierarchy of states of being, ranging from disembodied spirits to human souls (Endicott 1970). For the animist, the natural environment is populated with a plethora of malevolent and beneficent spirits accessible through ritual manipulation. Shamanism and the cult of the ancestors were probably central to animistic practice on the peninsula during the pre-Indianized period (Wales 1957). Fundamental animistic beliefs and rituals were widely shared among groups throughout Southeast Asia and pre-Aryan India (Coedès 1968). The pre-Aryan substratum of cultural similarity may have facilitated the spread of India's great religious traditions into the Malay Peninsula's Neolithic coastal societies.

The religious traditions transmitted through trade and cultural contacts with India—Buddhism, Hinduism, and later Islam—transformed rather than superseded animism. The coastal-dwelling Dong-So'n peoples accepted Indian doctrines and ceremonies, interpreting the new religious elements within the framework of animism. The shifting cultivators and hunting and gathering tribes inhabiting the interior rarely came within the sway of the Indianized coastal states. Through trade relations with the peoples of the coast, they were exposed to popular traditions associated with Indian religions. Some nomadic and semi-nomadic tribal groups, such as the Batek Negritos, have incorporated elements of Hinduism and Islam into the myths and rituals comprising their animistic religion (Endicott 1979). On the whole, the animism of the forest peoples, unlike that of the coastal dwellers, reflects fleeting and superficial contacts with the imported religions.

Along with the successive adoption of Buddhism, Hinduism, and Islam, the animistic world view persisted among the Indianized peoples of the coastal settlements. Animism appropriated elements from the new religions and coexisted alongside them as folk religion (Coedès 1968). With the rise of Islam in fifteenth-century Melaka—the foremost peninsular state in precolonial times—animism adopted Islamic invocations, superimposing them on the earlier Buddhist and Hindu accretions (Winstedt 1951).

The animistic folk religion of the Malays—focused on the magical practitioner *(bomoh* or *pawang)*—continues to be an integral part of the peninsula's religious tradition. The fusion of animism with Hindu and Islamic elements is clearly seen in the complex of Malay magic involving the worship of saints and their graves *(keramat);* preparation of charms, divination, exorcism, propitiation of spirits; and shamanic seances (Winstedt 1951). Malay animistic folk religion is concerned with the pragmatics of everyday life: economic activities such as agriculture, hunting, collecting forest products, fishing, mining, trading; selecting and preparing propitious building sites; rites of passage; curing; competitive entertainments; personal power or attractiveness; and interpersonal relations, particularly love and revenge (Endicott 1970). While orthodox Muslims condemn animistic magic, many Malays regard these folk practices as complementing Islam, which deals more with ethics and salvation than with the specifics of man's worldly welfare.

Malay folk religion has also influenced the beliefs and practices of the Chinese, Indians, and Eurasians. Practical religion and everyday problem-solving among Malaysians of all ethnic groups is permeated by the animistic world view. Visits to Malay *keramat* and *bomoh* have become part of the widespread practical religion that crosscuts formal religious affiliations and ethnic and class boundaries. The significance of animistic practical religion will become more obvious in chapters 3, 4, and 5, where the motivations, understandings, and personal experiences of the devotees involved in new religious movements are examined.

Indianization and State Formation

The adoption of Indian religions and conceptions of state and kingship among the coastal Malays of the peninsula and archipelago followed the growth of supravillage-level political organization. Buddhism and Hinduism spread among the Malay elites as their economic and political activities became farther-reaching in scope. Religious ideas and practices originating in India were introduced to the Malay settlements located along the overland and maritime trade routes that linked Southeast Asia with India and China. The causal relationship between Indianization and state formation on the peninsula and elsewhere in Southeast Asia remains an issue of debate and speculation. Accounts of the emergence of states on the peninsula and in the archipelago generally focus on the interaction of trade with the diffusion of Indian ritual, religion, and political models but give differential emphasis to Indian versus local initiative in these contacts. There is, nevertheless, broad consensus concerning the role of Buddhism in pioneering the maritime trade route between India, Southeast Asia, and China (Coedès 1968; Paranavitana 1966; Wheatley 1975; Hall 1981).

The influence of Buddhism in relaxing religious taboos on overseas travel and commerce contributed much to quickening the tempo of trade between India and Southeast Asia during the first centuries of the Christian era.[3] The popularity of Buddhism, particularly the cult of Dipankara Buddha, among the Indian and Sri Lankan seagoing merchants started the diffusion of Indian religious forms throughout the Southeast Asian maritime networks (Coedès 1968). Dipankara Buddha was the patron of a corporation of bankers in Anuradhapura that financed trading voyages to Southeast Asia (Paranavitana 1966: 176). As a missionary religion initially introduced by merchants and later by religious specialists, Buddhism spread rapidly throughout the ports of the peninsula and archipelago. By the late seventh century, Chinese Buddhist pilgrims traveling to India on merchant vessels recognized the Malay maritime empire of Srivijaya as a center of Buddhism and recommended it as an essential stop for a year or two of study before proceeding on to central India (Coedès 1968:81).[4] Srivijaya, based in Palembang on the southeastern coast of Sumatra, expanded to the Malay Peninsula in the last quarter of the eighth century, at which time the Mahayana school of Buddhism was ascendant at the royal court.[5] The Srivijayan rulers firmly established Mahayana Buddhism in Kedah and the isthmian states of the peninsula. This part of the peninsula, according to H. G. Q. Wales, absorbed the full impact of the new religious influences and most clearly reflected "the fully fledged Mahayanist culture of the Sumatran metropolis" (Wales 1976:82).

The expansion of Indian culture into Southeast Asia has been characterized as a continuation overseas of the Brahmanization that began in northwest India (Coedès 1968:15–16). Southeast Asia, in G. Coedès' view, was a passive recipient of Indian influence transmitted through Indian merchants and migrants. J. C. Van Leur, on the other hand, argues that the coming of Indian civilization "emanated from Indonesian ruling groups, or was at least an affair of both Indonesian dynasties and the Indian hierocracy" (1955:103–104) in which the indigenous elite actively initiated cultural and commercial relations with India. O. W. Wolters (1970) further extends the thesis of local initative in his attribution of the Indianized Srivijaya empire's origin to Malay maritime achievements, which occurred independently of Indian influence.[6] The economic basis of state formation in the archipelago and on the peninsula was the result of internal developmental processes rather than contacts with India per se. Indigenous irrigation agriculture and maritime commerce, both pioneered by the Malays, generated complex political organization that transcended the village community.

The attainment of a supravillage level of organization enabled the Malays to respond effectively to the new opportunities accompanying the expansion of maritime trade in the Indian Ocean in the fourth and early fifth centuries. In a provocative account of the role of seaborne trade in stimulating the emergence of states from tribal societies in Southeast Asia, Kenneth R. Hall (1981:134) suggests that local chiefs sought to accumulate wealth by providing support services for international merchants at the ports that the chiefs controlled. The revenue obtained from these port operations increased the income of the coastal chiefs to an extent that would allow them to support large retinues of followers who could be called upon to protect or provision the port. The chiefs' enlarged labor resources, Hall argues, made possible the maintenance of security—policing the sea lanes to control piracy or stabilizing the hinterland—and the guarantee of regular supplies of food and desired merchandise to the traders. The Malay chiefs who controlled the ports of southeastern Sumatra and the peninsula extended their authority through mediating the international trading community's transactions with the local peoples of the coasts and the interior forests (Wheatley 1975).

Participation in international trade, as Paul Wheatley (1975:241–242) has hypothesized, created pressures for new authority structures in the Southeast Asian tribal societies. The coastal chiefs may have sought new political models to enhance their prestige and power among the foreigners as well as among their own people. The Indian institution of divine kingship centered around a sacred city identified with the cosmos would have been, as Wheatley (1975:239) has pointed out, the most appealing model available within the cultural horizon of the local chieftains. The Indian theory of divine kingship, elaborated in both Hindu and Buddhist thought, was introduced to Southeast Asian ports by Brahmin priests and Buddhist monks who traveled the eastern trade route in merchant ships. While the Buddhist traders who preceded the priests and monks aroused the local chieftains' initial interest in Indian religious practices, it was the Brahmins' and Mahayana monks' propagation of the royal cults of the god-king that eventually had the greatest impact on the Malay trading societies on the peninsula and in the archipelago. These cults instituted the worship of the local rulers as divine incarnations of such Hindu deities as Siva and Vishnu or the Mahayana bodhisattvas Avalokitesvara and Manjusri, overshadowing the earlier, less-explicitly aristocratic forms of Buddhism introduced by the merchants.

The Malay chiefs' assimilation of Sanskritized styles of kingship embodied in the royal cults transformed the coastal trading settlements into royal city-states by facilitating consolidation of the rulers' authority. The chiefs obtained recognition as god-kings through ritual consecration performed by Brahmins (Wheatley 1975). Ambitious chieftains highly prized the Brahmins' ritual services and summoned them to Malay courts on the peninsula and in the archipelago to legitimate dynastic interests (Van Leur 1955). The reports of Chinese envoys to Southeast Asia indicate that by the third century more than one thousand Brahmins were resident in one of the courts of the isthmian region of the Malay Peninsula (Wheatley 1975). Subsequent Chinese envoys to the region during the fifth through seventh centuries described the importance that the local rulers attached to the ceremonies and rituals performed by Brahmins in the isthmian royal courts. The possibility that at least some of the Brahmins serving Southeast Asian rulers were simultaneously both merchants and experts on ritual has been suggested by Wheatley (1975:245), who emphasizes that numerous records from medieval India document the involvement of Brahmins in commerce. Chinese texts also describe the Brahmins as coming from India "to seek wealth by serving the king[s]" of the peninsular courts (Wheatley 1975:243).

The practice of Brahminic ritual in the royal courts of Southeast Asia was complementary with rather than antagonistic to Buddhism, unlike the case in India. Neither Buddhism nor Hinduism penetrated deeply into indigenous Southeast Asian social life. In India, however, as Sylvain Levi (cited in Coedès 1968:121) perceptively observed, Brahminic doctrines defined the entire social order such that Buddhism and Hinduism were necessarily opposed. The character of Buddhism and Hinduism in the Malay trading kingdoms, as elsewhere in Indianized Southeast Asia, was highly syncretic.

The religious doctrines, symbolism, and ritual practices adopted during particular phases of contact with India became, in Wales' words (1976), a composite product reflecting successive influences.[7] Mahayana Buddhism, which predominated on the Malay Peninsula and in the Indonesian archipelago in the last quarter of the eighth century, tended to fuse with Hindu cults and indigenous ancestor worship. This syncretic process, which blurred the distinction between Buddhism and Hinduism, culminated in the royal cults of the god-king. These cults entailed elaboration of pre-Indian ancestor worship by drawing elements from the Mahayana cults of Avalokitesvara and other bodhisattvas and the Hindu cults of Siva and Vishnu.

By the late eighth century, the Malay rulers of Srivijaya had adopted the Mahayana Buddhist symbolism of sovereignty as attested by the construction of a sanctuary of the Buddha and the bodhisattvas Padmapani and Vajrapani at Ligor in A.D. 775 (Wolters 1970).[8] Tantric ritual, practiced in Palembang since at least the seventh century, was a significant element in the royal cult of the divine king.[9] Palembang, the seat of the Srivijaya empire, became a famous Mahayana Buddhist center that was known to both Nepal and Tibet by the eleventh century. Mahayana tantric practices associated with Srivijaya court ritual centered around the mystical identification of the ruler with Avalokitesvara, the sovereign bodhisattva and source of fertility. Through the course of its evolution, the Mahayana cult of Avalokitesvara gradually absorbed Saivite features.

The *Sejarah Melayu*, a mythical genealogy of the Islamized Malay rulers of the Melaka Sultanate, sought to establish Melaka's origins in the divine sovereignty of Srivijaya. The Muslim-Malay rulers of the fifteenth and sixteenth centuries, regarding themselves as the heirs of Srivijaya, held Buddhist-Saivite conceptions of kingship as expressed in the *Sejarah Melayu*'s description of the founder of the Melaka dynasty (Wolters 1970). The legendary ancestor of the Melaka sultans miraculously appears on Bukit Si-Guntang Mahameru in Palembang manifesting the attributes of the Mahayana divinity, Avalokitesvara, and is later given the title *Sri Tri Buana*, which, as Wolters notes, is a Saivite name (Wolters 1970:132; Brown 1970:13–15). *Sri Tri Buana*'s marriage to the daughter of the Palembang ruler, the only one of forty women who does not suffer from skin discoloration after sleeping with him, and his subsequent installation ceremony are strongly suggestive of tantric rites enacting a mystical union of Siva and Sakti (Brown 1970:16–17; Wolters 1970:132).

The syncretic Hindu-Buddhist worship of the ruler as a divinity was essentially a court-centered cult for the elite rather than an expansive missionary religion directed toward the masses (Coedès 1968:33). Elements of this tradition, however, filtered down to the common people through the oral transmission of such popular Indian epics as the *Ramayana* and the *Mahabharata* (Taib 1967). On the whole, however, indigenous social life beyond the confines of the royal courts was unaffected by Indianization because Indian social structures associated with Hinduism, particularly the caste system, were not transplanted to Southeast Asia. Although the common people had some awareness of tantric court rituals,[10] their religious life mainly focused on animism and the cult of ancestors. It was not until the thirteenth century that imported religions made a significant impact at the village level. Sinhalese Buddhism in the isthmian area of the Malay Peninsula and Islam in the Indonesian archipelago rapidly gained ascendancy over the tantric Hindu-Buddhist royal cults after the thirteenth century.

During the period of Srivijaya's decline in the last quarter of the twelfth century until its final disintegration in the fifteenth century, Islam began gradually to spread through the archipelago. The Islamization of northeast Sumatra appears to be contemporaneous with the dismemberment of Srivijaya, although, as Wheatley (1964:98-99) cautions, the relationship between these processes is problematic because the extent to which Srivijaya's power had waned before the coming of Islam is unknown. The growing strength of Islam in Sumatra by the late thirteenth century, as attested by Jambi's employment of Muslims as envoys to China, as well as Marco Polo's reports of the conversions of Perlak and Samudra to Islam, does suggest that the prestige of Srivijaya's Hindu-Buddhist cults was challenged by these developments.

Islam and the Malay Polity

Hindu and Buddhist contacts with the Indonesian archipelago and the Malay Peninsula dwindled as Muslim merchants extended their control over the Indian Ocean trade routes. Although Arab traders bound for China had been making regular stops at the ports of Srivijaya since at least the eighth century,[11] Islam did not make a noticeable impact in the region before the eleventh or twelfth century.[12] The role of the Arabs as propagators of Islam in Indonesian ports is undoubtedly significant, nevertheless the contribution of Indian traders to the spread of Islam in the area cannot be overlooked. The Islamization of Gujerat in western India resulted in the port of Cambay falling into Muslim hands in 1298, an event that was to have far-reaching consequences in the Malay world. Cambay, a renowned emporium on the Arabian Sea, had long-standing trade relations with Indonesia, which Muslim merchants who had settled there were readily able to turn to their advantage. Arab and Persian merchants, established in Cambay since the ninth century (Hall 1964:191), had engaged in trade and proselytization in the ports of northern Sumatra for several centuries preceding the Muslim domination of Gujerat. Together with the Arabs and Persians, Gujerati Muslim merchants played a major part in the development of Islamized port cities in northern Sumatra. A late thirteenth-century royal mausoleum of Cambay origin is the earliest evidence attesting to the presence of Muslim states in this region of the archipelago (Hall 1964:191).

The diffusion of Islam among the Malay trading states of north Sumatra cannot be considered in isolation from the maritime history of the Indian Ocean and the South China Sea, as A. H. Johns (1975:38) has emphasized. The sea routes pioneered by Arab merchants connecting the east coast of Africa with southeastern China developed into an extensive trading system in which by the fifteenth century the Arabic language was the major medium of communication. The Indian Ocean trade routes, which J. R. Hale (cited in Johns 1975:38) has characterized as comprising "an Arabic-speaking Mediterranean," gave rise to a cosmopolitan Muslim social milieu where profession of Islam enhanced cooperation among traders of diverse nationalities. The coastal Malays' involvement in maritime commerce drew them into the sphere of Muslim cultural influence. The predominantly Muslim foreign merchants who frequented the parts of the north Sumatran trading states encouraged local conversions to Islam. The growing strength of Islam in the port kingdoms exerted pressures on the rulers to present their authority in terms understood and respected by their Muslim subjects (Milner 1981:58). The conversion of local rulers to Islam enabled them to deal more effectively with the increasingly powerful foreign trading community whose commercial activities generated much revenue for the port kingdoms.

The *shahbandar,* a port official responsible for the collection of anchorage fees and import and export duties, may have served as a major channel through which the importance of Islam in the network of trade relations was communicated to the local rulers, according to B. Schrieke's (1957:238) hypothesis. Because the functions of the *shahbandar* required a knowledge of foreign languages, foreigners were generally appointed to this post. After the end of the thirteenth century, when Muslim merchants dominated the flow of trade between Cambay, Aden, and Sumatra, the local rulers found it convenient to employ mainly Muslim foreigners for the post of *shahbandar.* It is not unlikely that the *shahbandar,* in his position as a broker between the ruler and the Muslim merchant community, did not hesitate to bring to the ruler's attention the commercial significance of conversion to Islam. Through the *shahbandar,* the Malay rulers of the Sumatran port states had ready access to information about opulent Muslim courts beyond the archipelago, particularly those of Mughal India, and were no doubt encouraged to emulate these renowned Muslim sovereigns. Models of kingship in the Muslim world also would have been conveyed to the Malay rulers by religious scholars who accompanied Muslim traders to Southeast Asian ports, where the *shahbandar* arranged introductions to the rulers (Schrieke 1957:238; Milner 1981:54).

According to local tradition, Perlak was the first of the maritime Malay states of north Sumatra to be Islamized. Chinese sources indicate that Perlak's neighbor, Samudra, which converted to Islam somewhat later than Perlak, sent Muslim ambassadors to the Chinese court as early as 1282 (De Graaf 1970:125). The tomb of Sultan al-Malik al-Salih, reported to be the first ruler of Samudra, has been dated 1297 (De Graaf 1970:125). Islam must have set down roots in Perlak and Samudra before 1282.

Samudra, later known as Pasai, developed into a leading religious and commercial center frequented by numerous wealthy foreign merchants, including Arabs. Pasai sent embassies to India; and its royal court, as described by the Arab writer Ibn Battuta, who visited the area in 1345–1346, was Indian in cultural style and imported royal mausoleums from Gujerat (Schrieke 1957:261). Persian and Arab Muslim scholars found favor with the rulers of Pasai, whom Ibn Battuta reported as taking delight in discussing religious and mystical questions with foreign scholars (Schrieke 1957:261). Pasai, a flourishing pepper port, attracted much Javanese and Chinese shipping. The Javanese came to trade rice and spices for Pasai's pepper, which they then sold to the Chinese (Meilink-Roelofsz 1970:147).

On the peninsula, the Malay rulers of the new port kingdom, Melaka, eagerly sought a share of Pasai's international commerce and tried to form an alliance with Pasai. As the Malay maritime empire of Srivijaya relinquished its control of the Straits of Melaka in the face of the expansion of the Java-based kingdom of Majapahit, the remnants of the Srivijayan dynasty sought to restore its glory on the peninsula (Wolters 1970:174). Paramesvara, a prince of Palembang, took refuge on the Malay Peninsula as the Javanese invaded the remaining domain of Srivijaya and in 1403 founded Melaka as a trading emporium. It was Melaka's goal to attract international trade to its port. This, however, would be possible only when a regular supply of spices was guaranteed. The spice trade was controlled by the Javanese, who preferred to direct their shipping to Pasai where they enjoyed the privilege of exemption from import and export duties (Meilink-Roelofsz 1970:147). The king of Pasai responded to Paramesvara's request to participate in Pasai's trade with Java by sending ambassadors to Melaka to urge Paramesvara to convert to Islam as a condition for a political and commercial alliance (Cortesão 1944:239–240).

Muslim scholars who enjoyed the king of Pasai's patronage also ingratiated themselves at the court of Melaka where they won Paramesvara's favor. They persuaded him of the advantages of conversion to Islam and a marriage alliance with the Sultan of Pasai's daughter (Cortesão 1944:242). Paramesvara converted to Islam in 1414 and changed his name to Iskandar Shah upon marriage to the Pasai princess. Thus adoption of Islam became widespread among the population of Melaka. Through the alliance with Pasai, Islam was made the official religion of the Melaka Sultanate, which propagated it throughout the Malay Peninsula.[13] Although Islam had already been introduced to the peninsula during the fourteenth century, as attested by the discovery of a tombstone bearing an Arabic inscription dating back to 1386 in Terengganu on the northeast coast (Di Meglio 1970:120), it made little visible impact until the emergence of Melaka as a powerful Muslim trading state.

The power of Melaka's ruler to monopolize trade passing through the straits with his fleet of patrol boats, which forced all maritime traffic to call at the port for payment of tolls (Wheatley 1964:121, 127), as well as its favorable geographical location, enabled Melaka eventually to surpass Pasai as the leading Malay entrepôt in the region. Islamic scholars and missionaries were attracted to Melaka in increasing numbers as the population of foreign Muslim merchants resident in Melaka grew. Melaka's influence as a religious center was further enhanced by its commercial and political expansion on the peninsula and along the east coast of Sumatra (Meilink-Roelofsz 1970:148). On becoming vassals of Melaka, the peninsular states of Pahang, Terengganu, and Kedah converted to Islam (De Graaf, 1970:126). The isthmian state of Patani and its vassal, Kelantan, also adopted Islam under the influence of Melaka (De Graaf 1970:126). Melaka's Sumatran dependencies, Rokan, Kampar, Siak, and Indragiri, all became Islamized through their clientage in the fifteenth century (De Graaf

1970:126). After the Portuguese conquest of Melaka in 1511, Aceh became the new Malay center of trade and Islam.

The Islamization of the Malay Peninsula reflected developments in the Muslim world beyond Southeast Asia. During the earlier period of Islamic influence among the Malay states (eleventh through seventeenth centuries A.D.), the predominant doctrines of the mainstream of Muslim thought at that time particularly appealed to the Malay rulers, as Milner (1981:57) has argued. Persianized conceptions of kingship endowing royal authority with divine sanction, as well as Sufi mystical doctrines preached by itinerant Muslim missionaries in Malay port kingdoms, were compatible with the prevailing Hindu-Buddhist religious and political culture (Milner 1981:57–58). Adoption of medieval Islamic doctrines did not entail a radical departure from the tradition of divine kingship but rather represented a recasting of it in Muslim terms. The version of Islam initially presented to the Malay rulers reinforced royal authority at the expense of *Shari'ah* law.

The Wahabi reform movement, which swept through the eighteenth-century Muslim world, challenged the medieval Islamic concepts of royal authority that had been enshrined as the basis of the Malay polity. Persianized kingship and mysticism, regarded as orthodox during the preceding period of Islamization, were now attacked as heretical by reformers seeking to establish a *Shari'ah*-centered polity (Milner 1981:56). Muslim reformers of the eighteenth and nineteenth centuries proclaimed *Shari'ah* law as the foundation of the state, employing the new definition of Islamic orthodoxy to subvert the position of the Malay rulers. The influence of radical reformist doctrines emphasizing strict compliance with *Shari'ah* law was increasingly felt among the Malays during the second half of the nineteenth century (Roff 1970:167–168). It was at this time that the Malays intensified their direct contacts with Islamic centers in the Middle East.

Through greatly increased participation in the pilgrimage to Mecca *(haj)* beginning in the mid-nineteenth century, the Malays became aware of reformist doctrines current in the wider Muslim world. After completing the *haj*, Malay pilgrims occasionally remained in Mecca for an extended period of study under well-known Islamic scholars, some of whom were leaders of Sufi mystical orders *(tarekat)*. The Nakshabandiya *tarekat*, which was influential among Malay pilgrims, taught an orthodox form of mysticism that strongly emphasized obedience to *Shari'ah* law (Dobbin 1974:319). Malay *tarekat* teachers (often pilgrims returned from Mecca) who combined mysticism with reformist fundamentalism became the foci of political opposition in Sumatra (Dobbin 1974:319). Migrant Arab traders during the second half of the nineteenth century also served as channels for the transmission of Wahabi reformism to the Malay communities on the peninsula and in the archipelago (Roff 1970:164–170). Traveling Muslim scholars of local and foreign origin disseminated the new trends in Islamic thought on both sides of the Straits of Melaka, linking the Malays of Sumatra and the peninsula to the sources of Islamic reformism in the Middle East.

Islamic reformism inspired violent opposition to the traditional political order in several areas of the Indonesian archipelago, most notably in the Minangkabau region of Sumatra,[14] but had a considerably more subdued impact on the peninsula where some Malay rulers successfully compromised with the fundamentalists to defuse their attacks (Milner 1981:59–60). Pre-Islamic royal titles and court ceremonial were abolished in several of the peninsular Malay states. The nature of the relationship between the British colonial authorities and the Malay rulers, established during the "Forward Movement" of the 1870s, was based on recognition of the rulers' undisputed authority over Malay religion and custom (Roff 1970:175). As the Malay rulers found themselves bereft of any real decision-making power, they increasingly turned to the religious sphere to assert their power (Roff 1970:175). The British not only refrained from interfering with Islam but also supported the rulers' prerogatives in this domain by providing them with the bureaucratic and legal machinery to systematize Islamic law and practice (Roff 1970:176). By the end of the nineteenth century, a complex religious bureaucracy under the control of the traditional elite was assembled in the Malay states with the assistance of the colonial authorities (Roff 1970:176).

The creation of religious bureaucracies staffed by rural *ulama* (Islamic scholars) appointed by the ruler, most of whom were proponents of syncretistic Islam, provided a bulwark against fundamentalist reformers known as the *Kaum Muda* (Young Group) (Benda 1970: 186–187). British recognition of the Malay rulers' authority, as based on the control and administration of Islam, empowered each ruler to define what was to constitute Islamic orthodoxy within the borders of his state. During the period in which the ruling elites of Malaya were centralizing Islamic administration under their auspices, a second wave of religious reform was making its influence felt among Muslim pilgrims and students from the Malay world. The modernist teachings of Shaykh Mohamad Abduh of Cairo inspired and aroused Malay students pursuing their education in the Middle East during the late nineteenth and early twentieth centuries.[15] Returned pilgrims and students attempting to expound Abduh's modernist reform teachings in the peninsular Malay states were thwarted by the recently established Islamic administrative machinery.

The modernists, who sought to strengthen and uplift the Muslim community through purifying Islam from accretions of custom and tradition not in accord with the Quran and Hadith, propagated their ideas through new educational institutions known as *madrasah,* which were modeled after those in Cairo, and through the publication of newspapers.[16] In this regard the Straits Settlements of Singapore and Penang played an important role in the spread of modernist or *Kaum Muda* teachings.[17] In the Straits Settlements, governed directly as crown colonies, Islam was not under the control of a traditional Malay elite and *Kaum Muda* proponents were thus free to disseminate the new teachings without constraint. *Kaum Muda* newspapers, often banned from the peninsular Malay states, nevertheless reached the rural Malay community through the new style *madrasah* established on the peninsula and in the Straits Settlements. The *madrasah* relied heavily on the *Kaum Muda* newspapers for teaching material. Religious teachers trained in the new *madrasah* returned to their rural communities where their views generated much interest.

The *Kaum Muda* reformers extended their attack on the traditional rural *ulama* to include criticism of the colonial order (Benda 1970: 185). They denounced the colonial authorities for preserving Malay traditional social systems while at the same time creating a plural society in which Westerners and Asian immigrants enjoyed economic dominance. They also drew attention to the threat of Western values promoted by colonial educational institutions and Christian missionary activity. Although the *Kaum Muda* religio-political critique was not without influence in the Malay community, its challenge to the traditional Malay polity was effectively contained by the alliance between the rulers and the rural *ulama* employed in the state religious bureaucracies, a development indirectly supported by colonial policies. The close tie between Malay sovereignty and Islamic administration continued throughout the colonial period and was given constitutional status upon independence.

Christianity and the Colonial State

Christian evangelism accompanied European penetration of the Malay Peninsula. The Roman Catholics, the earliest of the Christian missionaries, arrived in the wake of the Portuguese conquest of Melaka in 1511. Alfonso d'Albuquerque, the Portuguese Viceroy at Goa, began to promote Catholicism soon after his victory over the Melaka Sultanate. The Portuguese Crown sponsored the missionaries who followed Albuquerque, as church and state were united in the pursuit of trade and converts in Asia. Opposition to Islam infused the Portuguese commercial and evangelical enterprises. The Muslim merchants who controlled the Indian Ocean trade routes were the chief rivals of the Portuguese for supremacy in the spice trade. Propagation of the Catholic faith was at once an instrument for the destruction of Muslim commercial power in key harbors where the Portuguese sought to establish naval bases and trading posts, as well as the symbol of the empire that the Portuguese aspired to build.

Continuous conflict between the Portuguese and Muslim merchants created implacable antagonism toward Christianity on the part of the Malays. Neighboring Muslim states, Aceh, Java, and Johor, challenged Portuguese commercial power. Between 1568 and 1587 these states attacked Melaka eight times. The Portuguese destroyed Johor Lama (the old capital of Johor kingdom) in 1587 but were unable to defeat their more tenacious rival, Aceh, until 1629. Protracted warfare between Melaka and its neighbor heightened the animosity between Muslims and Christians, reinforcing the Malays' already unfavorable impression of Christianity (Williams 1976:77). Portuguese Catholic missionaries in Melaka succeeded in converting only the Eurasians, and profession of Roman Catholicism became synonymous with the Eurasian community (Haines 1962).

Despite the failure of the Portuguese missionaries to evangelize the Malays, Melaka rapidly developed into a Catholic city. Catholic institutions proliferated in Melaka and by the late sixteenth century the city became a major center of missionary activities in Asia. The missionaries, who belonged to four religious orders based in Melaka—the Jesuits, Franciscans, Dominicans, and Augustinians—moved around Asia to Cambodia, Siam, Indo-China, Indonesia, China, and Japan to spread the faith (Teixeira 1961:100). Rivalry between these orders was rampant in the seventeenth century and diminished the effectiveness of the Portuguese missions (Haines 1962). The rise of Dutch naval power at the expense of the Portuguese also constrained Catholic evangelism at this time.

Dutch pressure on the Portuguese, which began in the late sixteenth century, culminated in the final Dutch siege of Melaka in June 1640 and was followed by the Portuguese surrender seven months later in January 1641. At the time of Melaka's fall to the Dutch after 130 years of Portuguese rule, its Catholic community had grown to 20,000 and was served by nineteen churches and chapels, including a cathedral (Lee 1963:43). The Dutch lost no time in dismantling Melaka's Roman Catholic establishment through deportations of priests and other Portuguese residents and through a severe persecution campaign. Churches were demolished or closed, Catholics were forbidden to hold public religious gatherings, priests on passing ships were barred from landing in Melaka, and banishment orders were issued against all those who refused to renounce Catholicism (Lee 1963:44).

Some of the Eurasians nevertheless continued to practice the Catholic faith in the surrounding jungles (Teixeira 1961:101). Portuguese priests from Goa and Macao smuggled themselves into Melaka and hid in the jungles where they ministered to the remnants of the Catholic community. The Eurasians also maintained their Portuguese and Catholic identity by absorbing non-Catholic Eurasian families who intermarried with them and by perpetuating their own language—a creolized form of sixteenth-century Portuguese known as *lingua do Christam*. The association between Portuguese and Catholic identity was such that anyone baptized during the Portuguese or Dutch occupation of Melaka, a period of 284 years, received a Portuguese surname (Teixeira 1961:101). Eurasians with Dutch surnames, regarded as converts to Calvinism, often became Catholic and adopted elements of Portuguese culture through intermarriage with Eurasian Catholics.

Although the Dutch East India Company encouraged promotion of Calvinist Christianity in the areas under its influence, no significant missionary work was carried out in Melaka (Williams 1976:79). The clergy of the Dutch Reformed Church were mainly concerned with ministering to the company's employees. Despite the lack of missionary zeal on the part of the Dutch, some of the local people nevertheless converted to Calvinism. The influence of Calvinism was ephemeral, and the Dutch Reformed Church did not survive the retreat of Dutch commercial and political power from the Malay Peninsula in 1824 when the British took control of Melaka.

The Roman Catholic Church, on the other hand, proved itself resilient to the political decline of Portugal in maritime Asia. Rome formulated a new policy toward missionary work in 1622 that aimed to eliminate the system of royal patronage through placing the missions directly under the control of a central organization, the Sacred Congregation for the Propagation of the Faith. The Catholic missions' ties with particular colonial and commercial powers were severed, and their relationship with Rome was correspondingly strengthened (Williams 1976:81).

French missionaries, under the close supervision of Rome, began to play a prominent role in Catholic evangelism on the Malay Peninsula as Portuguese mission activity declined. The new era of Catholic missions on the peninsula was initiated around 1662 with the work of French priests in Ayuthia, then the capital of Siam (Lee 1963:45). An outbreak of persecution in Siam in 1779 resulted in the expulsion of the missionaries, who then moved southward along the peninsula to continue their work. Two French missionaries expelled from Siam settled in Kedah in 1781 where they ministered to eighty Christians from Siam and Melaka (Lee 1963:46). Under the leadership of one of these missionaries, the small Catholic community in Kedah moved to Penang in 1786 when the island became a possession of the British Crown. The governor provided a building for the use of the mission. At the beginning of the nineteenth century, other French missionaries came to Penang in search of a new site for the Asian Seminary, which had been transferred from Ayuthia.

The British authorities in Penang supported the proposal by the French missionaries to set up the seminary. In 1809, the seminary, known as the College General, was established and the French missionaries proceeded to train native priests for countries throughout Asia (Lee 1963:47). The Society of Paris Foreign Missions, an arm of the Sacred Congregation for the Propagation of the Faith, steadily gained influence on the Malay Peninsula at the expense of the Portuguese missions during the nineteenth century. In 1888, Rome recognized the authority of the Paris Foreign Missions over the entire peninsula, including Singapore. The Portuguese were, however, allowed to maintain control of their churches and parishes in Melaka and Singapore within the organizational structure dominated by the Paris Foreign Missions (Williams 1976:99). The Paris Foreign Missions was assigned the responsibility of bringing the missions firmly under the control of Rome through its Vicars Apostolic and through training a native clergy.

Protestant missionaries became active on the peninsula after the eighteenth century. The London Missionary Society (LMS), which pioneered Protestant evangelism on the peninsula, directed its efforts toward the Malay and Chinese communities in the Straits Settlements from 1815 until 1846. Because missionary work among the Malays produced few converts, the LMS shifted its interest to the Chinese. In 1846, the LMS decided to abandon its work in the Straits Settlements to take advantage of the opening of China, a result of the British military victories over the Chinese government (Haines 1962). The new policy of the LMS was to concentrate its resources on China itself rather than on the less encouraging work in the Straits Settlements, where the transience of the Chinese immigrant communities hindered the formation of a stable Christian community. Although independent Protestant missionaries continued to work in the Straits Settlements, the LMS policy change resulted in the Malay Peninsula remaining outside of the mainstream of Protestant missionary activity throughout the period 1846 through 1881. During the period of the LMS's withdrawal, the Roman Catholic missionaries continued actively to evangelize in Singapore and on the peninsula (Haines 1962).

Education became a major force for Catholic evangelization by the mid-nineteenth century. With the entry in 1852 of the Brothers of the Christian Schools and the Sisters of the Holy Infant Jesus, the Catholic missionaries became more actively involved in the field of education. Non-Christians came into contact with the Catholic faith mainly through the new English-medium schools founded in urban centers (Williams 1976:103–104).

Christian missions, both Catholic and Protestant, rarely expanded their activities beyond the Straits Settlements before the last quarter of the nineteenth century. Chaotic conditions in the civil war-torn Malay states discouraged the missionaries from venturing farther into the interior. British intervention in the Malay states and subsequent establishment of protectorates over them brought about orderly political conditions and security of person and property conducive to missionary work. While the "British Forward Movement" on the peninsula broadened the field for missionary enterprise, the nature of the treaties between the British and the Malay rulers limited the scope of Christian evangelization to the non-Malay immigrant population. The British colonial administration, which had by 1874 committed itself to the policy of upholding the status of Islam in the Malay states, unofficially discouraged any missionary work among the Malays. The effect of this policy was to confer legal recognition of the social fact of Islam as the basis of the Malay polity and cultural identity.

Christian missionaries, responding to the new opportunities provided by the "British Forward Movement," founded churches and schools during the late nineteenth and early twentieth centuries in the larger towns that developed in the western Malay states. Evangelization centered mainly on the urban population comprising Chinese and Indian immigrant workers brought to the Malay states to fill the demand for labor generated by expanding British commercial interests.[18] The diversity of languages and dialects among the immigrant groups compelled the missionaries to structure their work along ethnic and linguistic lines. Catholic and Protestant missionaries alike allocated separate personnel and facilities to cater to the particular needs of the various groups. The linguistic specialization of missionary work led to the institutionalization of distinct sections within the Christian churches. Speakers of Chinese dialects and Tamil generally attended separate branches or services of the same church. Only the English-speaking sections of the churches were multiethnic.

The concentration of Christian evangelization through English-medium schools located in the Straits Settlements and large towns in the western Malay states led to formation of middle-class, English-speaking sections within the churches. In particular, the Catholics, Anglicans, and Methodists viewed the English school as an important means for propagating Christianity (Loh 1975:56). Missionaries from these churches contributed much to the expansion of English education in the late nineteenth and early twentieth centuries. At this time demand for English-educated, white-collar workers in the growing European-dominated commercial sector and in the colonial bureaucracy had become pressing (Loh 1975:50). The colonial authorities welcomed the development of English-medium mission schools and assisted these schools with grants-in-aid and occasional donations of land (Loh 1975:57, 62). The role of the mission schools in training English-speaking clerks complemented the colonial economy.

As mission-school education provided access to prestigious white-collar jobs, middle-class families or those who aspired to attain middle-class status eagerly sent their children to these schools. Christian schools offered a strong academic curriculum within which religious indoctrination was secondary. Generally, the missionaries sought to introduce students to Christian values indirectly rather than to proselytize aggressively among them (Loh 1975). Through their role in educating the urban elite, the mission schools enjoyed widespread influence that far exceeded mere baptism statistics. Some degree of familiarity with Christian teachings and values is common throughout the English-educated Malaysian middle class, although only a minority of mission-school students actually converted to Christianity. Christian converts recruited through mission schools were an elite group in colonial society. Conversion to Christianity came to be seen as an emblem of middle-class status.

The smaller Protestant denominations played a limited role in the field of education. The Lutherans, Seventh Day Adventists, Baptists, Pentecostals, and various independent evangelical Christian groups were overshadowed by the Roman Catholics, Anglicans, Presbyterians, and Methodists whose association with educational institutions attracted the attention of the urban public.

Throughout the colonial period the Christian missions were essentially foreign in character, although lip service was given to the goal of training indigenous church leadership. French, British, and American missionary organizations financed and controlled the major institutions through which Christianity was propagated on the peninsula. Despite the Paris Foreign Missions' explicit policy of training an Asian clergy, the French missionaries failed to significantly indigenize the Catholic Church before the Second World War. Although the College General had been established in Penang since the beginning of the nineteenth century, few local priests had been ordained. The first indigenous priest was not ordained until 1911, and from 1920 until 1950 only thirty-six had been ordained (Williams 1976:107). The recruitment and training of a native clergy was inhibited by the missionaries' negative view of the moral and intellectual standards of Asians. Moreover, the requirement of proficiency in Latin posed an obstacle to ordination of native priests.

In the case of the Protestant churches, the Asian clergy exercised little authority before the Second World War. Treated as subordinates of the foreign missionaries, the local Christian leaders were rarely included in policy formulation, which remained the domain of the foreign personnel. The status of the foreign missionaries was also reflected in salaries, allowances, and housing, enabling them to enjoy a markedly higher standard of living than their Asian counterparts.[19] The Asian clergy resented the foreign missionaries' prerogatives, yet at the same time recognized their dependence on the financial support, expertise, and direction that the missionaries provided. World War II and the Japanese occupation of Malaya abruptly ended the domination of foreign missionaries over local clergy. The Japanese internment of foreign missionaries created a vacuum in church leadership that enabled Asians to assume authority for the first time.

During their internment by the Japanese in Singapore's Changi Prison, foreign missionaries affiliated with the main Protestant denominations—Anglican, Methodist, Presbyterian, and Lutheran—became acutely aware of the importance of indigenous church leadership and made plans to establish an interdenominational seminary in Singapore after the war. Accelerated efforts to indigenize Christian leadership took effect after the Japanese occupation ended and preparations for eventual independence began.

Only a small proportion of the influx of Chinese and Indian immigrant laborers to the Malay Peninsula in the late nineteenth and early twentieth centuries was evangelized by Christian missionaries. The vast majority continued to adhere to various traditions of folk religion brought over from southern India and southern China.[20] The Chinese immigrants eclectically engaged in diverse practices drawn from the traditions of Mahayana Buddhism and Taoism. A strong concern with divination and spirit mediumship is characteristic of Chinese folk religion. In the case of the Indians, who were mainly low-caste, Tamil-speaking Hindus, scripturally based religion was similarly of little interest. The Tamil plantation laborers were immersed in South Indian folk Hindu practices that higher-caste, better-educated Hindus condemned as unorthodox. Isolated on rubber estates, the Tamil laborers persisted in such disapproved practices as spirit mediumship, animal sacrifice, and rituals of self-mortification. The South Indian folk Hinduism brought by Indian plantation laborers began a new phase of Hinduism on the peninsula that was discontinuous with the Hindu cults of the Indianized period lasting from the eighth until the fourteenth century. Unlike the Hindu-Buddhist cults adopted by the Malay rulers during the Indianized period, South Indian folk Hinduism had no point of articulation with the state.

The imported non-Muslim religions common among the immigrant population—Buddhism, Taoism, South Indian Hinduism, and Christianity—were peripheral to the colonial state. Only Islam enjoyed political recognition and a legally defined relationship with the colonial authorities.

CHAPTER TWO

The Cauldron of Change: Politics and Religious Organization in Contemporary Malaysia

RELIGIOUS developments in Malaya on the eve of the Second World War cannot be separated from the wider political events on the peninsula during the prewar years. In view of the rising tide of anticolonialism throughout Southeast Asia in the first quarter of the twentieth century (von der Mehden 1963), the emergence of Malay nationalist organizations was by no means an isolated phenomenon. The first stirrings of Malay nationalism were articulated through the activities of several secular and religious movements. Nationalist ideologies were espoused by aristocratic bureaucrats, vernacular-educated teachers, and Islamic reformers with Arab, Indian, and Sumatran backgrounds (Roff 1967). Unlike Islam, Christianity did not become associated with any nationalist movement on the peninsula. Christianity received no sponsorship from the colonial state and it was not identified with any major ethnic community. Rather, it attracted only a small number of followers from the transient non-Malay population in the urban areas. Consequently, the opportunity for Christianity to develop into a convenient means of political expression was limited. Hindu activism, on the other hand, was strongly associated with the Tamil Reform Movement, which represented a strand of Dravidian nationalism imported from the Indian subcontinent. The reform movement was mainly concerned with purifying Hindu practices and promoting particular Hindu festivals to heighten Tamil consciousness. The numerous campaigns launched by these reformers may be considered parochial efforts at redefining Hinduism, because their activities did not extend beyond the boundaries of the minority South Indian community.¹

In sum, Islam gained ascendancy in political affairs as the Malays strove to carve out a distinct identity in an evolving plural society, while Christianity, Hinduism, and other religions associated with the immigrant groups took a back seat in the political arena.² As precursors of the religious mosaic in contemporary Malaysia, these prewar developments established incontrovertibly the political juxtaposition between Islam and the non-Islamic religions. This chapter will focus on the ramifications of a politically laden dichotomy in religious organization in the postwar era and their implications for potential conflict in a rapidly changing society.

Religion as Political Instrument in the Postwar Era

The Japanese occupation of the Malay Peninsula from 1942 to 1945 defused to a certain extent the conflict between the traditional Malay elites and the young Malay radicals. Some of the elites fled the country while others collaborated with the Japanese. The radicals were either co-opted into nationalist organizations that were closely supervised by the Japanese, or they withdrew from political activity altogether. Malay political and religious fervor of the prewar years was reduced to a silent simmer during this period. About the only significant religious event that occurred during the war years was the convention of a pan-Malayan religious council at Kuala Kangsar in December 1944, which was attended by members of the Malay traditional elite (Stockwell 1979:7). Japanese sponsorship of this convention may be construed as a strategy to increase local cooperation at a time when the tide of the war was turning in favor of the Allies.

Following Japan's defeat in 1945, the occurrence of three separate events marked the reawakening of Islam as a major political force that the returning British authorities and non-Malays had to contend with. During the interregnum between the Japanese surrender and the establishment of the British military administration in the closing months of 1945, a whole spate of Malay atrocities against the Chinese caused considerable alarm throughout the country. Immediately after the Japanese surrender, guerillas of the Chinese-dominated Malayan Peoples' Anti-Japanese Army (MPAJA) emerged from the jungles and began a campaign of terror among the civilian population. Many Malays who had collaborated with the Japanese were summarily arrested, tried, and executed by the MPAJA. Because of the disorganized state of Malay national leadership, the terrified Malay population turned to the *penghulu* (village headman) and *ulama* for guidance and protection. As the MPAJA relentlessly delivered swift justice to its perceived enemies, the Malays organized themselves under the banner of various invulnerability *(kebal)* cults to retaliate against the Chinese (Burridge 1957; Stockwell 1979; Cheah 1981). The most renowned of these cults was the *Sabil'ullah* (Road to God) movement led by Panglima Salleh (also known as Kiyai Salleh) who directed many attacks against Chinese settlers, particularly in the Batu Pahat area in Johor. Members of these cults, while professing Islam as their rallying point, engaged in a variety of magical practices normally forbidden in Islamic teachings allegedly to gain an easy victory in their holy war against the Chinese infidels. Charms *(azimat)*, incantations *(jampi)*, and various esoteric rituals became the standard spiritual weapons sought by cult members in their battle preparations. In the ensuing skirmishes many Chinese and Malays lost their lives, but the Chinese (many of whom had no connections with the MPAJA) suffered the worst casualties (Cheah 1981).

The emergence of these cults must be interpreted against the background of various Sufi and other mystical Islamic orders *(tarekat)* in Malaya. According to al-Attas (1963:31), Sufi teachings had already reached the Malay Peninsula as early as 1488, mainly through pilgrims returning from the Middle East, or through Arab and Indian missionaries. At least nine Sufi orders have been identified by al-Attas as active on the peninsula. The leadership of these *tarekat* is decentralized, with members owing their allegiance to a specific leader *(shaykh)* in a particular locality. Panglima Salleh was such a leader during the 1945 Batu Pahat massacres. A *tarekat* is potentially a grass-roots movement that can be politically inspired to meet any perceived threat. Because of the *tarekat* leaders' ability to mobilize village support, many of them were feared not only by the Chinese but also by the Malay traditional elite. The latter were concerned that the militant cults could be manipulated by Malay radicals in an attempt at insurrection. Many Malay traditional leaders felt obliged to work with *tarekat* members in order to assert their influence in the villages. However, the threat posed by these cults to the stability of Malay society was neutralized in 1946 when the ordinary Malay folk rallied behind their traditional leaders to vehemently oppose the Malayan Union plan. The target of Malay hostility was switched from the Chinese to the British architects of the Malayan Union plan;[3] thus the powers of these *tarekat* were arrested but not totally eliminated. Nevertheless, for the first time in five years since the Japanese regulated Malay political and religious activities, the Malays were reminded that they could turn to Islam spontaneously to summon and demonstrate their political strength.

The violence perpetrated by these cults continued sporadically until early 1948 but none of it was directed by a national Islamic leadership. These incidents were mainly local affairs watched closely by the British security services. Meanwhile, the political development of Islam entered another phase with the formation in early 1947 of the *Majlis Agama Tertinggi SeMalaya* (MATA, or the Supreme Religious Council). Although MATA was established with the explicit purpose of reforming Islam, it was in fact sponsored by elements of the Malay left who had resumed their activities in such bodies as the Malay Nationalist Party (MNP) and *Pusat Tenaga Rakyat* (PUTERA, or Center of People's Power). A year later at a conference organized by MATA, the first Islamic political party, Hizbul Muslimin, was formed. This party represented the convergence of prewar radical movements in a loose alliance to oppose the Malay traditional elite and British colonialism. Its demands for the establishment of an Islamic state shorn of feudal arrangements and pre-Islamic accretions were seriously viewed by the leadership of the United Malay National Organization (UMNO),[4] which formed its own Islamic bodies to meet this challenge. The development of Hizbul Muslimin and its allies was cut short in 1948 during the Communist Emergency, when many radical organizations were outlawed and their leaders placed under arrest by British authorities. Ironically, the seeds of Islamic radicalism that germinated in MATA were sown within the ranks of UMNO, resulting in a breakaway group that founded the Pan-Malayan Islamic Party (PAS) in 1951. Members of Hizbul Muslimin and other banned parties soon found their niches within the ranks of PAS. Thus, the continuity of a politicized Islam was maintained during this turbulent period, despite religious alternatives provided by the Malay traditional elite and obstacles erected by the British colonial authorities.[5]

As the cultic frenzy became overshadowed by an organized front of Islamic radicals and reformers, another significant event occurred in

1950 that contributed to a growing Islamic consciousness among the Malays. This event, which involved a legal contest between a Malay woman and a Dutch couple over the custody of the couple's daughter, Maria Hertogh, eventually ended in three days of rioting in Singapore. Maria Hertogh was born in Java in 1937 to a Dutch soldier and an Eurasian woman. During the Japanese occupation, she was separated from her parents and came under the care a Malay woman who later brought her up as a Muslim in Terengganu on the east coast of Malaya. After the war her parents returned to Holland but continued to trace Maria's whereabouts through the Dutch authorities in Java and Singapore. In April 1950, Maria and her Malay guardian traveled to Singapore where they were embroiled in eight months of bitter legal proceedings as the Dutch authorities attempted to wrest her from her guardian's control. Publicity and controversy were heightened in August 1950 when Maria married a Kelantanese Malay resident in Singapore under Muslim law. In December, when the High Court of Singapore decreed Maria's marriage invalid and declared that she be repatriated to her parents in Holland, Malay rioters took to the streets and attacked both Europeans and Eurasians. Order was restored only after three days of street violence and after 18 people lost their lives and 173 were injured.[6]

The most significant aspect of this case was its transformation from a legal dispute into a religious conflict. Many Muslims perceived the decision of the court as a direct attack on Islam by Christian colonialists and sought to avenge their pride by open violence against the white infidels. But it was the organized protests just prior to the riots that suggest the political manipulations of Muslim sentiments common during the period. The Nadra Action Committee (Nadra was Maria's Muslim name) was formally constituted to represent the voice of Muslim protest against the court's ruling. Some members of this committee used their connections with the mass media to incite Malay resentment toward an alleged abuse of Muslim rights (Hughes 1980: 49–51).[7] The conflict between Muslim law and English common law in this case must be viewed in the broader context of the evolution of Malay-Muslim identity in the region. Malay ethnic sensitivity had already been aroused by what they saw as the humiliating conditions of the Malayan Union plan. The assertion of British authority in the Maria Hertogh case, occurring so soon after the Malayan Union fiasco, inflamed Malay suspicions that an insidious plot was in the making to undermine Malay-Muslim rights. The resulting anxieties and paranoia served only to accelerate the consolidation of Malay identity among a diverse group of people.[8] No doubt some Malay politicians assiduously capitalized on the religious aspects of this case to mobilize the masses (Means 1969:277), but among the Malays it was the growing realization of the shrinking boundaries of Islamic authority that played an important part in cementing their religious pride with ethnic consciousness.

The five years between the Japanese surrender and the Maria Hertogh riots saw the quickening tempo of Malay-Muslim assertiveness aided, ironically, by several events that were beyond the Malays' control. On the other hand, the non-Muslim religions were not enveloped in experiences that were likely to propel them into the political arena. There are at least three reasons for the apolitical direction taken by these religions. First, the non-Muslims on the peninsula were ethnically heterogeneous with no single ethnic group claiming total membership in a specific religion. Christianity was identified with the Chinese, Indians, and Eurasians. But many Chinese remained within the folds of Taoism and Mahayana Buddhism, just as many Indians acknowledged Hinduism and Islam as their traditional religions. Compared with the Malays, who are all Muslims by birth, none of the non-Malays could realistically attempt to attain political integration within and between ethnic groups through religious symbols. Second, the establishment of two non-Malay political parties (the Malayan Chinese Association, or MCA, and the Malayan Indian Congress, or MIC) after the war was not religiously inspired. Neither party had explicit ties to religious organizations. Unlike UMNO, which had to maintain a religious program to compete with PAS, the MCA and MIC felt no pressure to fortify their religious quarters because their rivals had yet to appear on the horizon. Non-Malay opposition parties that were formed after 1950 had no religious bases and therefore did not evoke any religious response from the MCA and MIC. Third, the British, on their return to the peninsula after the war, attempted to introduce a more uniform system of government through the Malayan Union plan. One of the conditions of this plan was the extension of Malay privileges to the non-Malays. Had this condition been carried through, the constitutional arrangements of Islam vis-à-vis the other religions would have been different. It may be speculated that the political weight of Islam would have been forcibly lessened to accommodate the non-Muslim religions as commensurate with the increased political status of the non-Malays. Whether the non-Muslim religions would have then become politicized is equivocal but their raised status could have been a catalyst to such politicization. In actuality, the Malayan Union plan was abruptly curtailed and Islam retained its superior position in relation to the other religions.

The Malayan Constitution of 1957 (the year of the country's independence) brought to a logical conclusion the consecration of Muslim rights and the enshrinement of Islam as the state religion. The marriage between mosque and state[9] in this legal maneuver conferred on Islam a special status that had far-reaching consequences for the Malays' relationship with the non-Malays. Through this legal charter, the special privileges that the Malays enjoyed during the colonial era (such as land entitlement, civil service jobs, and education) were now given a religious twist with the implication that apostasy entailed the loss of these privileges. For the non-Muslims (who in this case were non-Malays), the enforcement of Islamic law placed severe restrictions on their religious liberties. As noted by Gordon P. Means (1978:390), stringent changes in Islamic law were effected in nearly all Malayan states between 1952 and 1960 for the explicit purpose of defining the religious obligations of Muslims as well as controlling the activities of non-Muslims. Muslim sensitivities had gradually acquired a legitimate base from which punishment could be meted out to non-Muslims who attempted to proselytize Muslims and whose activities were considered insulting to Islam.

The question of why non-Muslims did not challenge the implementation of these laws must be examined in relation to the political negotiations preceding the country's independence. Up to the Second World War, the Chinese and Indians who had emigrated to Malay were considered a transient population. Many of them treated Malaya as an "El Dorado" that provided opportunities for employment and business ventures, but they did not consider it a permanent home. Consequently, they did not regard citizenship privileges and political participation as urgent matters.[10] After the war, the non-Malays who had become a part of the settled population realized the necessity of full citizenship rights as a guarantee of their domiciled status in Malaya. Had the Malayan Union plan been successful, they would have secured equal citizenship rights with the Malays. The Malays, on the other hand, feared that the Malayan Union plan would only increase the numerical strength of the non-Malay citizens, thus obliterating the Malay character of their country. Opposition to the Malayan Union plan resulted in the Federation of Malaya Agreement of 1948. Under this agreement, federal citizenship was automatically granted to the Malays but not to the non-Malays. It was in the context of this political development that a Malay came to be defined legally as someone who habitually spoke the Malay language, professed the Muslim faith and conformed to Malay customs. The rules of citizenship legislation, however, were not sufficiently rigid to cause extreme polarization between the Malays and non-Malays. As Malaya approached independence, the conditions for citizenship were reworked to meet certain demands of the non-Malays but without seriously antagonizing the Malays.[11] In short, the bargain over citizenship rights and privileges became a fundamental principle of ethnic compromise that carried a recognition of Islamic supremacy in exchange for the legitimation of non-Malay status.

The political achievement of Islam in postwar Malaya symbolizes the triumph of Malay nationalism in an era of unceasing encroachments and interventions by the non-Muslims. The apolitical nature of the non-Muslim religions, however, does not imply an absence of religious mobilization among the non-Muslims. In the postindependence period, the intrusions of Islam into non-Muslim affairs have precipitated moves to seek non-Muslim unity. But the impression that the gathering storm is a one-dimensional conflict between Muslims and non-Muslims is not wholly accurate. Each religious community in contemporary Malaysia is experiencing a high degree of experimentation and innovation, often resulting in the formation of many competing movements. Yet at the national level this religious diversity is resolved into an image of conflict between Muslims and non-Muslims. To analyze the dialectics of this religious phenomenon, we will examine the variety of religious organizations in contemporary urban Malaysia before locating their relevance in the Muslim versus non-Muslim conflict. Since our study focuses on religious movements in the capital city of Kuala Lumpur, we will first provide a brief description of that city as a religious center.

Contemporary Urban Religious Organizations

Kuala Lumpur first gained political importance in 1896 when it was established by the British as the capital of the Federated Malay

States.[12] As the administrative center of British colonialism, Kuala Lumpur developed quickly from a frontier town into a bustling city that commanded wide prestige and political resources. After the war, Kuala Lumpur continued to maintain its political status as the capital of the Federation of Malaya (and later of Malaysia). By the 1960s, the concentration of administrative, commercial, and transportation functions in Kuala Lumpur had transformed it into a city that dominated not only its immediate tributary areas but the whole of Malaysia. As an important center of cultural dissemination and political networks, events in Kuala Lumpur have far-reaching effects in various parts of the country.[13] As the seat of the federal government, its administrative jurisdiction includes the screening and registration of religious bodies. The location of major religious institutions in Kuala Lumpur underscores its role in the coordination and control of religious affairs throughout the country. It is within the context of Kuala Lumpur's transcendence over the rest of the country that religious change in the city can be construed as having significant national implications. We will briefly describe the ethnic-religious structure of Kuala Lumpur as a prelude to analyzing the organized forms of religious activities in the city.

According to the 1980 census, the population of Kuala Lumpur and its satellite town of Petaling Jaya[14] exceeds one million people, of which more than fifty percent are Chinese, about a quarter are Malays, and the remainder are Indians, Eurasians, or Europeans. Chinese predominance in Kuala Lumpur can be traced to the city's origin as a Chinese mining camp that was later transformed into a center of trade and British political administration (Lim 1978). The existence of ethnic enclaves in the city is a remnant of the colonial past that saw the imprint of British policy on living arrangements and the spread of mutual segregation. The spatial polarization of Chinatowns, Indian settlements, and Malay reserves in Kuala Lumpur provides an interesting history of social distances maintained in an ethnically plural city that is now gradually feeling the impact of urban renewal programs aimed at ethnic desegregation. Until these programs succeed in altering the ethnic structure of the city, Kuala Lumpur remains very much a neocolonial city characterized by large pockets of ethnic enclaves that are interspersed occasionally by areas of multiethnic residence.

The complex ethnic divisions within Kuala Lumpur pose immense difficulties for urban planners who are attempting to create for the city an image of cultural uniformity, as was first observed by Terence G. McGee (1963).[15] Ethnic fragmentation in the city, in addition to a long history of ethnic competition, has not produced conditions favorable to the realization of the ideal of cultural integration. It is in the cultural separateness of Kuala Lumpur that Islam, despite its elevated status as an official religion, has not come to dominate the religious character of the city. The large number of mosques, churches, temples, and shrines scattered throughout Kuala Lumpur reflects a vibrant religious pluralism that defies efforts at cultural amalgamation. The rapid growth of Kuala Lumpur has also contributed to changes in the religious profile of the city. In a reanalysis of census data extending over a forty-year period, M. S. Sidhu and Gavin W. Jones (1981) showed that between 1931 and 1970 the Muslim population in Selangor (Kuala Lumpur and Petaling Jaya are located within this state) had quadrupled, mainly as a result of the large influx of Malays into the city and its environs. In the same period, the city's Hindu population trebled while increases in the Christian population, mainly from Chinese conversions, accounted for a quarter of the country's Christians living in Kuala Lumpur alone. Similarly, adherents of the Chinese religious complex[16] in the city had also increased, although no figures were provided by the authors. The overall pattern emerging from these figures suggests that each religious group in the city is maintaining its own pace of development and ethnic identification, instead of moving toward religious assimilation or the acceptance of one particular religion as dominant. The organized expression of this religious diversity in Kuala Lumpur requires further explication.

Islam

Although Islam is the official religion of Malaysia, there is no head of the Muslim religion nor a national priesthood for the entire country. The *Yang Dipertuan Agong*[17] continues to be the nominal head of Islam in his own state, the former Straits Settlements of Melaka and Penang, the Federal Territory,[18] and the east Malaysian states of Sabah and Sarawak.[19] He has no jurisdiction over Islamic affairs in the other states, which come under the constitutional domain of individual sultans. In other words, Islam provides a symbol of unity for all Malays but its administration is controlled at the state level and not through a central religious body. Nevertheless, Islamic orthodoxy in Malaysia is maintained by adherence to the *Shafi'i* school of law recognized by the *Sunni* sect (see Mackeen 1969). In various states, religious decisions pertaining to Islam are made by the sultan who is advised by the *Majlis Ugama,* a consultative body comprising aristocrats and various high Muslim officials. The daily administration of Islamic matters is handled by the State Religious Department while the *Shari'ah* court is responsible for the administration of Islamic law. *Shari'ah* law, however, is not applicable to non-Muslims and is legally separate from the civil judiciary system. The decentralization of Islamic administration in Malaysia is favored by the sultans, most of whom view their positions as religious heads as one of their remaining vestiges of traditional authority. This guarded attitude of the sultans has brought some of them into conflict with the federal government, which has initiated some attempts at centralizing Islamic administration.[20]

Islamic bureaucracy in the Federal Territory is controlled by an autonomous Religious Council through the offices of the Religious Department. A National Council for Muslim Affairs is also located in the city. This council, which is officially headed by the prime minister, was formed in 1968 to coordinate the administration of Islamic affairs through the participation of representatives from each state, with the exception of three recalcitrant states (Johor, Kedah, and Pahang). Although the National Council cannot interfere directly with state Islamic matters, it can in its advisory capacity exert limited influence on their course of development. The National Council is housed within the Islamic Center, which is a division of the prime minister's department. The Islamic Center is staffed mainly by government functionaries who supervise the administration of the National Mosque in Kuala Lumpur,[21] as well as direct the activities of the Islamic Research Center and various missionary and consultative bodies. Another city-based Muslim organization, the Islamic Missionary Foundation, was created in 1974 by the federal government for the purpose of raising Islamic consciousness among the Malays. The needs of the non-Malay Muslims are managed by a voluntary organization, the Muslim Welfare Association, headed by a former prime minister. Several other independent Muslim organizations also have their headquarters in the city. Although these organizations do not receive regular government aid, some continue to liaise with government-sponsored Islamic bodies. This brief overview of Islamic organizational complexity suggests that the problem of administrative and policy control continues to plague the foundations of Islamic consensus, an ideal that has been cultivated by the government to promote Malay ethnic distinctiveness.

Christianity

Christianity in peninsular Malaysia is a minority religion where only 2 percent of the population is Christian, as compared to 56 percent Muslims, 19 percent Buddhists, and 8 percent Hindus (1980 census of Malaysia). Despite its minority status, the Christian presence is strongly felt, especially in the urban areas where non-Malays predominate. According to a survey conducted by Duain Vierow and Jack M. Shelby (1979), at least twelve denominations are established in Malaysia, each being an independent organization that controls a number of churches throughout the country.[22] The larger denominations (such as the Roman Catholics, Methodists, and Anglicans) and those with a substantial membership (such as the Assemblies of God) have decentralized their organizational functions into several administrative units known either as dioceses, districts, or divisions, but with their headquarters centered in Kuala Lumpur or Petaling Jaya. Because many Christians are Chinese and Indians who have received either an English or vernacular education, some denominations (particularly the Methodist church) have organized their churches along ethnic-linguistic lines, with, for example, sections in English, Chinese, and Tamil to meet specific needs. Although each denomination maintains an organization separate from the others, the older and more established Protestant churches have formed a joint council based in Petaling Jaya to promote the ideal of ecumenism in Malaysia. In February 1985, this council together with the Catholic church and the newer evangelical churches established the Christian Federation of Malaysia.

Running parallel to these formal church organizations are several voluntary Christian bodies run mainly by the laity. Many of these voluntary organizations, which are based in the Kuala Lumpur and Petaling Jaya area, are engaged in missionary and evangelical activities or in providing counseling and training services to the general public. In addition to the missionary programs conducted by various local churches, there are several denominational and interdenominational associations of foreign missionaries that manage their own programs throughout Malaysia. In recent years, however, a restrictive government policy on foreign missionaries has reduced the activities of these associations. The local voluntary organizations comprise largely interdenominational groups that are involved in spreading the gospel, recruiting members, and fostering Christian fellowship. Some of these groups (such as the Navigators and the Campus Crusade for Christ) were recently introduced into Malaysia to evangelize among the urban youth. Other lay Christians have established a telephone counseling service for the emotionally disturbed. These voluntary organizations provide an alternative source of religious gratification for Christians who are not totally satisfied with formal church services. The absence of a central coordinating body for these organizations implies that members have greater flexibility in making decisions and planning programs. Unlike Islam, which is a state-controlled religion, many church authorities do not have direct influence over the affairs of these organizations, unless the organizations are dependent on particular churches for funds. The relative autonomy enjoyed by these voluntary bodies further undermines the precarious cohesion of a Christian community that is characterized by competing denominations.

Hinduism

Slightly more than 80 percent of the Indian population in peninsular Malaysia is Hindu, with the largest concentration residing in the states of Selangor and Perak (Sidhu and Jones 1981). The Hindu religious system in Malaysia is as complex as its counterpart on the Indian subcontinent and can be broadly arranged into three categories. First, many of the Indian immigrants to Malaya continued their worship of various village deities in shrines that are still popular today. These shrines are usually maintained by individual devotees or families. Over the years, some shrines have been upgraded into temples through financial donations and ritual refurbishment. These larger temples dedicated to the universal deities of the Hindu pantheon comprise the second category. These are generally more elaborate and elegant structures managed by lay committees and attended to by full-time priests, many of whom are engaged on a contract basis from India. Most of the Hindu temples in Malaysia are of the Saivite tradition, although some Vaisnavite temples are found scattered throughout the country.[23] The Sri Maha Mariyamman Temple in Kuala Lumpur is recognized as the most prestigious and affluent Hindu temple in Malaysia. Although it is dedicated to the village deity, Mariyamman, it is one of the few Hindu temples in Malaysia that has been successfully "Sanskritized."[24] The third category of Hindu organizations comprises the newer nonsectarian movements, such as the Ramakrishna Mission, that are more reform-oriented in their approach and tend to attract mainly middle-class urban Indians. In addition to holding religious classes, these nonsectarian organizations run orphanages, children's homes, and meditation centers.

As in the case of Christianity, there is no centralized system of temple management in Malaysian Hinduism. Temples and shrines are run independently by family members, members of a particular caste, or volunteers from a group of regular worshippers. *Ashram* are managed by committees or spiritual heads with affiliations to meditation centers in India. In the 1950s, several members of the Indian community formed a national Hindu body, now known as the Malaysian Hindu Sangam, in an attempt to unify and systematize various Hindu temples and organizations throughout the country. The Hindu Sangam has not fully achieved this goal, especially in Kuala Lumpur where it has met with stiff resistance from its chief rival, the committee *(Devastanam)* of the Sri Maha Mariyamman Temple. The *Devastanam* has also embarked on a similar goal of bringing other Hindu temples and organizations under its wings.[25] The Hindu Sangam's efforts to organize religious classes, cultural performances, and conferences have been almost equally matched by the avid participation of *Devastanam* and other Hindu groups in similar activities. While Kuala Lumpur remains a center of Hindu religious learning and activities, it is also a city that exemplifies organizational disparateness in Malaysian Hinduism.

Buddhism

According to the 1980 census, Buddhists comprise 19 percent of the population in peninsular Malaysia, making it the second-largest religious group in the country. Although the census did not distinguish between Mahayana and Theravada Buddhists, it can be safely assumed that most are Chinese adherents of the Mahayana tradition that has long-established roots in China. The Mahayana temples are largely independent bodies maintained by public donations and run by monks with or without the assistance of a lay committee.[26] There are some Mahayana organizations that are strictly under control of the laity, such as the Malaysian Buddhist Society in Kuala Lumpur where members perform the functions of ordained monks. Many Mahayana temples are affiliated with the Malaysian Buddhist Association (MBA), an umbrella Mahayana organization founded at the Kek Lok Si Temple (a Pure Land sect temple) in Penang in the early 1960s. The headship of the MBA is an elected position held by a monk. Although the current head is a monk based in Melaka, an elaborate building was constructed in the late 1970s in Kuala Lumpur as the central venue for national and international Buddhist activities. Intense factionalism within the Mahayana circle arose when the Selangor branch of the MBA attempted to wrest control of this building from the parent body in Penang, resulting in protracted litigation. This conflict over the building suggests its significance, aside from its property value, as an unfolding symbol of Buddhist prestige. Control of the building has now been returned to the Penang group.

Unlike the Mahayanists, the Theravadins do not have central organization such as the MBA. The oldest and most widely known Theravada temple is the Buddhist Vihara in the Brickfields section of Kuala Lumpur, which has been controlled by a Sinhalese organization, the Sasana Abhiwurdhi Wardhana Society, since the turn of the century. Within the grounds of the Buddhist Vihara stands the Wisma Dhamma, the headquarters of the Buddhist Missionary Society (BMS), a lay organization involved in active proselytization among the English-speaking non-Malays, especially on university campuses throughout the country. The BMS was formed in 1963 and is run by a group of middle-class, English-educated Sinhalese and Chinese. The laity is also active in the Selangor Buddhist Association, which controls a Theravada temple in Kuala Lumpur served by monks from Kedah state and from Thailand. A family-run Theravada temple is located in Kampung Siam, an urban village in Kuala Lumpur. A group of Thai monks, however, controls the Wat Chettawan Buddhist Temple in Petaling Jaya that was built in the 1960s with the assistance of the Thai government.

Aside from the Mahayana and Theravada temples, there are several independent, non-sectarian Buddhist organizations based in the urban areas of Malaysia. The oldest of these is the Penang Buddhist Association, originally formed in the 1920s by a Theravada monk for purposes of advocating religious reforms. The Young Buddhist Association of Malaysia, also a Penang-based organization, is active in Buddhist ecumenism, having recently suggested the formation of a joint Buddhist council to coordinate Mahayana and Theravada activities in the country. A non-sectarian Buddhist center was recently established in Petaling Jaya by a Thai-trained monk involved in missionary activities through the Dharmafarers' Movement. The Japan-based Nichiren Daishonin Buddhist movement is also active in Malaysia. Like the other religions described heretofore, Malaysian Buddhism is characterized by a plethora of individual organizations that lack central leadership. The relative autonomy of the laity in these organizations suggests that they experience fewer constraints in introducing innovations and that clerical interference can be resisted more effectively. Whether the formation of a national Buddhist council will limit this independence has yet to be determined.

Other Religions

Although Sikhism is a minority religion in Malaysia, it has a relatively long history in the Kuala Lumpur area. Sikhs form an exclusive community in the city, having first arrived in Malaya in the 1870s and eventually establishing themselves in Kuala Lumpur in the 1880s (Amarjit Kaur 1973). The Sikh organizations that were founded in Malaya in the early twentieth century were strongly influenced by Sikh reform movements in the Punjab. They were also concerned with improving Sikh welfare and maintaining Sikh identity in Malaya. Most of these organizations, however, were torn by regional and ideological differences, with the result that few survived by the end of the Second World War. In the postwar period, several new Sikh religious organizations were formed that also had regional or ideological concerns (Malhi 1976). Similarly, many of the sixteen Sikh temples *(gurudwaras)* in Kuala Lumpur are factionalized by regional loyalties. Regional rivalry, especially between the Malwa and Mahja Sikhs, is further promoted by the independent administration enjoyed by each Sikh religious organization or temple in the country. To date there is no national Sikh organization that collectively represents Sikh religious interests in Malaysia, although the Malwa-controlled Tatt Khalsa Diwan Selangor in Kuala Lumpur is considered the most influential Sikh religious organization and is consulted by the government on Sikh religious matters (Malhi 1976:148).

Another minority religion that has a moderately large following in Malaysia is the Baha'i faith, which was introduced by an Indian missionary who made his first conversions among middle-class non-Malays in the early 1950s (Murthi 1969). Baha'i centers in Malaya were first established in Seremban (Negri Sembilan) and Melaka. It was only in the 1960s that full-scale missionary activities were launched throughout the country, particularly among the estate Indians and Chinese new villagers. In 1964 the Baha'is in Malaysia elected their own National Spiritual Assembly (NSA) in Kuala Lumpur and thereby became independent of the Regional Spiritual Assembly in Jakarta, Indonesia. The NSA is responsible for the overall administration of more than fifty local spiritual assemblies established throughout the peninsula. Each local assembly is run by nine elected members in an assigned district and is to a certain extent independent of other local assemblies.

Taoism is probably the least organized religion on the peninsula, although it has the largest number of Chinese adherents. In the 1980 census, 13 percent of the population was identified as Confucianist, presumably taken to mean practitioners of rituals and beliefs derived from a combination of Buddhist, Taoist, and various traditional Chinese philosophies. In other words, few Chinese are exclusively Confucianists, Buddhists, or Taoists. For purposes of convenience, we use the word "Taoism" to describe this complex of Chinese religious beliefs. Despite Buddhist influences on Taoism, it is possible to distinguish between Buddhist and Taoist temples. The former tends to have only Buddha images, especially in Theravada temples. On the other hand, there is a large spectrum of Mahayana temples ranging from those with Buddha and bodhisattva images to those with a mixture of Buddha, bodhisattva, and Taoist images. But in the Taoist temples, the main deities are largely those of traditional Chinese origins. Generally, most Taoist temples are managed by a committee of worshippers, while a resident spirit-medium attends to the needs of the supplicants. No national-level Taoist temple or organization exists in Malaysia today. Each temple is an independent body but may have some ties with other temples. Because the spirit-medium is the thaumaturgical focus in most Taoist temples, it is sometimes difficult to impose strict distinctions between spirit-medium cults and Taoist practices. The borderland between these two religious practices will be discussed further in the next section and in chapter 5.

Competing Religious Alternatives

None of the religions described so far are indigenous to the Malay Peninsula, although some are the traditional religions of immigrant groups. The peninsula has always been, in a sense, a religious marketplace that offers a wide range of alternative beliefs, with the ascendancy of one religion being dependent on the changing political forms in the region. This process was discussed in the previous chapter, but what needs to be emphasized here is the lack of an enduring primary religion on the peninsula. This differs from a politically dominant religion where a government legitimates its claim to rule through the selection of particular religious symbols. Historically, it is rare to find members of any one society adhering to a fixed, immutable set of religious beliefs, because religious change is a constant rather than a variable. But such change has been amplified on the peninsula by the multiple intercultural contacts that have occurred over the ages. The result is that all religions on the peninsula are rapidly evolving systems open to foreign influences and indigenous innovations. We argue that a politically dominant religion, such as Islam in contemporary Malaysia, does not necessarily constitute an established primary religion that provides a fundamental model of the sacred. Although Islam is constitutionally the official religion of Malaysia, it is also in many respects an ethnic religion that is specifically crucial to the maintenance of Malay identity. The other religions also have relatively strong ethnic affiliations, except for Christianity, Baha'i, and Theravada Buddhism, which are less exclusively ethnic in character. Thus, ethnicity may be seen as a confounding factor in the Malaysian religious system, for it contributes to the plural nature of religious expression on the peninsula. Furthermore, the lack of a unified tradition in many of these religions seriously inhibits the formation of an ecclesiastical authority that wields considerable power in centralizing religious beliefs and practices.

Given the complex diversity of religious systems on the peninsula, it is difficult, if not impossible, to apply the church-sect typology[27] to the Malaysian situation. At best, we can speak of the degree of tension experienced by groups within a religious tradition or of tensions between different religious traditions (Glock and Stark 1965). Even then, not all groups within a religious tradition are necessarily in tension. Consider, for example, Hinduism and Taoism, which can be described as loose collections of mutually tolerant cults[28] rather than coherent religions. These cults usually involve the worship of a constellation of deities. In some Hindu and Taoist temples, these deities are believed to manifest themselves through the trance performances of resident spirit mediums. Spirit-medium cults are therefore an intrinsic aspect of these two religious systems. Exclusive membership is generally not a characteristic of these popular cults; there is relatively free movement of worshippers between cults within each system. This suggests that if there are tensions between cults in the Hindu or Taoist system, they are not similar to the sectarian tensions envisaged by W. S. Bainbridge and R. Stark (1980). Tensions within the cultic milieu in the Hindu or Taoist tradition may result from competition for membership, personal antagonisms, and so on, but they do not necessarily represent a break or separation from the larger religious system.

The amorphous organization of worship peculiar to Hinduism and Taoism is not readily found in Christianity, Islam, Theravada Buddhism, Sikhism, and the Baha'i faith. Since the latter religions are not polytheistic in orientation, like Hinduism and Taoism, they are less likely to develop into structures of individualized cultic worship. One exception, however, is Catholicism, which condones special devotion to saints although not all the saints assume a deified status similar to that of gods and goddesses in the Hindu or Taoist pantheon. Tensions generated within the tighter structures of religions such as Christianity and Islam are more likely to result in sect formation. This is because monotheistic religions tend to be more exclusivist than the polytheistic traditions and are therefore limited in providing within the system cultic alternatives to the religiously dissatisfied. Even this pattern is now changing. There is evidence to suggest that multiple religious membership can dampen the sectarianization process. Simultaneous participation in several groups within and across religious systems is not an uncommon phenomenon in Malaysia where there is little centralized control over non-Muslim religious activities. For example, the neo-Pentecostal Movement (or the Charismatic Renewal) in Malaysia attracts members from all Christian denominations, yet it cannot be treated as a sect because it is not a schismatic Christian movement. Many Christians who are involved in the Charismatic Renewal are also members of their respective churches. Similarly, many Islamic revivalist movements in Malaysia do not fit neatly into the church-sect framework. Few such movements have openly declared a break with the dominant Islamic organizations and some maintain an open-door policy to Muslim outsiders (mainly Malays) who may not totally reject their connections with other Islamic bodies. These new religious phenomena may at best be categorized as cultic movements or alternatives that lack elaborate organizational structures and are sustained by the enthusiastic participation of their followers. Although these cultic movements are not explicitly schismatic, their status is highly vulnerable to the vicissitudes of the parent systems, unlike the Hindu and Taoist cults whose existence is generally taken for granted within their respective systems. The precarious character of Christian and Islamic cultic movements will be discussed at length later.

In view of the difficulties in applying the Eurocentric, church-sect typology to the Malaysian situation, we suggest two broader and less unwieldy concepts—formal religious organizations and competing religious alternatives—in organizing our observations of religious phenomena on the peninsula. There are at least two reasons for using these concepts. First, they do not imply the existence of a primary religion from which all religious deviations are evaluated. There is, rather, inordinate flexibility between the two concepts: a formal religious organization can also be treated as a religious alternative. These concepts therefore provide a sense of perpetual mobility between religious systems on the peninsula, a situation that has been generated and sustained by continuous intercultural contacts over the centuries. Second, the word "alternatives" allows us to avoid the value-loaded terms—church, sect, and cult—that connote conventionality and deviance. In circumventing this problem by a more neutral choice of words, we are able somewhat objectively to compare competing religious groups without having to make irrelevant distinctions regarding their status on the church-sect-cult continuum. This approach also gives us much latitude in making comparisons across religious systems. A cult in a polytheistic religion is merely treated as an alternative to various establishments in the monotheistic traditions. Obviously, such broad concepts have their own set of problems, particularly the problem of progressive explanation. We cannot use them to explain the processes of religious transformation, although we could describe the natural history of each religious group separately. These concepts, however, are empirically useful to the extent that we emphasize the fluidity of religious phenomena in contemporary Malaysia.

Formal religious organizations in our conceptual scheme can be conveniently defined as legitimate bodies endorsed by the Malaysian government through registration under various legal statutes.[29] Thus most of the religious organizations outlined in the preceding section are included within this definition. All formal religious organizations are required to submit regular financial and other documents to the government. In short, an open declaration of their activities and resources is a prerequisite to maintaining legitimacy. In adopting a legal approach to formal religious organizations, we avoid the problem of conventionality and deviance since contending groups within the same religious tradition or between different traditions are similarly recognized by an outside secular body. Competing religious alternatives is a much broader concept and embraces two levels of meaning. It can be taken to mean formal religious organizations to indicate the variety of choices that individuals can make among legitimate religious groups. On another level, it can mean cultic alternatives or innovative religious groups that have yet to attain formal recognition from the government. These alternatives may include imported religious groups that have become popular in other countries or homegrown innovations that are striving for recognition and expansion. Cultic alternatives become formal religious organizations when their applications for legal status are approved by the government. In assessing such applications, the government sometimes consults various established religious bodies, implying that the latter may have indirect influence in the legitimation process.

By using these concepts, we can identify three levels of religious competition in contemporary Malaysia: (1) among organizational alternatives; (2) among cultic alternatives; and (3) between organizational and cultic alternatives. While these conceptual categories suggest the continuous movement of individuals among alternatives within and between various religious traditions, in actuality the scope of religious experimentation is limited by the ethnic factor. Since all Malays are Muslims by birth, they are restricted to alternatives within the Islamic tradition. Aside from participating in recognized Islamic organizations, Muslims have the choice of joining various *tarekat* or revivalist movements. This choice, however, has become circumscribed as a result of recent government campaigns against Islamic cultic alternatives. Although Malays are legally prohibited from joining non-Muslim religious alternatives, some have nevertheless shown passing interest in them or even obtained covert assistance from non-

Muslim thaumaturgists without ostensibly committing apostasy.[30] Non-Malays, on the other hand, have greater freedom in trafficking between a large variety of religious alternatives since they are not subjected to legal restrictions similar to those affecting the Malays. Even then, difficulties in converting to Islam are experienced by non-Malays who are not Muslims by birth, because they face ostracism from their families and respective communities, or because they are not easily accepted into exclusivist Islamic organizations and movements (see Nagata 1978). There is a greater tendency for non-Malays to experiment with non-Islamic alternatives. In recent years, many Chinese have turned to various Hindu and Christian alternatives, while many Indians have converted to Christianity and some have begun exploring various Taoist and Hindu alternatives. The Baha'i faith has also increased its missionary activities among the Chinese, Indians, and some aboriginal groups. Multiple participation in several non-Islamic alternatives is a growing trend among the more adventurous non-Malay seekers.[31] The gradual erosion of religious boundaries among the non-Malays forms a strong contrast to the relatively encapsulated religious activities of the Malays. These differences in religious experimentation reinforce ethnic patterns in religious participation and therefore continue to perpetuate the gulf between Muslim and non-Muslim affairs, a problem that we will elaborate in the following section.

Islamic Activism and the Non-Muslim Response

The apparent polarization between the Muslims and non-Muslims masks many crucial developments within the Malay-Muslim community that need to be examined before the wider religious tensions can be fully understood. The continuing struggle between UMNO and PAS for Malay political supremacy, as well as the spread of international Islamic fundamentalism, are two important sources of religious activism that have affected the development of Malay identity in the 1970s.

Since independence in 1957, PAS has become increasingly critical of UMNO on the question of the Islamic state. While UMNO supports Islam as the state religion, it has always been adamantly secular in its outlook. The model of statecraft adopted by UMNO leaders is undoubtedly influenced by modern Western secularism, yet UMNO has to maintain an edge over PAS in Islamic matters to compete for the support of the Malay masses. Since its formation, PAS has vowed to strive toward the realization of an Islamic state. Its program of action in reaching this goal, however, has not been too explicit, particularly on the relationship between Islam and the political structure of the state (Funston 1980:148). Despite this, PAS had managed to entrench itself as the state government of Kelantan in northeastern Malaysia for nearly twenty years until its ouster by UMNO in 1977. Kessler (1978) has argued convincingly that the long-standing popularity of PAS among the Malay peasantry in Kelantan mirrors a recurring division in Malay society where the interests of a Westernized aristocratic elite, represented by UMNO, are pitted against those of the rural masses. In other words, class tensions in Malay society readily find expression in the contest of Islamic ideologies.

In this contest, the strategy of one-upmanship is employed by both sides to demonstrate their religious concern and fervor. Each party attempts to outdo the other by projecting a more puritanical image of itself. PAS has publicly announced its opposition to the importation of various cultural forms from the "decadent West," such as dancing, gambling, the consumption of alcohol, wild parties, sexual exhibitionism, and so on. UMNO leaders, on the other hand, have not only spoken out on the alleged moral decline in the West, but also have made apparent moves to control moral behavior by legal means, such as attempts to introduce a morals law applicable to Muslims and non-Muslims alike,[32] and a law to ban Muslims from entering or working in Malaysia's only casino. In terms of actual power, however, UMNO has the upper hand in implementing Islamic policies because it has more political and financial resources at its disposal than does PAS. As pointed out earlier, Islamic bureaucracy at the national level has been expanding since independence, but particularly after the establishment of the Federal Territory, with the effect of increased Islamic activities sponsored by the UMNO-dominated government. Furthermore, the teaching of Islam is limited only to those who have obtained official certification *(tauliah)* from the State Religious Department. Similarly, the Friday sermons *(khutbah)* are prepared by the State Religious Department and delivered by recognized mosque officials. Despite the tight control the federal and state governments have over Islamic activities, there is still much anxiety over the ability of PAS to influence the Muslim public with its rhetoric. Hence, UMNO and its supporters are prepared to accelerate Islamic activities to prevent PAS from overshadowing them at the public level.

The rise of Islamic fundamentalism in recent years has posed additional challenges to the image of UMNO as the chief guardian of Muslim morals. The formation of Islamic movements that seek to redress moral and other grievances is not an unusual phenomenon in Malaysia's history, as was noted in the previous chapter. The current wave of Islamic reformism, popularly known as the *dakwah*[33] movement, differs from the earlier movements in its public style and political orientation. Inspired by the Iranian Revolution and other developments in the Middle East, and with the renewed influence of Muslim missionaries from the Indian subcontinent, the *dakwah* movement has become the most visible and publicized form of religious assertion in contemporary Malaysia. The common sight of many Muslims dressed in an ostentatious Arabic style—turbans and long flowing robes for men and full- or semi-*purdah* (veils) for women—and their uniform rejection of Western materialism tend to give the impression that *dakwah* is a unified movement. On the contrary, a closer examination of the movement reveals that it actually comprises several independent groups that have limited political commitments and are somewhat inward-looking in their religious orientation. The largest of these groups is ABIM (*Angkatan Belia Islam Malaysia,* or the Muslim Youth Movement of Malaysia) which claims a membership of nearly 35,000 throughout the country. ABIM has been most vociferous in propagating the ideal of *Shari'ah* law and other aspects of Islamic culture, but like many of its urban counterparts it has yet to resolve its ambivalences toward Western secularism. These contradictory attitudes are vividly brought into relief in ABIM's concern for the importance of secular education—a concern that has resulted in its establishment of several schools whose programs are oriented toward the national examination system.[34] Similarly, *Darul Arqam,* an Islamic fundamentalist commune located on the outskirts of Kuala Lumpur, pursues the ideal of economic self-sufficiency with much vigor but has not totally rejected the use of modern Western technology.

Most researchers who have written on the *dakwah* movement would agree that these ambivalences reflect the Malays' uneasiness with the West, the appeal of which continues to exercise a certain influence on their search for a more satisfying identity, especially among the recently urbanized Malay youth. Others may argue that these ambivalences suggest the secondary importance of Westernization as an issue but principally provide a concealed means of articulating popular protest against the postcolonial state. Nevertheless, these ambivalences nurtured within an Islamic milieu find expression in a separate stream of moral entrepreneurship that is somewhat at odds with government religious policies. Like PAS, many *dakwah* members are openly critical of the declining piety of a secular government and stress the need for the Islamization of the whole society. Since the larger *dakwah* organizations are registered bodies, the only legitimate recourse the government has in countering their claims is to launch its own *dakwah* activities. On the other hand, the government has intensified its campaign to label smaller, unregistered *dakwah* groups as deviant and heretical in an effort to control their influences. The recent violence perpetrated by a band of Muslim fundamentalists in Batu Pahat has provided the government with a legitimate reason to increase its vigilance over the *dakwah* movement.[35] Although the government has the power to withhold legal recognition from any religious group, it has until now not instituted laws to prosecute hostile religious groups. The increased threat from PAS and the *dakwah* movement, however, has induced the government to seek more stringent measures to reinforce its legal authority in religious matters. In early 1983, new amendments to the penal and criminal codes were passed by the Malaysian Parliament that bestowed wider powers on the government in controlling religious dissent (Das 1983). These amendments were obviously legislated to curb Islamic activities that are antagonistic to the interests of the state, but non-Muslims are equally affected by these changes since they were made within the context of the civil law.

Non-Muslim concern over the effect of these legal amendments on their religious freedom was further aroused when all state governments agreed at a Chief Ministers' Conference in early 1983 to institute controls over the apparently indiscriminate building of shrines and temples.[36] There is already much resentment among non-Muslims that the allocation of land for churches and temples has been declining in recent years. The proposal to regulate non-Muslim places of worship is likely to exacerbate tensions between Muslims and non-Muslims. The spillover of tensions within the Muslim community into the non-Muslim community was seen in 1978, when a spate of Hindu temple desecrations initiated by a group of Muslim fundamentalists ended in violence.[37] This event alerted many non-Muslims to the likelihood of increasing Muslim encroachments on non-Muslim territories. Suspicions among the non-Muslims of *dakwah* activities are now extended to the government whose attempts at religious control are treated as part of an undifferentiated trend of Islamic activism. Whether non-Muslims are aware of the schisms within the Muslim community is no longer an important issue, because they have now developed a heightened sensitivity to the defense of their religious rights. A logical outcome of this incipient wariness is the growing urgency to establish alliances across the non-Muslim religions. The preparation by the heads of various non-Muslim religions to build a common front in response to perceived Islamic challenges suggests the possible emergence of a pressure group to guard non-Muslim religious interests. In other words, an unforeseen consequence of intra-Muslim rivalries has been the mobilization of non-Muslims despite the wide differences between them. To what extent this non-Muslim alliance of convenience will become politicized depends on the future religious policies of the government and the developments within Malaysian Islam.

The arousal of non-Muslim sentiments may be treated as an aspect of the larger problem of ethnic identity formation in Malaysia. Since religious differences in Malaysia coincide with ethnic distinctions, it can be surmised that the religious mobilization of non-Muslims represents another form of ethnic alignment. Historically, the conflict between the Malays and non-Malays has always revolved around political and economic issues. Although these issues continue to structure ethnic relations in Malaysia, their saliency has been somewhat reduced since 1969 when the Malay political establishment withstood serious challenges from the non-Malays and remained unshaken.[38] Instead, the government turned the 1969 race riots into a reason for adopting a hard-line policy in advancing Malay economic interests. Non-Malays were further deterred from openly using the question of Malay privileges as an ethnic issue by the enactment of sedition laws. The government strategy of expanding its coalition base in 1974 to include several non-Malay opposition parties was employed primarily to contain ethnic mobilization hostile to Malay interests. These political developments of the 1970s have severely limited the opportunities of overt non-Malay dissent. The expression of non-Malay ethnicity via political symbols has become too much of a liability for any lasting public effect. However, the political constraints imposed by the government have until recently left relatively unhindered the development of ethnic sentiments within the non-Muslim religions. The Islamic ferment of the 1970s also has been partly instrumental in widening the scope for ethnic mobilization within the non-Muslim religions. In short, the political and religious events of the last decade have ineluctably channelled the direction of non-Malay ethnic expression into the religious arena. We do not imply that at this time there is a conscious effort by the non-Malays to promote actively their ethnic interests behind religious banners. Rather, we suggest that many non-Malays have retreated into various religious activities as convenient alternatives for ethnic expression. The structure of some of these alternatives and the complexities of ethnic expression within them will be analyzed in the following three chapters.

CHAPTER THREE

The New Pentecost: Crisis and Renewal in the Charismatic Movement

THE adoption of the charismatic movement, an American religious innovation, by Malaysian Christians expresses the dialectic between reactions to secularization and Islamization. This chapter is concerned with the transformation of an imported religious movement within a social milieu strikingly different from that where the movement originated. The neo-Pentecostal, or Charismatic Renewal, movement initially emerged in response to conditions prevailing in American society in the late nineteenth and early twentieth centuries. Shortly thereafter, the movement was exported with remarkable success to diverse types of societies where it became a vehicle of particular local needs and aspirations. For Malaysian Christians, the meaning of participation in the Charismatic Renewal has been shaped by Malaysia's attempts to attain a Western standard of living through rapid urban and industrial development, concurrent with a program of accelerated Islamization.

Charismatic Christians seek to affirm the relevance of religious definitions of reality within secular society. At the same time, they respond with a sense of crisis to postindependence political changes affecting the status and prerogatives of non-Muslim religions. The reaction of the Charismatic Renewal to secularization and Islamization will be examined in this chapter in relation to the local situation in which Malaysian Christians find themselves increasingly excluded from the public domain. The Christian community is uncomfortably aware of itself as a marginal minority in the Muslim-dominated Malaysian society. The difficulties of consolidation and expansion within what Christians regard as a hostile political environment engender apprehensiveness toward the future. Christians view their unsatisfactory situation from an ethnic perspective. Although Christianity is not an ethnic identifier—except in the case of the Eurasians—it is politically classified as a non-Malay religion. The Christians, who include Chinese, Indians, and Eurasians, perceive themselves collectively as non-Malays deprived of political power and prestige. Through the charismatic movement, a new sense of Christian and non-Malay identity is emerging.

Christianity in Postindependence Malaysia

The indigenization of Christianity began during the Japanese occupation of Malaya and gained momentum as preparations for independence proceeded in the wake of World War II. Earlier, Christian institutions on the peninsula were financed and controlled by foreign missionaries who demonstrated little commitment to training an Asian clergy. In anticipation of their eventual departure after independence, the foreign missionaries exerted more serious efforts to train local Christians for church leadership positions in the postwar period. The churches nevertheless faced a severe lack of indigenous personnel as the colonial era drew to a close in 1957. At the same time, relentless political pressures for indigenization of all spheres of social life, including Christian organizations, continued. Attainment of independence was followed by the imposition of strict conditions on issuing visas to foreign missionaries. Limited numbers of foreign religious personnel were granted visas, and they were issued with the understanding that the sponsoring Christian organization would train local citizens to fill the positions upon the expiration of the visas held by the foreign missionaries.

During the years following independence, the shortage of trained local clergy persisted as a problem for the churches. Even today, local seminaries established in response to the need for indigenous Christian leadership are not yet able to provide sufficient numbers of trained staff for the churches. This situation compels church leaders to request special permission from the government to recruit more missionaries from abroad and to extend the visas of those presently serving in the country. The immigration authorities usually review these requests on a case-by-case basis—when sufficiently strong justification is demonstrated, the request may be granted.

With the passing of the colonial era, Christian organizations and activities became subject to greater governmental regulation. This change particularly affected Christian educational institutions. Soon after independence, the mission schools were absorbed into the government educational system. In effect, the mission schools continued to exist in name only, as the Christian organizations lost administrative control and previously compulsory religious subjects in the curriculum at first were made optional, then were eliminated altogether. The now entirely secularized schools no longer afforded opportunities for evangelism or indirect transmission of Christian values. Loss of influence in education dramatically reduced the prestige Christians enjoyed during the colonial period. Secularization of the mission schools signaled the marginal position Christianity would occupy in Malaysian society.

The steady advance of administrative obstacles inhibiting church expansion followed the decline of Christian influence in education. Restricted access to land for Christian churches and cemeteries is one instance of this trend. In the view of Christian leaders, recent urban development plans formulated at the federal and state levels allocate inadequate amounts of land for Christian needs. The land issue, regarded as a serious threat to the survival and growth of Christianity in Malaysia, has drawn Roman Catholics and the larger Protestant denominations together into an informal cooperative relationship.

The postindependence acceleration of Islamization has aroused much apprehension among Catholics and Protestants. Islam's predominance in the public domain is reflected in generous allocations of prime urban land for the construction of mosques; regular interruption of radio and television programs for Quran readings and prayers; and extensive newspaper coverage of Islamic activities and affairs. Furthermore, Islamic studies are incorporated into the curriculum of government schools and all Muslim students are required to study Islam as a regular academic subject. Non-Muslim religious instruction is not included in the school curriculum and can be held only outside school hours. Propagation of Islamic values is now government policy. In accordance with this policy, the government sponsors annual televised Quran reading contests during the Muslim fasting month.

The government has also reaffirmed legal recognition of non-Muslim religious freedom in the context of its Islamization policy; nevertheless, Christians feel pressured to conduct their activities circumspectly.

The perceptions of the current religious crisis held by peninsular Malaysian Christians reflect the anxieties of middle-class, non-Muslim urbanites. The significance of this group can be seen in examining the distribution of Christians by ethnic group and region. The 1980 census revealed that Christians constitute 7 percent of the population of Malaysia as a whole. On the peninsula, however, Christians are only 2 percent, while in the Borneo states of Sarawak and Sabah they are 29 percent and 27 percent of the population, respectively.[1] The membership of peninsular Christian churches is concentrated in urban areas, especially in the largest west-coast cities.[2] The Christian population is largely middle-class, and overwhelmingly of Chinese or Indian origin. Slightly more than 51 percent of the Christian population is Chinese and about 35 percent is Indian.[3]

The postindependence developments described heretofore have provoked defensive reactions among the Christian community. Church leaders have come to view Christian unity as an urgent necessity in light of Christianity's progressive marginalization since independence. The leaders of the Council of Churches of Malaysia (CCM), an ecumenical organization comprising nine denominations,[4] and the Roman Catholic hierarchy have aspired to form a broad-based umbrella organization to enable Christians to take a unified public stand on national issues affecting non-Muslims. The proposed umbrella organization would not only bring Roman Catholics and Protestants together but also non-Christian groups such as the Hindus and Buddhists. At the same time, the CCM has attempted to serve as an organizational basis for greater unity among Christians. The CCM's overtures to other Christian groups have, however, met with resistance. The CCM is affiliated with the World Council of Churches (WCC), a liberal ecumenical body dominated by doctrinally flexible Protestants,[5] and has attempted to enlist the membership of fundamentalist, evangelical, or Pentecostal churches. The Roman Catholic church has shied away from a formal affiliation with the CCM because of the latter's connection with the WCC.

The Roman Catholic church represents the mainstream of Christianity in peninsular Malaysia, where almost 80 percent of all Christians are Catholic. Among the Protestants, who account for 19.4 percent of Christians, the Methodists are the largest and most influential denomination. The Methodists include 42 percent of the Protestants, while the next largest denominations, the Anglicans and Seventh Day Adventists, represent 17.5 percent and 7 percent of the Protestants, respectively. Pentecostal denominations account for about 9 percent of the Protestants (Thomas 1978).

All the Christian groups standing outside the CCM nevertheless demonstrate genuine interest in developing an interreligious umbrella organization that would include the CCM yet maintain an identity separate from it. This interest was reflected in the positive response of non-CCM Christian groups toward two national Christian conferences sponsored by the CCM. In 1979, at the first of these conferences, 150 representatives of 42 churches (including Roman Catholics, evangelicals, and Pentecostals) attended, and in 1982 the second conference attracted 300 participants. The government's Islamization policy has made the various churches more willing to cooperate together; however, the growing assertiveness of Islam in Malaysia must be regarded as merely a catalyst rather than a cause of the local churches' ecumenical aspirations, as the international ecumenical movement has been in progress since the early twentieth century. In their antagonism toward the ecumenical movement under the auspices of the WCC, the evangelical and fundamentalist churches are attempting to form a National Evangelical Council as an alternative to the CCM, but are nevertheless willing to cooperate with the CCM to a limited extent. In 1985 cooperation between the CCM, Catholics, and evangelicals was formalized as the Christian Federation of Malaysia.

In addition to efforts to forge a degree of Christian unity on the national level and to cooperate with non-Christian religious leaders, new approaches to local-level Christian organization have been adopted. Christian solidarity and expansion are increasingly pursued in informal, private settings. The bureaucratic obstacles in constructing additional church buildings have encouraged Christians to gather in private homes. Catholic and Protestant cell groups meeting in private homes have proved highly effective in revitalizing existing church membership and evangelizing non-Christians. Along with the formation of cell groups, Christians are relying on lay leadership to a much greater extent. This flexible style of organization is less subject to government controls and provides a solution to the problem of the lack of trained clergy.

The forms of organization of the charismatic movement are also largely unaffected by the lack of access to land and the restrictions on visas for missionaries. Prayer meetings in private homes and lay leadership are features of charismatic organization that minimize the movement's need to deal with government officials. In the case of the Catholic charismatics, incorporation of the movement within the structure of the Catholic church eliminates the requirement of registration under the Societies Act, since the church is already a legally recognized body. Because the Catholic charismatic movement does not have a legal existence separate from the Catholic church, it enjoys invisibility.

Before the mid-1970s, the neo-Pentecostal—or charismatic—movement had only limited influence among Malaysian Christians, although denominational Pentecostalism was introduced as early as 1930. The largest Pentecostal denominations in Malaysia—the Pentecostal Church of Malaya, the Independent Pentecostal Church, and the Assemblies of God—founded between 1930 and 1952 together embraced a membership of four thousand by 1970 (Thomas 1978: 38). The Roman Catholics, Methodists, and Anglicans, who comprise the mainstream of the Christian community, had little or no contact with the Pentecostal denominations. The Christian mainstream was largely unaware of Pentecostal doctrines and forms of worship until the interdenominational charismatic movement reached Malaysia around 1975. Although participation in the charismatic movement cuts across all the divisions within the Christian community, the focus of this chapter is on Roman Catholic charismatics in view of the predominance of Catholics among Malaysian Christians.

Origins of the Charismatic Movement in the United States

The significance of the Catholic charismatic movement in Malaysia must first be understood in relation to its American origins. It is from the American Protestant tradition of revivalism that the Catholic Charismatic Renewal found its inspiration and models. This tradition has generated ecstatic, emotional sectarian movements in the United States since the early eighteenth century.[6] One of the most influential Protestant sectarian movements, Pentecostalism, emerged at the beginning of the twentieth century as an expansive and dynamic trend in

American Christianity. Pentecostalism seeks to revive the apostolic phase of Christianity through special emphasis on the third person of the Trinity, the Holy Spirit. The "outpouring of the Holy Spirit," manifested in the performance of miracles, distinguished apostolic from institutional Christianity. The early Christians "filled" with the Holy Spirit spoke in tongues, healed the sick, exorcised demons, prophesied, and beheld visions. Among these ecstatic behaviors, glossolalia,[7] or speaking in tongues, is given particular importance as the initial evidence of the Baptism of the Holy Spirit, the fundamental religious experience sought by Pentecostals. Although ecstasy has been a force throughout Christian history, Pentecostalism as an organized international movement is a twentieth-century phenomenon.[8]

Dissatisfaction with the traditional American Protestant churches in the early twentieth century was articulated through the rhetoric of a return to apostolic Christianity. The attempt to return to apostolic Christianity was expressed in a series of revival meetings beginning in Kansas in 1900, which spread to Missouri, Texas, and California by 1906. The Pentecostal movement emerged from the revival meetings of this period. Charles Parham, an itinerant lay Holiness preacher, and his Bible school students in Topeka, Kansas, convened camp meetings where performances of glossolalia and miraculous healings were featured as evidence of the power of the Holy Spirit (Williams and Waldvogel 1975:97–98). Widespread newspaper coverage of the ecstatic happenings at the revival meetings fanned public excitement, contributing to the incipient movement's propagation. The Azusa Street revival of 1906 in Los Angeles, California, was the most spectacular among the turn-of-the-century revival meetings. The publicity accompanying the Azusa Street gatherings attracted people from all over the United States and even inspired a few European evangelists to come to Los Angeles to observe the "new Pentecost." Fervent missionary activity followed in the wake of the Azusa Street revival as the participants believed they had been empowered by the Baptism of the Holy Spirit for evangelism and Christian service. After dispersing from Azusa Street to preach the "full gospel" at home and abroad, the missionaries rapidly formed Pentecostal churches in several major American, Canadian, and European cities (Nichol 1966:34–35).

Although Pentecostalism became an international movement almost immediately and took root in diverse settings, its origins in the United States are intimately related to the process of secularization.

The Pentecostal movement offered a solution to the crisis of faith provoked by challenges to the literal truth of the Bible as the prestige of natural science rose in the late nineteenth and early twentieth centuries. In the attempt to deal with discrepancies between the Bible and scientific discoveries, liberal theologians adopted a critical historical approach to the Bible and abandoned any insistence on the literal truth of the scriptures. The development of secularized theology profoundly disturbed many Christians. The Pentecostal claim to having found the proof of scriptural truth in the experience of Spirit Baptism as evidenced by glossolalia was deeply convincing to many who had begun to doubt the basis of their faith in Christian teachings. Pentecostalism focused on leading Christians to individual ecstatic experience culminating in euphoria that imparted a sense of certainty and power. An experiential as opposed to a formal theological approach to the crisis of faith proved impressive to large numbers of Christians (Bloch-Hoell 1964:11-12).

The initial phase of the Pentecostal movement was distinctively lower-class in character, appealing to European immigrants and economically depressed, uneducated, native-born Americans, both black and white.[9] Pentecostalism also attracted women, who in large numbers participated in the movement as evangelists as well as followers. The decentralized, individualistic nature of authority in the movement minimized institutional barriers to women assuming leadership roles. Pentecostalism rapidly evolved into a more middle-class-oriented movement. Some of the Pentecostal congregations stabilized, became wealthier, and began to take on features of respectable Protestant denominations—impressive church buildings, an educated ministry, and less emotional worship styles. The "left wing" of the movement reacted against these "worldly" tendencies with an uncompromising sectarian stance, while the "right wing" moved toward cooperation with the mainstream evangelical and fundamentalist denominations (Nichol 1966). The revival campaign in more sophisticated and middle-class style continued to be the major vehicle of Pentecostal evangelism. At present, well-publicized mass meetings are held in expensive hotels and feature traveling evangelists who direct their message to an affluent audience. Such updated revival campaigns are no less effective in drawing large crowds than the late nineteenth- and early twentieth-century camp meetings.

The Pentecostal movement includes a broad spectrum of groups whose organizational forms range from isolationist, sectarian, and decentralized congregations with a local or at most regional membership to large denominations with elaborate ecclesiastical machinery, educational institutions, and an international membership.[10] Revival ministries, independent of any Pentecostal sect or denomination, are particularly important organizational forms. The nonchurch-based revival ministries continuously launch mass campaigns worldwide, generating and sustaining the movement's evangelistic zeal. One of the best-known evangelists associated with this form of Pentecostal organization is Oral Roberts of Tulsa, Oklahoma. The Healing Wings Revival Ministry, founded by Roberts in the early 1950s, has pioneered radio and television evangelism and adopted the use of audiovisual media in conducting mass meetings that have attracted as many as eighteen thousand people (Nichol 1966:223).

No less influential in spreading the Pentecostal message is another revival organization founded by Oral Roberts. In 1951, Roberts, together with a wealthy California dairyman, Demos Shakarian,[11] created the Full Gospel Businessmen's Fellowship International (FGBMFI) to introduce Pentecostalism to businessmen and professionals who are generally members of mainline Protestant denominations. To approach the new Pentecostal constituency, FGBMFI conducts banquet meetings at well-known hotels (Nichol 1966:242). FGBMFI's dinner meetings throughout the United States and overseas, where laymen evangelize other laymen by testifying about their personal experiences with the Baptism of the Holy Spirit, reached a class of people previously unreceptive to Pentecostalism. The success of Roberts and Shakarian in drawing middle- and upper-class businessmen and professionals into the Pentecostal experience has contributed significantly to the emergence of neo-Pentecostalism; that is, the spread of Pentecostalism into the mainline Christian churches, both Roman Catholic and Protestant. The activities of FGBMFI have transformed Pentecostalism from a stigmatized lower-class religious expression into a respectable, middle-class movement.[12]

The neo-Pentecostal message reached Roman Catholics through several influential Pentecostal publications, most notably David Wilkerson's *The Cross and the Switchblade* and John Sherrill's *They Speak with Other Tongues*. These books were introduced to Catholic laymen attending the 1966 National Cursillo Convention (Gromacki 1967:153–154).[13] Members of the Cursillo movement became interested in learning more about the Pentecostal experience. Four Catholic laymen on the staff of Duquesne University, who were active in the Cursillo movement, pursued their interest in Pentecostalism by joining a Pentecostal prayer group held at the home of an Anglican layman. The four Catholic academics reported receiving the Baptism of the Holy Spirit accompanied by glossolalia after attending several of the home prayer meetings. Not long after their initiation into Pentecostalism, the academics led a weekend spiritual retreat in 1967 for a group of university students. Under their direction, the students were baptized in the Holy Spirit and spoke in tongues. This retreat, known as the Duquesne Weekend, served as a model for other Catholics attracted to Pentecostalism. The Duquesne Weekend was soon followed by the Michigan State Weekend, a spiritual retreat organized by University of Notre Dame lay staff members for students and staff at Michigan State and Notre Dame universities (Gromacki 1967:153–154).

The two university-based weekend retreats launched the Catholic Charismatic Renewal (CCR). CCR prayer groups rapidly formed throughout the United States in the wake of extensive mass media coverage of the Michigan State Weekend. CCR participants stress interpersonal sharing of feelings and experiences within a face-to-face group, as well as development of a sense of community. The new movement seeks a personalization of traditional Catholic belief and practice, as well as miracles and gifts of the Holy Spirit. Expressive and improvised styles of worship are encouraged.

The new lay movement also attracted the participation of nuns and priests, although the reaction of the Roman Catholic hierarchy toward the CCR has been ambivalent. Some bishops endorsed the movement while others discouraged or barely tolerated it. The obvious Protestant influence in the CCR aroused the suspicions of bishops unfriendly to the movement (Fichter 1975). Although a lay-controlled movement, the CCR not only welcomes clerical participation but also eagerly seeks endorsement from the church hierarchy, while not wishing to be controlled by it.

Despite the Protestant Pentecostal influence on the CCR, it nevertheless operates within the structure of the Roman Catholic church and is not a schismatic or separatist group. The movement promotes the Pentecostal experience as a means of renewing and strengthening the sacramental life of the church. Participants in the movement testify that they have become more involved with the sacraments and devotional practices of the church since receiving the Baptism of the Holy Spirit. Insofar as the movement encourages participants to become better Catholics, as it claims to do, the church hierarchy regards it as commendable. The church hierarchy has found the theological basis of the CCR doctrinally sound and Pope Paul VI granted recognition to it (Fichter 1975:44–47).

The emergence of the CCR in the late 1960s reflected the responses of middle-class, well-educated Catholics to profound changes within the American Catholic community. The assimilation of Catholics into the mainstream American middle class, which became evident by the mid-1960s, generated new issues for the church. The American Catholic community had previously defined itself in terms of the immigrant experience of discrimination and exclusion from mainstream institutions. Catholics reacted to the Protestant majority's hostility by forming a distinctive Catholic subculture and ethnic ghettos. The new Catholic middle class' movement from city ghettos to the suburbs initiated the breakdown of the Catholic subculture. Religious discrimination became muted as secularization of American society intensified. Catholics found ready acceptance in middle-class, suburban society and mainstream institutions, and separate Catholic educational, health, recreational, publishing, and social welfare institutions became obsolete (Devine 1975:11, 39).

The Catholic church in America recognized in the 1960s that it had fulfilled its mission to Catholic immigrants and needed to find a new direction. At the same time, the church as a whole was engaged in the self-conscious period of renewal set into motion by the Second Vatican Council (1962–1965). Following the reforms of the Second Vatican Council, many Catholic orders in America began to redefine their goals and identity. Many externals of Catholic worship that had symbolically differentiated Catholics from Protestants—abstention from meat on Fridays, obligatory fast days, and legalist approaches to sin and penance—were dropped for the purpose of encouraging a more mature, less parochial level of religious understanding and practice. These reforms bewildered the average layman, but did not go far enough to satisfy some of the sophisticated intellectual groups within the church. The aftermath of the Second Vatican Council was characterized by much infighting and dissension within the American Catholic community. The church no longer appeared to speak with one voice as various groups attempted to formulate a new version of Catholic identity within American society (Devine 1975:9).

The problem of identity was more acutely felt by middle-class Catholic intellectuals. No longer tied to ethnic ghettos or dependent upon the Catholic subculture to meet their social needs, the middle class sought a new basis of American Catholic identity. For these Catholics, the external markers separating Catholics from Protestants were no longer essential. However, the stripping away of many familiar Catholic devotional practices, particularly the implicit downgrading of the cult of the Virgin Mary, left a vacuum that the reforms of the Second Vatican Council did not concretely fill. Neo-Pentecostalism provided a new experiential approach to devotion and to the redefinition of Catholicism in America. The lay-initiated CCR took up several of the themes of the Second Vatican Council: a wider role for laymen in the church, a stronger biblical orientation, and a greater willingness to communicate with non-Catholic Christians.

These concerns of American Catholics, which find expression in the CCR, are also meaningful to the Catholic community in Malaysia, although for rather different reasons. The local significance of the CCR and the broad issues it addresses are examined next.

Urban Charismatic Organizations in Malaysia

The spread of the neo-Pentecostal movement among mainstream Protestants and Roman Catholics in Malaysia has taken place outside the organizational structures of the classical Pentecostal denominations. The Malaysian Christian community was introduced to the Charismatic Renewal through a series of well-publicized, interdenominational revival meetings held in first-class hotels in Kuala Lumpur and other major cities on the west coast of peninsular Malaysia. These charismatic revival meetings, which became frequent events in the mid-1970s, were conducted by visiting foreign evangelists, usually sponsored by the FGBMFI, the Assemblies of God, Oral Roberts' Abundant Life Center, and other American-based Pentecostal revivalist organizations. The Assemblies of God, although a classical Pentecostal denomination, has adopted an interdenominational approach modeled after that of the FGBMFI in promoting the Pentecostal experience within mainline Christian churches. The interdenominational revival meetings attracted large numbers of middle-class Catholics, Anglicans, Methodists, and members of other established Protestant denominations who demonstrated an interest in seeking Spirit Baptism. The performance of spiritual healings at the revival meetings also appealed to these Christians.

Roman Catholics felt little inhibition in attending the prayer meetings sponsored by Protestant charismatic organizations. They learned of the CCR during the same period Protestant charismatics became active in Malaysia; foreign clergy returning from home leave overseas and Malaysians traveling and living abroad were channels of information about the CCR. Malaysian Catholics were also influenced by Protestant charismatics and CCR literature.

Several leaders of the CCR in Kuala Lumpur and Petaling Jaya were involved with the movement before 1975. The CCR, however, did not become widespread among Malaysian Catholics until 1976 when the archbishop of Kuala Lumpur officially adopted a policy of encouraging more lay participation in church leadership, and also endorsed the CCR in this connection. The new policy regarding the role of the laity was initiated when the church hierarchy decided to convene a month-long Pastoral Renewal Conference in Penang in August 1976. All the priests in the country were requested to prepare the laity of their parishes to take over the running of the church for the duration of the Pastoral Renewal Conference. This unprecedented radical action on the part of the church hierarchy was intended to rouse the laity from its traditional passivity. Implementing the reforms of the Second Vatican Council and charting a new direction for the church in relation to the rapid changes in Malaysian society were the principal items on the agenda of the Pastoral Renewal Conference. Central to this agenda was a new emphasis on lay leadership at the grassroots level (Williams 1976:242).

The attempt to bring the local Catholic church into line with the reforms of the Second Vatican Council concerning lay participation coincided with the need for an effective response to the lack of ordained priests in Malaysia. The difficulties in providing sufficient local or missionary priests were seen as presenting the church with a crisis of survival. In view of this situation, the Pastoral Renewal Conference adopted an explicit policy toward the laity. Promising lay leaders, particularly among Catholic youth, were to be identified and given special guidance along with increased responsibility. The Catholic laity as a whole was to be mobilized through the development of dynamic lay leaders. Promotion of the CCR was intended to further the new lay-oriented policy. The Catholic hierarchy also looked to the CCR as a counterweight to the charismatic prayer meetings sponsored by Protestants, especially the Assemblies of God. It was well known that Catholics regularly attended the Sunday afternoon interdenominational prayer meetings that the Assemblies of God held at a large hotel in Kuala Lumpur. The Catholic clergy viewed this development with misgiving, as they suspected the Assemblies of God were surreptitiously proselytizing Catholics and other mainline Christians under the guise of holding interdenominational gatherings.[14] Concern over the activities of Protestant charismatics persisted through the years following the 1976 Pastoral Renewal Conference in Penang.[15] Seven years later, the archbishop of Kuala Lumpur publicly referred to undesirable Protestant influence on Catholics, expressing concern about Catholic youths who were being "led astray" by new Christian sects. He explicitly highlighted the function of the CCR "to counteract the effects of the new sects" and "to gather the lost sheep."[16]

Official support of the CCR was also encouraged by the recognition on the part of the Catholic clergy that Protestant charismatics and folk occultists were meeting the thaumaturgical needs of Catholics. Belief in spirit possession in Chinese, Indian, and Malay folk religious practices is widespread in Malaysia among Christians and non-Christians alike. It is not uncommon for Catholics to consult spirit mediums and other folk religious practitioners for supernatural assistance with a broad range of personal troubles.[17] The failure of the church to provide effective pragmatic assistance with such personal crises led Catholics to resort to occult folk practices condemned by the church. The CCR addresses the unmet thaumaturgical needs among Catholics in its attempt to institutionalize exorcism and spiritual healing within the framework of the Catholic church.

Appropriately enough, the CCR was first introduced to the Archdiocese of Kuala Lumpur by a French priest acknowledged by his superiors as having the gift of exorcism. Around 1975 this priest, a longtime resident in Malaysia, began holding charismatic prayer meetings on Friday evenings in a large Catholic church in Kuala Lumpur. His reputation as an exorcist and healer drew crowds of both Christians and non-Christians to the CCR meetings where petitioners were given spiritual treatment irrespective of their religious affiliations. The priest asserted the lay character of the movement in defining his role as merely advisory and appointing a service team of six married couples to take charge of the CCR group. He also trained a group of laymen to assist with exorcisms. Soon after the priest initiated the movement in Kuala Lumpur, CCR prayer groups were organized in private homes and on church premises in nearby Petaling Jaya. Some of the more enthusiastic members attempted to spread the CCR message to troubled youth in Petaling Jaya. This gradually became the work of a young exorcist of Chinese and Sri Lankan ancestry who had acquired his skills through close association with an American Protestant pastor active in the charismatic movement. This pastor had treated many Catholic cases of spirit possession, with the approval of Catholic priests active in the charismatic movement. Upon the encouragement of the archbishop and the French priest, the young exorcist took over the American pastor's role after the latter's departure and turned his "youth ministry" into a recruitment center for drug addicts, gangsters, and wayward youth who attributed their personal problems to spirit possession.

At the same time that the young exorcist was organizing CCR prayer groups with the help of his youth recruits, two other Catholic laymen also emerged as CCR activists. These were two Eurasian brothers, one of whom formed a large CCR prayer group that met regularly in a Catholic church in Petaling Jaya. The other brother, together with an Indian doctor from the Anglican church, organized an ecumenical charismatic prayer group known as the Christian Revival Society.[18] The group met weekly at the home of the Indian doctor in a fashionable area of Kuala Lumpur, with Roman Catholics comprising about one-quarter of the participants. In addition to the Christian Revival Society, the Indian doctor was involved in the Holiness Center, an Oral Roberts revival ministry established in Kuala Lumpur in 1978. The doctor and several of his colleagues formed a group of "spirit-filled doctors," organizing their medical practice around charismatic ideals. These doctors and several other professionals, all of whom were Protestants inspired by Oral Roberts' work, joined together to propagate the charismatic movement outside of the structures of the various churches to which they belonged. The lunch-hour prayer meetings held twice weekly at the Holiness Center, located near the Indian doctor's clinic, attracted Catholics, Protestants, and non-Christians. Oral Roberts' books and other charismatic literature were usually displayed for sale after the meetings ended. Although CCR activists participated informally in the Holiness Center meetings, the official leadership was entirely Protestant.

Most of the charismatic groups described above attract somewhat large, impersonal followings. There are, however, several smaller groups characterized by an exclusive membership based on specific social ties. One such example is the Hallelujah Fellowship, a tightly-knit group of ten white-collar employees from a large department in the government. Since 1977, the group has been meeting weekly during the lunch hour in the basement of a Catholic church in Petaling Jaya. The founder and leader of the group is a 35-year-old government clerk who has been involved in Catholic lay activities for more than a decade. Hallelujah Fellowship, similar to other charismatic groups, conducts its meetings in English—catering to people who have attained or aspire to attain middle-class status.

On the periphery of the charismatic movement is an innovative Catholic prayer community known as the Servants of the Cross. The official establishment of this community in 1982 was the outcome of lay Catholic experimentation since the mid-1970s. Servants of the Cross recruits its members through the Life in the Spirit Seminar, as does the CCR, but gives greater emphasis to the less-dramatic gifts of the Spirit, such as wisdom, knowledge, teaching, patience, and discernment. Servants of the Cross aims for gradual, long-term spiritual growth rather than enthusiastic performances of thaumaturgy. Members of Servants of the Cross meet in a Catholic church in Kuala Lumpur. The membership, which now numbers about one hundred, includes a core group concentrated in Petaling Jaya. The core group tends to interact frequently on an informal basis, and in this way shapes the movement's policies. Servants of the Cross is only one of many experimental Catholic evangelistic lay communities—known as Covenant Communities—throughout the world. These communities differ from the CCR in that they require greater commitment from their members. The model for these communities is derived from Acts of the Apostles in the New Testament, and is based on commitment expressed in terms of service, obedience to the group's leadership, tithing on a voluntary basis, counseling, evangelization, prayer, sharing, and brotherhood.

The diversity of urban charismatic organizations suggests that Malaysian Christians are no longer restricted to church-based activities but have the opportunity to participate in a wide range of lay-oriented alternatives. Indeed, the popularity of these organizations is attested by their multiple memberships and overlapping followings. Despite the increase in innovative options, there is a distinct difference between Catholic and Protestant charismatics in the accountability of their actions, a problem that we will examine next.

Authority Structures and Group Processes

Catholic charismatics differ from their Protestant counterparts in their relationship with the church hierarchy. Whereas Protestant charismatics tend to enjoy more autonomy from church authorities, the Catholics are relatively more constrained in their actions. Even then, Catholic charismatics continue to experiment with various CCR and interdenominational Protestant charismatic groups. CCR participants are not necessarily committed to any particular prayer group and often "shop around" comparing different groups. Under these circumstances, prayer groups sometimes compete among themselves to attract and retain a following. Mobility between alternative prayer groups results in fluctuating followings centered around particular personalities. The relative stability of the core leaders, however, maintains the CCR's structural continuity.

The larger CCR groups meet in churches and are controlled by parish-level service teams with priests as advisors. The parish service teams function within a hierarchy of state- and national-level service teams in accordance with the model of organization developed by the CCR in the United States. The parish-based CCR groups, unlike the groups meeting in private homes, are embedded within a well-defined structure of organization and authority. CCR groups under the jurisdiction of service teams in parishes in Kuala Lumpur and Petaling Jaya are supervised by the Selangor Catholic Charismatic Renewal (SCCR), the state-level service team. The SCCR oversees about thirty-five CCR groups throughout Selangor's parishes, and advises and instructs newly organized CCR groups in charismatic doctrines. While the service teams comprise mainly laymen, consultation with priests is actively sought and valued. Within the framework of the service teams, laymen exercise authority clearly delegated by the priests who act as advisors to the CCR groups.

In the case of CCR groups meeting in private homes, the legitimate delegation of clerical authority and the groups' relationship to the church can be ambiguous. These groups are more loosely structured because they are not under the direct supervision of a service team and a priest. Consequently, the lay leaders of home-based CCR groups have greater scope to experiment along lines not prescribed by the church. The lay leaders' individual personalities and interpretations of the movement are more prominent in the home-based CCR groups.

Problems of commitment, leadership, and innovation are often reflected in the rivalry between parish- and home-based CCR prayer groups, as in the case of the Praise and Glory Community and the Walk in the Spirit group in Petaling Jaya. The parish-based Praise and Glory Community (PGC), led by a Eurasian man in his forties, had been holding large, somewhat formally structured charismatic meetings on Friday evenings at a Catholic church for about a year, when another Eurasian man in his thirties, a reformed gangster who was trained as a CCR leader, moved into a house two doors away from the church. The younger man began to conduct small, intimate prayer meetings in his home, and the boisterous singing and guitar-playing at his meetings attracted some of the PGC members. During its first year, the home-based Walk in the Spirit (WITS) group recruited a following of 35 to 40 participants. The WITS's leader sought to project a unique identity for his group through an innovative program of group therapy, sharing his home and possessions with the members, and issuing T-shirts bearing the group's "tongues of fire" logo. He attempted to actualize his concept of Christian community-building in creating a personalized family environment within which intimate problems were freely shared and solved. The spontaneous, unstructured meetings made WITS seem more dynamic and inspiring than PGC's routinized formal prayer meetings held at the church. WITS envisioned itself as carrying out an active mission rather than merely offering a supplemental church service as appeared the case with PGC. Its leader's reputation as a healer and exorcist drew troubled persons and their families to WITS for relief from a broad spectrum of sufferings that included homosexuality, drug addiction, lack of direction in life, family conflicts, legal problems, sorcery, and spirit possession. WITS came to focus its activities around the resocialization of deviants within a respectable religious setting. Provision of therapy and a new way of life, as well as home visits to the sick, were the main features of the mission to which WITS had dedicated itself.

In operating autonomously from the church and refusing to defer to the authority of the leader of the PGC as the senior CCR member in the parish, WITS's actions provoked strong criticism among conservative Catholics in the parish. Members of the parish advised WITS members to slow down their activities. Dissension also developed within WITS itself over allegations that personal confidences revealed in the group had been violated. The group therapy fiasco and the possibility of his group's imminent disintegration eventually forced the leader of WITS to seek the support of PGC. The return of WITS to the fold of the parish-based CCR organizational structure was marked by four activities—resumption of regular attendance at the local CCR leaders' meetings, termination of group therapy sessions, regular attendance at Mass at the nearby Catholic church, and offers of voluntary services to the church. In its reabsorption into the larger CCR structure, WITS lost its unique identity but regained a semblance of stability in its operations. The WITS-PGC type of conflict is not uncommon within the CCR, and suggests the constant pressure on home-based prayer groups to conform to the church-directed leadership of the CCR.

Another experiment involving CCR lay leaders also provoked conflict. Several active CCR lay leaders were inspired by the potential of the charismatic movement for promoting Christian unity, and became interested in fostering closer cooperation with Protestant charismatics. Some CCR lay leaders joined the Christian Revival Society (CRS) charismatic meetings to support the ecumenical aspirations of the group. Between eighty to one hundred people—mostly Indians, Eurasians, and some Chinese—attended the weekly CRS meetings at the house of an Indian doctor. The emotional intensity and inspirational quality of these meetings impressed many participants. Dramatic personal testimonies bearing witness to miracles worked by the Holy Spirit in individual lives were the focus of CRS meetings. The host often had an implicit agenda prepared for the weekly gatherings: several interest-catching testimonies, as well as visits by itinerant charismatic evangelists from overseas, formed the main attractions of the evening. These arrangements effectively sustained the group's enthusiasm.

The greater degree of excitement and freedom to experiment with new styles of charismatic behavior offered by CRS strongly appealed to the CCR leaders who participated. Nevertheless, their ecumenical experiment with the Indian doctor and his colleagues terminated abruptly after seven months. Doctrinal differences between the Catholic and Protestant charismatic leaders became more pronounced over time. The Protestant charismatics accused the Catholics of worshipping Mary rather than the Holy Trinity. The CCR leaders claimed that the Catholic position on Marian devotion was unfairly exaggerated and that Protestants dogmatically viewed all Catholics as Mary worshippers.[19] The Protestants, in turn, were regarded as having self-righteous attitudes concerning salvation. At the time the Catholic charismatics severed their ties with CRS, the archbishop of Kuala Lumpur issued a directive to CCR leaders to withdraw from close interaction with Protestant charismatics. While CCR leaders complied with the archbishop's directive, the ordinary participants in the movement were under less pressure to do so. Some were unaware of the new policy while others chose to ignore it. Catholics thus continued to participate in Protestant charismatic groups unofficially and on an individual basis.

This case study illustrates the underlying tensions between Catholic and Protestant charismatics. The Catholic church hierarchy is suspicious of Protestant intentions, and, at present, merely gives lip service to Christian unity while actually discouraging close contacts between Catholic laymen and their Protestant counterparts. The withdrawal of the CCR leaders from ecumenical charismatic groups reflects their deference to church authority, and in this way their identity as Catholics as opposed to charismatics is emphasized. The "Catholicness" of the CCR is further reinforced by changes in the Life in the Spirit Seminar, its main channel of recruitment and initiation. The Seminar's former emphasis on a basic Christian message cutting across denominational lines has shifted to explicitly relating charismatic teachings to Roman Catholic doctrines, suggesting that the Catholic church is reluctant to relinquish control of charismatic ideology to the Protestants.

Charismatic Ideology

The ideology of the CCR is codified in the Life in the Spirit Seminar, a seven-week series of lectures and discussions that serve to recruit and initiate new participants to the movement. The Seminar, which is conducted by a team of laymen, originated from the collective efforts of members of the Word of God charismatic community in Ann Arbor, Michigan. To formalize instruction and recruitment into their community, the Word of God members prepared a manual that has been the basis of the Seminar since 1971. The manual provides CCR prayer groups throughout the United States and elsewhere in the world with a guide for evangelism and initiation. Initially, the basic Christian message, a summary of the essential points of New Testament teaching, comprised the content of the Seminar. Until 1980, the Seminar's presentation was ecumenical in its approach, emphasizing Christian consensus through the core teachings of the New Testament, without reference to the theological controversies. The presentation of the basic Christian message was directed toward Roman Catholics, Protestants, and non-Christians. In recent years, however, the Seminar has become unequivocally Roman Catholic in its orientation.

The Seminar offers instruction in Christian living as a response to what its originators saw as the growing tendency of the church toward secular humanism and the decreasing awareness of the Christian message in the aftermath of the Second Vatican Council.[20] In its rejection of secularism, the Seminar directs participants to return to original Christianity through adoption of the apostles' lifestyle as described in the New Testament. The Seminar gives greater attention to scriptural study than previously has been customary in Roman Catholic tradition. Knowledge of the scriptures, along with prayer, participation in the sacraments of the church, and Christian fellowship, are emphasized as the means of encouraging Christian living in a non-Christian, secular world. The Seminar proceeds from a consideration of the relationship between Christians and the secular world. The participants are urged to reflect on the condition of the contemporary world and are made aware that the ills of the world are beyond secular solutions and that much of what is wrong in the world must be attributed to demonic forces. Seminar participants are guided to renounce secular society through repentance, faith, and living in the life of the Spirit. To adopt the lifestyle of the apostles requires that one enter into a new relationship with Jesus by receiving the Holy Spirit and asking for charisms and strength to lead a new life, and then to join in a Christian prayer community with others who have committed their lives to Christ. The formation of apostolic prayer communities is the goal of the Life in the Spirit Seminar. The charisms of the Holy Spirit are bestowed as tools for building up "the body of Christ," that is, the church, while apostolic prayer communities of Spirit-baptized Christians revitalize and strengthen it.

In the eyes of the charismatics, the gift of the Holy Spirit is an overwhelming experience of God's saving power and forgiving love through surrender to Christ. Particular spiritual gifts, such as prophecies, healings, or speaking in tongues (glossolalia) must all be seen as secondary to the fundamental gift, the total surrender to Christ under the guidance of the Holy Spirit. The secondary gifts, however, are the means and opportunities of a continuing experience of the fundamental gift. Charismatics also believe that the gift of tongues is the doorway to the other gifts, as it arouses the faith required to receive and use them. Glossolalia is referred to in the Seminar as an act of surrender to God and an exemplary experience of faith. According to the charismatic interpretation of the New Testament, speaking in tongues is a phenomenon that includes, but is not restricted to, preaching God's word in a human language of which one has no previous knowledge. In charismatic doctrine, glossolalia can function as a sign, a message from God to the assembly, or an aid to prayer, depending on the particular circumstances in which it occurs.

The functions of sign and message are fulfilled in the public use of glossolalia. The gift serves as a sign when the strange sounds uttered are miraculously intelligible in and of themselves, without need for interpretation. The one for whom the sign is intended will understand the utterance since it is a genuine human language known to him. As a message, tongues are uttered aloud and interpreted. The person given the gift of interpretation will not understand the strange sounds spoken, but will be inspired by the Spirit to share in faith an insight or idea about the meaning of the message. When more than one person in a prayer group receives and shares a similar message, although expressed in different words, the gift is confirmed as authentic.

The private use of tongues, on the other hand, enhances the prayer life of the individual. Tongues is an aid to prayer that does not rely on concepts or discursive thought. This gift enables one to pray under any conditions. Distractions, fatigue, and work are no barrier to prayer, as the conscious, rational mind is transcended through tongues and only the faith experience of God remains. The charism of tongues is also used to praise God when one has exhausted all words and ideas. In the prayer of intercession when one does not know what to ask for or for whom to pray, the Spirit is ready to intercede through the utterance of inarticulate sounds. Praying in tongues, furthermore, is a means of tapping the power of faith to wage spiritual warfare against demonic forces.

The formal charismatic ideology imparted in the Life in the Spirit Seminar is often received and interpreted by Malaysian Catholic charismatics in terms of spirit possession and exorcism. For Malaysian Catholic charismatics, spiritual gifts not only symbolize union with divine forces, but also represent attainment of supernatural power to solve pressing problems of everyday life, such as sorcery, illness, unemployment, and family discord. This sense of personal power is expressed in the claims of CCR participants of having better control over every aspect of their lives since experiencing Spirit Baptism. The CCR itself is viewed by its Malaysian adherents as an instrument for solving immediate problems and for reducing future uncertainties. In other words, charismatic teachings constitute a practical religion that is more concerned with life at present than with life hereafter.

Protestant charismatics, like their Catholic counterparts, are preoccupied with the thaumaturgical implications of charismatic ideology. For both Protestants and Catholics, the movement's ideology offers a prestigious solution to the problem of sufferings attributed to malevolent supernatural forces. Charismatic ideology allows the diagnosis of spirit possession to be combined with, or distinguished from, secular categories of physical and mental illness, such that prayer and exorcism are regarded as complementary to medical treatment. Charismatic thaumaturgy addresses itself to the same situations as folk occultism, yet does so in the name of Christianity, and implicitly recognizes the relative validity of scientific knowledge in mental and physical healing. This approach to thaumaturgy is consistent with the aspirations of Malaysian Christians to a modern, Western lifestyle.

Catholic charismatic ideology places the practice of thaumaturgy clearly within the church's authority structure, while Protestants are not similarly constrained. The CCR teaches that only priests have the power and authority to exorcise demonic forces. Laymen are encouraged to assist priests in conducting exorcisms and may carry out what is known as "deliverances"—driving away evil spirits surrounding rather than possessing the sufferer. Protestant charismatics, on the other hand, require no clerical supervision or authorization in practicing spiritual healing and exorcism. These differences in ideology control run deep in the Charismatic Renewal and are important in understanding the future direction of the movement, a theme to be discussed in the next section.

The Impact of the Charismatic Movement on Malaysian Christianity

The charismatic movement is, paradoxically, a source of unity and dissension within the Malaysian Christian community. On one level of observation, the movement contributes to a sense of Christian identity that transcends lines of division between Catholics and Protestants and between the theologically liberal and conservative wings of Protestantism. The movement's success in promoting active and intense religious involvement on the part of laymen, and in evangelizing non-Christians, has infused the Christian community with a new vitality to respond to the pressures of rapid social change and greater Islamic assertiveness in Malaysian society. Yet observation on the level of mainstream Christian church organization reveals that the charismatic movement generates conflict and fissiparous tendencies. We will examine the movement in relation to the emergence of a superordinate Christian identity cutting across denominational and ethnic divisions, and in relation to its effects on traditional structures of organization within the Christian community.

Urban and industrial development in Malaysia has given rise to an increasingly secular, individualistic society that is highly receptive to the charismatic movement and other innovative forms of religion. The focus of the charismatic movement on individual ecstatic experience, within a diverse range of alternative prayer groups outside conventional church settings, has strong appeal within a social milieu that offers individuals greater freedom from traditional constraints, as well as a proliferation of choices. Participation in the movement offers expansion of choice for Christians, because exclusive commitment is not demanded. The movement encourages Christians to maintain affiliation with their regular churches and at the same time participate in one or more charismatic prayer groups. Christians may maintain their particular denominational identities as Catholics, Anglicans, Lutherans, and so forth, while also forming a broader, more inclusive sense of Christian identity as charismatics.

Many Malaysian Christians view the emergence of charismatic identity as a solution to the problem of Christian unity. The participation of both Catholics and Protestants in the charismatic movement is seen as evidence that the Holy Spirit is working to bring Christians together. The interdenominational dimension of the movement suggests to them that direct experience of the Holy Spirit transcends formal doctrinal differences between Christians. They also maintain that the movement is an expression of the Holy Spirit's response to the Christian community's need for revitalization in its encounter with politicized Islam.

Charismatic Christian identity entails not only the attenuation of denominational divisions but also the erosion of ethnic boundaries among non-Malays. The propagation of the movement mainly through the medium of the English language has shaped its multiethnic, middle-class character. Although some charismatic groups use local vernaculars—Chinese dialects and Tamil—the movement as a whole in Malaysia tends to be English-speaking. Identification as a charismatic Christian is associated with middle-class orientation and deemphasizes ethnic background. In Malaysia, middle-class orientation includes a preference for the use of English rather than the national language (Bahasa Malaysia) or other vernaculars, familiarity with English-language mass media, and aspiration to a Western style of life.

Urban Indians, Chinese, and Eurasians who have attained or seek to attain middle-class status avidly consume imported Western ideas and manufactured goods. Participation in religious and social movements of Western origin has become an emblem of middle-class status, as has acquisition of Western fashions and technology. The openness of middle-class-oriented non-Malays to Western influence of all varieties is reflected in the willingness of Christians to experiment with the new styles of behavior introduced in the charismatic movement. The movement's encouragement of uninhibited expression of emotion in public gatherings through personal sharing, testimony, confession, exuberant singing, and gestures presents Malaysians with a novel social situation requiring departure from their usual emotional reserve and guardedness in public interaction. Adoption of charismatic Christian identity involves a process of shedding traditional constraints on social behavior and assimilating Western forms of interaction characterized by emotional expressiveness.

Mainstream Christian organizations generally oppose the approach of the charismatics to Christian unity. Many Protestant churches, particularly those of fundamentalist and evangelical orientation, doctrinally reject Spirit Baptism, glossolalia, and other charisms as valid forms of Christian worship. The Roman Catholic church, on the other hand, acknowledges the theological soundness of the basic charismatic teachings, yet is wary of undesirable Protestant influences arising from Catholics interacting closely with Protestants in the context of interdenominational charismatic prayer groups. The Catholic and Protestant establishments view Christian unity as achievement of understanding and cooperation among church leaders who respect each other's institutional boundaries. From the perspective of church leaders, encouragement of interaction across denominational lines at the grassroots level is more likely to lead to doctrinal confusion and organizational disruption than to constructive Christian unity. The populist conception of unity held by the charismatics is thus regarded with apprehension and distaste among mainline church leaders.

The leaders of the mainline churches have not been able effectively to insulate their members from charismatic influences. Charismatic expertise in spiritual healing and exorcism has made a positive impression on many members of Roman Catholic and Protestant churches. The popularity of charismatic thaumaturgy among Malaysian Christian laymen has created strong pressures on the mainline churches. Christians who have been introduced to charismatic thaumaturgical practices often come to regard their own churches as deficient in these practices and look toward the movement for assistance with personal problems attributed to supernatural causation. Many Malaysian Christian laymen believe that demonstrations of control over malign supernatural forces are necessary for maintenance of faith and expect their churches to cater to this need. Their interaction with itinerant charismatics has stimulated attempts to introduce glossolalia, spiritual healing, and exorcism into the mainline churches. Many mainline Christian clergy disdain charismatic thaumaturgy as "primitive," emotional theatrics but are unable to ignore the widespread demand for this form of pastoral care. They are all too aware that unwillingness on the part of the churches to involve themselves with thaumaturgy strengthens the appeal of folk occultists and charismatic exorcists to their members.

The Catholic church, unlike other mainline churches, has made efforts to minister to the personal needs of its members in terms of the cultural idiom of spirit possession. Incorporation of thaumaturgy into the mainline churches, however, entails the realignment of authority relations between the clergy and laity. The perennial lack of trained clergy in Malaysia constrains the ability of the churches to provide intensive and personalized thaumaturgical services. For example, several lengthy, exhausting sessions may be required to complete a single exorcism. Few clergy have the time and energy to devote to the numerous alleged victims of spirit possession who seek exorcism. Delegation of much of this work to laymen is therefore inevitable. Encouragement of lay participation in thaumaturgy fosters both partnership and competition between clergy and laity. Some of the laymen active in healing and exorcism work under the clergy's supervision, while others perform thaumaturgy independently without authorization. The independent lay healers and exorcists attract their own clientele and followings, and tend to ignore or resist the clergy's authority.

The experience of the Catholic church in accommodating the demand for thaumaturgy has revealed unforeseen problems of control. The attempt to cater to needs for spiritual healing and exorcism has increased the clamor for such treatment to the point of overburdening priests and their lay assistants. This situation has encouraged unauthorized, selfappointed lay exorcists to offer their services to many alleged possession victims who are without ready access to similar experts recognized by the church. Several priests skeptical of the charismatic movement have also noted that the preoccupation of the laity with thaumaturgy has been allowed to divert attention from more substantial doctrinal matters. Critics within the church claim that the willingness to embrace the spirit possession idiom in the provision of pastoral care has retarded mature understanding and practice of Christian teachings among laymen.

Although the Roman Catholic hierarchy has officially endorsed the charismatic movement and integrated it within the main body of the church on a level similar to lay organizations such as the Legion of Mary, Young Christian Workers, or the Christian Family Movement, the reaction of the clergy at the parish level varies. Some parish priests have supported the movement, while others have discouraged or barely tolerated it. Aside from the controversies surrounding the practice of thaumaturgy, the strong Protestant influence on the charismatic movement is disquieting to the critical priests. The survival of the church, from the clergy's point of view, requires a defensive posture with respect to relations with the Protestants. Nevertheless, the Catholic church has been able to exert a reasonable degree of control over the charismatic movement through its highly centralized authority structure.

In contrast to the Catholics, many other mainline Christian churches have refused to accommodate the charismatic movement to any degree. Compared with the Catholic church, the relative weakness of centralized authority in Protestant churches reduces their ability to incorporate a diverse range of lay movements within their organizations. The Anglican bishop, for example, has officially discouraged Anglicans from participation in the movement. Despite the bishop's stand, many Anglican laymen are involved in charismatic groups yet maintain discretion for fear of being expelled from the church. The charismatic movement has also disturbed Methodist church leaders. Large numbers of young Methodists are attracted to the movement and some leave the church altogether, with the result that fewer young people are attending Methodist services. Along with the younger members of the Methodist church, there are also pastors who attend charismatic prayer meetings and are sympathetic toward the movement. The pastors participate only in an individual capacity and not as official representatives of the Methodist church. Few of the pastors attracted to the charismatic movement dare to identify themselves with it openly for fear of jeopardizing the comfortable and secure livelihood provided by the Methodist church. The Methodist bishop and other senior church officials, in their opposition to the charismatic movement, have taken disciplinary action during the past few years against several pastors who openly identified themselves with the movement. Although none of these pastors were expelled, all received stern warnings to conform to official Methodist doctrine.

The theologically conservative fundamentalist and evangelical Protestant churches are as hostile to the charismatic movement as the liberal Protestant churches. They have been similarly unsuccessful in isolating their members from charismatic influences. Charismatic factions have formed within some of these churches, generating dissent and divisiveness. Because these churches tend to be small, independent congregations without centralized authority structures, the ensuing disruptive factionalism is more difficult to contain than in the large, bureaucratically organized Catholic church and the liberal Protestant denominations. In some cases, the charismatic factions within fundamentalist and evangelical churches have been strong enough to take over the congregation, and the opposing minority have withdrawn to form a new group. On the other hand, numerically weak charismatic factions within these churches are sometimes expelled or pressured to renounce their ecstatic practices.

The schismatic tendencies set in motion by the charismatic movement within the mainline and fundamentalist churches are constrained, however, by the awareness of the church leaders of the marginal position of Christianity in Malaysian society. Islamization sets limits on the degree to which disintegrative forces are allowed to develop within the churches. Increased missionary work by the Muslims, together with government policies favorable to Islam, are perceived by church leaders as serious threats to the general welfare of Christians in Malaysia. Lacking the necessary political resources to resist Islamic expansionism, Malaysian church leaders can only direct their efforts inward to prevent the disintegration of their congregations and the weakening of their religious tradition. Thus, the practical need for more effective Christian organization and a greater sense of unity moderates the inclination of the church leaders to suppress the charismatic movement. Despite its divergent trends related to denominational differences, the charismatic movement continues to provide a vital bulwark against non-Christian encroachments. In short, the minority status of Christianity in Malaysia ensures to a certain extent the survival of the charismatic movement.

CHAPTER FOUR

Ashes and Avatar: Miracles and Identity in the Satya Sai Baba Movement

THE second coming of Hinduism to the Malay Peninsula had virtually no impact on the process of state formation, unlike its initial appearance in the region two millennia ago. The mass migration of Indians to Malaya in the first quarter of the twentieth century resulted in no significant religious transformations on the peninsula. Islam was already an established religion among the Malays, and Christian missionaries were actively spreading the gospel on the peninsula. The Indian immigrants were mainly laborers who worshipped Hindu deities of the "Little Tradition" in relative isolation in their estate settlements. Urbanization, however, has wrought great changes in the structure of Malaysian Hinduism, as village deities have been given new veneers of respectability in the context of expanding cities and suburbs. The process of Sanskritization specific to the peninsula forms a theme of analysis in this chapter, yet one that is related to the minority status of the Indians and their relationship with the other ethnic groups. Although Sanskritization is normally treated in conjunction with the question of social mobility, we are linking it to the problem of ethnic identity formation that is central to all forms of social interaction in Malaysia today.

Patterns of Hinduism in Contemporary Malaysia

If Hinduism is nominally dichotomized into the Sanskritic variety and the popular variety, with the former approximating the "Great Tradition" and the latter the "Little Tradition," a large proportion of Hindu practices in Malaysia may be considered as part of the popular category.[1] There are at least two reasons for this observation. First, a large proportion of the Indian immigrants who were recruited to work in the colonial economy were drawn from various village communities in South India. These early arrivals to the peninsula brought with them the worship of various non-Sanskritic deities, a practice that has continued to the present. These deities, however, have over time acquired Sanskritic attributes and have even generated much appeal among the higher-caste Hindus. Second, the absence of religious centers *(math)* and traditional monastic orders implies the limitation of sources of scriptural authority that are vital to the maintenance of Sanskritic Hinduism. Unlike the situation in India, where the complexities of Sanskritic Hinduism are expressed through a multitude of religious orders and priestly traditions, many Hindus in Malaysia depend on the *pandaram* and *pujari*—ritual specialists who have little or no Sanskritic training—to perform various religious functions. The larger urban temples may employ some initiated priests *(kurukkal)* from India on a short-term basis (considering government restrictions on the importation of foreign priests), but this does not necessarily ensure the continuation of a Sanskritic tradition. The shortage of priests with Sanskritic backgrounds has also resulted in the recruitment of some Smarta Brahmins for the dual role of temple and domestic ritual functionaries (Rajoo 1975:55).[2] In other words, the scope for innovation in Malaysian Hinduism seems to be wider than that in India, given the lack of scriptural control maintained by established priestly or monastic traditions.

The latitude for innovation within Malaysian Hinduism contradicts to an extent the rigid separation between the Sanskritic and popular traditions. The process of innovation connotes the mutability of Hindu orthodoxy to include both Sanskritic and non-Sanskritic elements. Even Milton Singer (1972:138) has noted that Hindu orthodoxy in urban Tamilnadu (South India) not only includes the learned Sanskritic tradition but has also incorporated many local customs and popular practices and beliefs.[3] This observation he defines as "the cultural drift of orthodoxy," an inherent flexibility in Hinduism that permits a variety of changes without destruction of its basic structure. The implications of Singer's findings are crucial for understanding the dynamics of religious change in Malaysian Hinduism. If Malaysian

Hinduism is characterized by a relative lack of textual authority, the sources of change are more likely to be found in the laity and non-Sanskritic priests. These people are the major practitioners of the faith, actively involved in defining and redefining the boundaries of Hinduism for themselves and others. Most of their religious activities, however, exemplify an earthbound pragmatism rather than the pursuit of transcendental ideals (Mandelbaum 1966). Yet the influence of Sanskritic Hinduism on the popular variety has been profound. This is most evident in the imitation of Sanskritic practices in popular rituals, or the adoption of Sanskritic deities for thaumaturgical purposes.

The first type of influence is most clearly manifested in the performance of temple rituals. Most priests serving in large Hindu temples dedicated to the higher deities are expected to conduct worship according to the rules prescribed by the scriptural *agama* (manuals of ritual in temple worship). Even then, many such priests (including Brahmins) are not well acquainted with the intricate technicalities of agamic worship and usually turn to visiting specialists from India for advanced instructions (Aveling 1978:175). These priests in turn become models of emulation for the non-Brahmin *pandaram* and *pujari*. In the absence of an authoritative body of trained ritual specialists, this hierarchy of imitation easily becomes an accepted mode of prestige acquisition that often accompanies the ritual upgrading of a temple. In many cases, however, the elimination of non-agamic forms of worship precedes ritual imitation, since the priest concerned may not have had the opportunity to acquire fully the requisite knowledge. A prime example of such ritual change, recorded by R. Rajoo (1981), concerns a Munisvaran[4] temple in an urban village in Kuala Lumpur. This temple was founded in the 1940s by a Tamil laborer who had erected a shrine in honor of the deity following a dream about him. Gradually, as the number of devotees increased, the shrine was turned into a small temple. In the 1960s, the temple came under the control of a local Indian politician who, with a Punjabi colleague, decided to raise its status by improving its structure as well as its social and financial position. In 1974, representatives of thirty Munisvaran temples throughout Malaysia organized a conference to which Indian politicians and community leaders were invited. At the conference, an association of Munisvaran temples was formed with the Punjabi appointed as its president. This association has received recognition from the government as a legitimate religious body representing Hindus in

Malaysia. More importantly, participants at the conference unanimously agreed that Munisvaran was indeed a manifestation of Siva, a Sanskritic deity. In accord with its raised status, an injunction was passed to terminate animal sacrifices, alcoholic offerings, and mediumship as a first step to introducing agamic worship in Munisvaran temples. In addition, the inclusion of *Sivarattri,* a major Saivite festival, in the calendrical ceremonies of the temple was accepted as a means of image enhancement.

Aside from ritual imitation, Malaysian Hindus who have the financial means may employ Brahmin priests from India to consecrate a temple in their efforts to promote a religious facade suggestive of Sanskritic Hinduism. This route to religious respectability had been adopted by the *Devastanam* (committee) of the Sri Maha Mariyamman temple in Kuala Lumpur.[5] From a small shrine built in the 1870s, it has grown into a large, powerful temple in the Indian community. In 1974, the *Devastanam* hired several Brahmin priests from South India to consecrate the temple with a Sanskritic fanfare that included performances of Indian classical dances and music. Even today, the *Devastanam* continues to employ Brahmin priests to maintain the agamic form of worship (Rajoo 1975:41).[6] But it is in the socioeconomic standing of this temple that the *Devastanam* is able to command the respect of a large part of the Indian community. As the wealthiest Hindu institution in the country, reinforced by strong political patronage, its adoption of agamic forms may be construed as the culmination of a long climb to religious respectability. However, the *Devastanam*'s sponsorship of *Taipusam,* an annual festival usually celebrated with extravagrant displays of self-mortification by devotees in fulfillment of personal vows, has moved reform-oriented Hindus to rebuke its efforts at agamization. These individuals regard the increasingly baroque trend of self-mutilation at *Taipusam* as lowly and degrading behavior that is inconsistent with the commitment to agamic worship. Yet, *kavadi*-bearing at *Taipusam* has become more spectacular with each passing year and has been identified as a significant Hindu event.[7] As a popular Hindu festival patronized by high-ranking politicians and sanctioned by an influential temple with claims to agamic status, the ecstatic rituals of penance at *Taipusam* have acquired a gloss of respectability often denied to the religious practices of the "Little Tradition." Thus, the *Devastanam* is able to introduce Sanskritic patterns of worship at the Sri Maha Mariyamman temple without completely severing its support of particular non-agamic practices, because the notion of orthodoxy in Malaysian Hinduism has never been clearly defined in the absence of a formal body of Hindu scriptural authority.

When we examine the phenomenon of spirit possession among Malaysian Hindus, we also see similar processes of ritual upgrading at work. Traditionally, practices associated with spirit possession are regarded as characteristic of village Hinduism (Harper 1957). Spirit possession may occur on two levels—individual devotees are possessed by a deity during a festival, or a spirit medium goes into trance to seek supernatural help for a client. In both types of possession, the descending spirit may be a local deity or a member of the scriptural pantheon. Since Sanskritic and non-Sanskritic deities play equally important roles in spirit possession, the question is not whether Sanskritization connotes the adoption of scriptural deities for thaumaturgical purposes, but rather how the adoption is actualized. In short, the process of Sanskritization in possession performances makes sense only if we focus on the rituals accompanying them. Status elevation in possession rituals, especially in mediumship, has been observed by several researchers. Lawrence Babb (1974:40), in his study of Hindu mediumship in Singapore, reports that "Most mediums, if they have the means, conduct their activities in their own temples which imitate, though on a diminutive scale, the large public temples of the city." These attempts by mediums at recreating temple worship in seances suggest their concern for seeking common grounds with the "higher" Sanskritic practices. Rajoo (1975:230) cites the case of a female medium who, during a seance, expelled a menstruating client. He interprets the medium's strict adherence to the rules of ritual pollution as an instance of emphasizing her high ritual status. We have also observed a Hindu medium in Petaling Jaya who applies similar rules of ritual pollution in his seances. Thus the continuing popularity of spirit mediumship among Malaysian Hindus of all castes and classes not only ensures its survival, but also prompts its practitioners to upgrade their ritual status as a means of asserting an agamic identity.

M. N. Srinivas' original formulation of Sanskritization treats ritual change as "a claim to a higher position in the caste hierarchy than that traditionally conceded to the claimant caste by the local community" (Srinivas 1968:6). In the Indian context, ritual change is both a symbolic claim to and assertion of caste superiority in various areas of ordered social interaction. In applying this model of Sanskritization to our data for Malaysia, it is necessary to consider the extent of change in the caste system on the peninsula and its relevance to the various forms of agamization described above. First, the complexities of the caste system in Malaysia are considerably different from those in India. In the absence of Brahmin domination among Malaysian Hindus, we may conveniently speak of a two-tier system with the non-Brahmins as "high" castes and the untouchables *(Adi Dravida)* as "low" castes. Although the hierarchical positions of subcastes within these two broad divisions are more or less recognized, the aspiration to agamic status in ritual worship is not limited only to members of a particular subcaste. Instead, non-Brahmins and the *Adi Dravida* compete eagerly for the attainment of agamic status in ritual worship. Second, the modern urban system in Malaysia is relatively open, in the sense that educational and occupational opportunities are widely available. Since independence, many non-Brahmins and *Adi Dravida* have improved their socioeconomic positions. Upward social mobility for Malaysian Indians, however, does not necessarily imply upward caste mobility because the urban system in Malaysia is not differentiated along corporate caste lines. For the Indians, at least, upward social mobility can be construed more as an individual achievement than an explicit measure of change in caste status.[8] Given these conditions, Sanskritization in Malaysian Hinduism has fewer caste connotations than in India.

One of the significant changes in the caste system in Malaysia has been the breakdown of prescribed communication across caste groupings. As pointed out by Marian Aveling (1978:189), ordered interaction between castes has become muted as a result of the mediation of other ethnic groups. In other words, the presence of non-Indian groups provides alternative fields of social transactions that preclude caste considerations. The dilution of these hierarchical relations renders ineffectual the assertion of caste superiority in agamization. Without a well-defined system of caste interactions, the demand for differential treatment by agamized groups is irrelevant. Stripped of its formal caste trappings, Sanskritization in Malaysian Hinduism is only symbolically meaningful as a claim for equal membership in the larger Hindu community. This claim presupposes a body of idealized ritual rules that agamic aspirants must master in order to reaffirm their communal bonds. If these are indications that suggest a loosening of caste functions in religious activities,[9] it is but a short step to argue that agamic rituals have now assumed other group functions, especially functions related to the consolidation of ethnic identity. As a minority ethnic group with low status in the political system, Malaysian Indians are acutely sensitive about their identity vis-à-vis the other ethnic groups. The pursuit of agamic worship with reduced caste implications therefore provides a new reference point in the expression of Indian ethnic identity. The accomplishment of agamic worship may be viewed as a symbolic endeavor to seek alliance with other Indian Hindus involved in similar worship. Our observations on the shifting meanings of Sanskritization in Malaysia suggest that the patterns of Hinduism in contemporary Malaysia cannot be analyzed in isolation from developments in the field of ethnic relations.

From the perspective of ethnic relations, the Indian reform movements that emerged in the 1920s and thereafter were particularly concerned with the presentation of an acceptable Hindu image to the Malaysian public. Leaders of these movements had hoped to improve Indian esteem by introducing reforms aimed at eliminating various kinds of Hindu practices thought to be despicable and degrading. Prior to the Second World War, the spread of these movements was greatly influenced by the rise of Dravidian nationalism in South India, which was anti-Brahmin and anti-Aryan in its outlook. The arrival on the peninsula in 1929 of E. V. Ramasamy Naicker, chief advocate of Dravidian nationalism, inspired his Malayan supporters to form the Tamil Reform Association, which sought to replicate South Indian reforms locally. One of the reforms that was vigorously pursued was the banning of animal sacrifice and self-mortification in Hindu worship. Purging Hinduism of these practices was considered an exercise in religious "spring cleaning" as well as a moral obligation to uphold the good name of the Indian community. However, the absence of state support for these movements, as well as their political fragmentation, limited their success in remolding the culture of popular Hinduism (Rajeswary 1969:216). Even after the war, members of the reform movements continued to press for legislative control of practices such as *kavadi*-bearing and fire-walking. As S. Arasaratnam (1970:174) points out, these postwar attempts at religious reform gradually lost momentum because Indian community leaders were concerned that the reformist activities might backfire and work against their interests.

Besides, many Hindus were reluctant to support these reforms and agitated for the continued practice of *kavadi*-bearing and fire-walking.

Clearly, then, religious reform as a technique of ethnic impression management was not very successful in the postwar years. Instead, many Indians turned inward to rediscover their ethnic identity during the Tamil cultural revival of the 1950s, a revival that was influenced by the effervescent Dravidian nationalist ideologies in South India. The Saiva Siddhanta school of southern Hinduism was greatly emphasized as an important source of religious learning because of its connections with Tamil traditions. The Tamilization of Hinduism became the order of the day as various urban religious movements took to organizing classes and devotional gatherings using Tamil as the principal medium of communication. Religious experts from Tamilnadu were invited to deliver lectures and instruct Malaysian Hindus on Saivite philosophy. This trend of Hindu activism contributed to the reinforcement of Tamil ethnic boundaries, especially at a time when politics in preindependent Malaya rapidly developed along ethnic lines.[10] As Indian politics in Malaysia became more cloistered and protectionist in orientation, major Hindu organizations began to turn to the Indian political establishment for patronage and support. Today, organizations such as the Malaysian Hindu Sangam are allied with Indian ministers and other political dignitaries as necessary connections to the government. Occasionally, these organizations function as pressure groups in negotiating with the government on various ethnic issues.[11] While many Hindu organizations in contemporary Malaysia enjoy legitimate status as religious groups, in actuality some have assumed the role of protectors of Indian interests. The other politically less-inclined groups have nevertheless introduced forms of worship that are central to the preservation of Indian identity, especially in the urban areas. One of these forms of worship is the collective prayer *(bhajan)*, which was first popularized by several Tamil-based urban Hindu movements (Rajoo n.d.),[12] and is somewhat reminiscent of the Radhakrishnan *bhajan* in Madras studied by Milton Singer (1972). As an aspect of the *bhakti* (devotion) tradition in Hinduism, these urban *bhajan* have instilled in many middle-class Indians, who are unfamiliar with their cultural heritage, a serious interest in rediscovering their ethnic background. It is in this urban environment that the Satya Sai Baba movement has taken root and gained a large following of Indian and Chinese devotees, a phenomenon that we will discuss in the next section.

In sum, we can think of Hinduism as always having been a primary ethnic identifier among the Indians in Malaysia. The complexities of Indian ethnic expression within the Hindu medium can be traced both historically and sociologically. In the first instance, the shift in emphasis from an extroverted reformism before the war to an introverted cultural revival after the war not only reflects nationalist influences emanating from the Indian subcontinent, but also the changing political conditions on the Malay Peninsula. Second, this interplay between extraneous influences and local conditions is further complicated by class divisions within the Malaysian Indian community. Where urban religious reforms have been spearheaded mainly by the middle class, the push toward agamic rituals in Hindu temples and shrines (especially those of the lower deities) has been championed by the lower class. This division is most vividly epitomized in the long-standing conflict between the Malaysian Hindu Sangam, an organization led by middle-class professionals, and the Sri Maha Mariyamman *Devastanam,* a committee of working-class Indians. These complexities continue to be played out today in the Satya Sai Baba movement.

The Advent of Satya Sai Baba

As an aspect of the salvationary philosophy in Hinduism, the holy person *(guru, swami, sadhu, paramahansa)* occupies a vital position in the lives of devotees seeking spiritual beneficence and knowledge or release from earthly desires. The guiding role of the holy person is rooted in the traditional belief that only a few spiritually enlightened individuals have the ability to mediate the chasm between the world of ordinary mortals and the planes of ultimate reality. To the extent that the *guru* is not only a liberated soul *(jivanmukta)* but also a preceptor to those who wish to tread the path to god-realization, he is often worshipped by his followers as a god or god-incarnate *(avatar).* As Joel Mlecko (1982) has noted, it was the *bhakti* movement—which began in the seventh century A.D. and continues to the present day—that decisively promoted the divine status and obsequious worship of the *guru.* Among such godmen in India today, Satya Sai Baba ranks high in popularity, rivaling the prestige of those whose names have become household words on the subcontinent and beyond. Pictures of Satya Sai Baba—a round-faced, bushy-haired man in ochre robes—adorn the walls of shops and homes of his Malaysian devotees, although he has yet to set foot on the peninsula. Other *guru* who have visited the peninsula have not been able to arouse so poignantly the enthusiasm of so many Hindu and non-Hindu Malaysians. Who is Satya Sai Baba and why is his appeal so magnetic?

Historical Background to the Satya Sai Baba Movement

According to his official biographer, N. Kasturi (1973-1975), Satya Sai Baba displayed extraordinary powers even as a child. Born as Satya Narayana Raju in 1926 in the village of Puttaparti in Andhra Pradesh (South India), he grew up in a landowning family that claimed descent from a chiefly lineage. Kasturi mentions that Satya Narayana's birth was heralded by a number of auspicious events and occurred on a day and month devoted to the worship of Siva. When he was a little older, he awed his companions with the ability to materialize from empty bags objects which he then distributed generously. His friends always turned to him in times of trouble, seeking advice and consolation from the boy *guru*. His innate concern for helpless animals, the sick, and the poor has been described as an integral aspect of his humane character. From an early age he demonstrated a flair for the dramatic, a trait for which his family was well known. It was reported that he had even written songs for the village opera at the age of eight.

Except for the revelations of these special talents, Satya Narayana's life was quite uneventful until the age of fourteen when he experienced an intense crisis. While on an excursion he suddenly collapsed and remained unconscious for several hours. The occurrence of this incident was attributed to several causes (ranging from snake or scorpion bite to an attack of hysteria), which were never clearly determined. Although he recovered consciousness, he immediately lapsed into episodes of strange behavior—laughing, weeping, and even reciting long Sanskrit passages uncontrollably. His parents believed that he had fallen victim to demonic possession and sought out several exorcists to treat the boy, but their efforts were without success. The crisis drew to a close two months later when Satya Narayana, seemingly in control of his emotions, made the announcement that he was a reincarnation of Sai Baba of Shirdi, a Maharashtrian saint who had died in 1918. Not long after that, he renounced the world and walked out of his family home to begin his divine mission. A Brahmin neighbor looked after him while he ministered to a growing crowd of devotees who addressed him as Satya Sai Baba. In 1950 two *ashram* (religious abode) were constructed; the first near his birthplace, and the second near Bangalore in the state of Karnataka. Both *ashram* have become important centers of pilgrimage for thousands of devotees from all over India and other countries. His fame as a miracleworker and healer spread beyond India in the late 1960s, at a time when the religious axis in the West was shifting toward the East.[13] As a saint for all seasons, he commutes regularly between his two *ashram* to give *darshan* (blessings by sight) and advice to his devotees, these activities being a continuation of his childhood performances on a grander scale.

Satya Sai Baba's life as recounted by his numerous biographers reflects in essence a pattern of mystical transformation typically ascribed to Indian ascetics who have renounced the world. The two most important themes of his life story—miracle performances and saintly reincarnation—are central to the beliefs of the Hindu world, resurfacing time and again to legitimize the divine status of the godmen of India. As a youth his divine status was not closely questioned, even though Sai Baba of Shirdi was virtually unknown to the people of Puttaparti. As an adult he upgraded his claim to avatarhood by publicly declaring in 1963 that he was an incarnation of the god Siva. We are not concerned, however, with the authenticity of these claims, but rather with the historical connections underlying them. These connections provide an understanding of the accessibility of past traditions in the legitimation of charismatic claims.

In the absence of detailed historical records, it is difficult, if not impossible, to establish Satya Narayana's motives for claiming a spiritual link with Sai Baba of Shirdi, unless the reincarnation hypothesis is accepted at face value. Nevertheless, Satya Narayana's link with the original Sai Baba is clearly manifested in his frequent use of sacred ash *(bhasma* or *vibhuti)* for healing and other ritual purposes. During his lifetime Sai Baba of Shirdi kept a fire burning perpetually in a clay hearth *(dhuni)*—a tradition that is often attributed to a sect of Saivite mystics known as the Nathpanthis (see Dasgupta 1969)—from which ashes were collected as thaumaturgical substances. Upon the death of

Shirdi Sai Baba, his disciples discontinued these practices, but it was Satya Sai Baba who revived the sacramental dispensation of *vibhuti*. However, because Shirdi Sai Baba had no successor to his name Satya Sai Baba cannot claim direct descent from a specific spiritual lineage. Among Shirdi Sai Baba's disciples, Upasani Baba was recognized as the most likely successor—yet he left Shirdi in 1915 to set up his own *ashram* at Sakuri (White 1972:870). The absence of a spiritual lineage has not prevented Satya Sai Baba from manipulating particular Hindu myths to establish for himself an acceptable religious past. His claim that both he and Shirdi Sai Baba are incarnations of Siva serves to reify various Siva myths recorded in the Purana (see Swallow 1982) as a justification of his avatarhood. But in seeking a permanent association with the god Siva, Satya Sai Baba has dropped all Islamic elements in the teachings and practices of his predecessor, although this does not imply his rejection of Islam.[14] He preaches a simple philosophy of love and devotion that is distinctly Hindu in form and content, with emphasis on the importance of Vedic literature and rituals.

This brief exegesis of Satya Sai Baba's background reveals that his particular claim to avatarhood and demonstration of supernatural powers *(siddhi)* are not startling innovations within the Hindu tradition. In fact, one of his greatest skills lies in his ability to bring old Hindu myths to life through the reenactment of various puranic lores. As Swallow (1982:154) argues, his choice of Saivism as an arena for dramatizing these religious concerns reflects that tradition's rich store of moral messages articulating the ironies and profundity of human existence. Those who have come to appreciate these skills are mainly individuals with an urban, middle-class background, who respond not only to his alleged siddhic abilities but also to his offer of salvation through a personal devotion to god. The *bhakti* resolution is intellectually and ritually undemanding, and is therefore most attractive to the urbane Indian who has little or no rigorous training in the scriptures, or to the non-Indian spiritual seeker whose understanding of Hinduism is somewhat superficial. These patterns of appeal are also evident among the Malaysian followers of Satya Sai Baba, but the consequences and expressions of this attraction are somewhat different from those on the Indian subcontinent and elsewhere. In the remainder of this chapter we will explore the social conditions peculiar to Malaysia that have given rise to this mass religious movement.

Urban *Bhajan* and Satya Sai Baba Organizations

One of the main activities of the Satya Sai Baba movement in Malaysia revolves around *bhajan* peformances. These are devotional groups that meet regularly for an hour or more in public halls and private homes to pray and sing. As mentioned earlier, this form of worship was quite popular among Hindu urbanites in the postwar years, but it blossomed into a distinct expression of middle-class Hindu piety in the mid 1970s at the height of growth of the Satya Sai Baba movement. The *bhajan* fever spread momentarily to estate and working-class Indians as their middle-class compatriots zealously organized Satya Sai Baba missionary activities throughout Malaysia. Many lower-class Indians, however, have shied away from these urban *bhajan*, regarding class barriers as difficult to bridge by mere attendance at ceremonies devoted to a rich man's godman. Consequently, most of the Satya Sai Baba *bhajan* are centered in urban areas, organized and attended mainly by middle-class Indian and Chinese devotees.

Prior to 1969, Satya Sai Baba was worshipped only by a small number of Indian devotees. The first public Satya Sai Baba *bhajan* was held in Kuala Lumpur in 1969, but dissension over leadership among the organizers led to the formation of a splinter group in Petaling Jaya. At the Petaling Jaya center, internal divisions again caused a split, resulting in the formation of a Chinese-dominated group that moved to a Kuala Lumpur suburb. These quarrels revolved around the question of access to control of resources: as a *bhajan* group gained considerable membership and wealth, contests over these resources usually resulted in the less-powerful faction breaking away to form its own group. These contests were taken so seriously that instances of rigged committee elections were reported. In 1980, we estimated that there were about fifty Satya Sai Baba centers spread throughout the country, with the largest number located in Kuala Lumpur and Petaling Jaya. With the exception of two, the major Satya Sai Baba centers are dominated by Sri Lankan Tamils. The leadership of these centers is almost exclusively male, although each center has a section concerned with women's activities. Some of these groups are run jointly by Sri Lankan Tamils and Malayalis. The dominance of the Sri Lankan Tamils in the Satya Sai Baba movement can be attributed to their middle-class status, their established background in organizational leadership, and their high concentration in urban areas.[15] Of the two groups not dominated by Sri Lankan Tamils, one is controlled by working-class Indian Tamils in Klang, a port city near Kuala Lumpur, and the other comprises mainly Chinese devotees in Ipoh, about two hundred kilometers north of Kuala Lumpur. The group of Chinese devotees worship in a Satya Sai Baba temple (the only one of its kind in Malaysia) built from funds donated by a Chinese philanthropist. Other Chinese devotees have also organized themselves in several groups located throughout Malaysia, ranging from Kuala Lumpur in peninsula Malaysia to Labuan Island, off the coast of Sabah in East Malaysia. Most of the larger *bhajan* groups are government-registered bodies, while many of the smaller ones are inconspicuous enough to remain free of government scrutiny. Since 1979, efforts have been made to organize a national council for coordinating Satya Sai Baba activities. The stipulated aim of this council is to provide a legal umbrella for all Satya Sai Baba centers in Malaysia. Preliminary attempts at integrating these centers in preparation for such a council resulted in the organization of two pan-Malaysian Satya Sai Baba camps held successively in 1979 and 1980 at a seaside resort, both of which attracted hundreds of Chinese and Indian devotees. These two camps foreshadow the emergence of a middle-class Hindu organization that is likely to become a radical alternative to the established Hindu bodies on the peninsula.

While all Satya Sai Baba organizations function essentially as discrete centers of worship, some are actively involved in proselytization and missionary work. Active recruitment of members to the movement is not only conducted through networks of kin and friends, but also by regular contacts with the sick and underprivileged. By organizing film shows on Satya Sai Baba, followed by personal narratives on his miracle performances and distribution of hagiographic literature, the curiosity of friends, colleagues, and relatives is aroused, turning them into easy targets for recruitment. The newcomers are urged to read the personal accounts of miracles compiled in local and foreign publications that are available at most Satya Sai Baba centers as well as from an Indian cloth merchant who doubles as an agent for such literature. Members of the *Seva Dal* (service group) in the Satya Sai Baba movement make frequent visits to hospitals, prisons, slums, orphanages, homes for the aged, and various rehabilitation centers to advertise their religious wares. For instance, during hospital visits the devotees engage in friendly conversation with non-Muslim patients to inquire about their backgrounds and ailments. Before leaving, they distribute packets of *vibhuti* to the patients, instructing them to ingest the holy ash or rub it on their bodies for healing purposes. Interested patients are given more information and invited to attend *bhajan*.

As part of a wider campaign to promote its image as a decent and respectable movement, *Seva Dal* volunteers have begun participating in an ambitious program of public service that ranges from blood donation to assistance during natural disasters. Satya Sai Baba devotees are concerned, however, that their altruistic excursions not be construed by the public as a membership drive. Not only have they avoided promoting Satya Sai Baba's name on these occasions, but also have refrained from singing his name at special *bhajan* held in various Christian churches and Hindu and Chinese temples. The latter activity may be viewed as a subtle effort in allaying the fears of other Hindus and non-Hindus of Satya Sai Baba as a religious threat. Devotees claim that practicing *namasmaran* (singing of God's name) outside Satya Sai Baba circles is consistent with their avatar's call for *sarvadharma bhajan,* that is, *bhajan* glorifying all the traditionally accepted god-forms, thus giving them grounds to refute allegations that they are launching a new religious movement. While the defensive front is maintained largely by the *Seva Dal* members, other groups have been formed in response to directives from the parent body in India—the World Council of Sri Satya Sai Organizations (WCSSSO)—for purposes of organizational cohesion. Two such groups are the *Bal Vikas* and the Study Circle. The former is an educational group that conducts weekly religious classes for devotees' children between the ages of six and thirteen. The teachers are local volunteers who have received special training arranged by the WCSSSO. They run these classes according to the guidelines provided by the parent body in India. The Study Circle, on the other hand, comprises small discussion groups that meet fortnightly in devotees' homes, places of work, or schools to study Satya Sai Baba's teachings and other spiritual matters according to a manual issued by the WCSSSO.

Despite their importance as bases of ideological indoctrination, these groups nevertheless assume a secondary place in the movement because the weekly *bhajan* continues to be regarded as the focus of all Satya Sai Baba activities. As the mainstay of the *bhakti* path to salvation, the *bhajan* provides the occasion for collective singing and prayer that recharges the devotees' faith in their *guru*'s mission on earth. This is done by recitation of the *guru*'s name or other divine names in hymns that can induce states of ecstasy when performed in unison and with sustained enthusiasm. Weekly *bhajan* are conducted mainly in private homes on Thursday, a day when Satya Sai Baba was alleged to have led his first *bhajan*. (Among Hindus, Thursday is also an auspicious day dedicated to the *guru*.) Monthly *bhajan* are usually held on the first Sunday of each month, while annual *bhajan* are held in conjunction with festive occasions such as the Tamil New Year, Christmas, or the birthday of Satya Sai Baba. The monthly and annual *bhajan* are normally staged in public halls and are financed by devotees on a rotating basis. In some respects, these *bhajan* have become arenas of competition where devotees attempt to outdo each other in staging lavish performances. Special *bhajan* are conducted occasionally to celebrate a devotee's birthday or the fulfillment of requests made to Satya Sai Baba, or to commemorate the passing of a devotee.

A typical *bhajan* comprises worship in three stages, the first being the preparation of the devotees for hymns and prayers. The second stage is the *bhajan* proper, where about twelve to fourteen hymns are sung. The third stage is the *puja* (religious offering) to Satya Sai Baba and other deities. The seating arrangement in a *bhajan* is characterized by sexual segregation with female devotees sitting on the left and male devotees on the right, separated by a path that leads to an altar. The *bhajan* leader sits close to the altar with the musicians who play a variety of instruments such as the harmonium, drum, cymbals, and *chipla* (a kind of castanet). All devotees sit facing the altar, which normally comprises a full-length, colored picture of Satya Sai Baba and a color picture of his feet *(patham)*.[16] A picture of Shirdi Sai Baba is placed next to the pictures of Satya Sai Baba. Images and pictures of other Hindu deities and saintly figures from other religions also crowd the altar, together with several brass lamps that are lit with coconut oil. An empty sofa draped in silver and blue cloth with flowers strewn around it is usually stationed in a corner near the altar. This unoccupied sofa is symbolic of Satya Sai Baba's presence.

At the beginning of the *bhajan* lamps are lit. A devotee rings a bell then says three words in Tamil, pausing after each word—*mounam* (silence), *thianam* (meditation), and *pranavam* (cosmic chant)—followed by three chants of the word *Aum* (the divine sound). The *namavali* (necklace of names or salutations) are next recited in unison, led by a devotee who is well versed in Sanskrit. Altogether, 108 *namavali* are recited, each embodying the essence of Satya Sai Baba's teachings and the properties of the divine.[17] At some centers, the *namavali* are omitted and are replaced by hymns. As the salutations are recited, a few devotees scatter fresh flowers on the altar. There is a general belief among the devotees that the chanting of sacred words and divine names creates an atmosphere of worship favorable to their well-being. The next stage of worship involves the singing of hymns dedicated to Satya Sai Baba and various deities. These hymns are sung mostly in Tamil, Sanskrit, and English. In *bhajan* groups comprising mainly Chinese devotees, hymns are sung in Mandarin, Hokkien, or Cantonese. Many Chinese devotees, however, are also familiar with the Tamil and Sanskrit versions of these devotional songs. *Bhajan* singing usually ends with the chanting of *Aum, shanti, shanti, shanti* (peace) and five minutes of silence. In the final stage of worship, special *mantra* (Sanskritic formulas for ritual invocation) are chanted, followed by the performance of the fire ritual *(arathi)* in which camphor lamps are waved in a clockwise direction before the pictures and images on the altar. When the *arathi* ends, *vibhuti*, milk, and *prasad* (sweetened food offerings) are passed around to each of the devotees. A dash of *vibhuti* is ritually smeared on the forehead and arms while small portions of milk and *prasad* are consumed. At the Chinese-dominated *bhajan*, however, elaborate vegetarian meals are served to the devotees at the end of the gathering. The *arathi* is taken around and the devotees bring their palms together near the flame and then touch their faces, doing it only once or thrice. Before the group disperses, a devotee delivers a short sermon on Satya Sai Baba's teachings and makes various public announcements. The *bhajan* closes with devotees greeting each other *Sai Ram* (an invocation of Rama's name).

The rituals in Satya Sai Baba *bhajan* are in actuality simplified versions of temple worship and resemble in certain ways the *bhakti* practices that originated in medieval India. As a devotional form of worship, they do not differ greatly from the other types of *bhajan* currently in vogue among Malaysian Hindus. These include *bhajan* that are based on the Vedantic tradition and those that are characteristically Tamil in orientation (Rajoo 1975:274). The former type emphasizes the recitation of names of Hindu deities, particular *guru*, and Sanskrit *mantra*, while devotional hymns composed by the Tamil Saivite saints are given more prominence in the Tamil-oriented *bhajan*. In this regard, Satya Sai Baba *bhajan* are closer in form to the Vedantic tradition. The promotion of *bhajan* as a veritable expression of Hindu piety in the Satya Sai Baba movement coincides with similar efforts made by other Hindu organizations to spread this form of worship throughout Malaysia. In competing with these organizations, the Satya Sai Baba movement has inadvertently contributed to the evolution of the *bhajan* as a distinct mode of worship among middle-class Hindus in Malaysia.

Becoming a Devotee

The increasing popularity of Satya Sai Baba in Malaysia prompts us to ask why and how people become attracted to the movement. We will attempt to answer these questions by examining the responses of forty-two devotees (thirty-seven Indians, four Chinese, and one Eurasian) who participated in our nonrandom survey. Table 1 shows the breakdown in percentage of responses indicating the devotees' motives for joining the movement. The majority of interviewees claimed that they joined the movement for salvationary reasons. These are people who allegedly sought spiritual emancipation through devotional worship and public service. They believe that peace of mind can be attained by strict adherence to the *bhakti* teachings of Satya Sai Baba. Only three respondents said that they were attracted to Satya Sai Baba because of his supernatural powers. All three described their personal observation of holy ash materializing on the pictures of Satya Sai Baba and other Hindu deities as the main reason for becoming devotees. One respondent became a devotee to help his wife find a cure for her arthritis. He also expressed his admiration for Satya Sai Baba's teachings. Another respondent said she joined because her husband was in the movement.

Table 1. Reasons for Joining the Satya Sai Baba Movement

	Percentage	Number
Ideological (concerning salvation)	85.7	36
Observed miracles	7.1	3
Health reasons	2.4	1
Spouse a devotee	2.4	1
No response	2.4	1

Contrary to our initial expectations that a concern with the miraculous is the prime motive for becoming a devotee, our survey findings suggest that most respondents had been moved by Satya Sai Baba's *bhakti* ideology and his calls for selfless service. There are two ways of explaining these results. First, our nonrandom sample may be biased in favor of the more ideological devotees. This can only be confirmed by results from a larger survey. Second, attraction to the ideals of *bhakti* does not necessarily preclude a concern with the miraculous. Exposure to miraculous events, either through firsthand experiences or secondhand accounts, is an inherent characteristic of the Satya Sai Baba movement. It is unlikely that our respondents are unaware of the extraordinary powers attributed to Satya Sai Baba. Indeed, more than half of our sample (69 percent or 29 respondents) reported that they had experienced miraculous healings, visions, and other supernatural phenomena that were in some way related to Satya Sai Baba. Our informal interviews lead us to speculate that ideological motives are often premised on direct experiences or vicarious knowledge of Satya Sai Baba's powers. Typically, devotees first become convinced of Satya Sai Baba's *siddhi* through personal experiences or experiences related by other people before they develop an interest in *bhajan* and other spiritual matters. For instance, a leading figure in the movement (a Sri Lankan Tamil) claimed that he had no interest or faith in Satya Sai Baba and other Hindu deities prior to his witnessing of *vibhuti* manifestations on religious pictures. Today, he actively participates in Satya Sai Baba *bhajan* (he even composes hymns) and *Seva Dal* activities, and has broadened his spiritual pursuits to include meditation and theosophical teachings. Other similar cases suggest that verbal reports of ideological motives should not be taken at face value, since further probing often reveals that these motives may have evolved from an individual's initial attraction to supernatural phenomena.

Table 2 provides the breakdown in percentage of the various sources of influence that bring individuals into the movement. A substantial proportion of our sample indicated that friends and colleagues had introduced them to the movement. Several said they became interested in the movement after reading Satya Sai Baba books or listening to tapes of his speeches that they had purchased or borrowed from friends and relatives. A small percentage were directly influenced by their relatives. Interestingly, about a quarter of our sample listed the combined influences of friends, relatives, and literature as crucial

Table 2. First Contact with the Satya Sai Baba Movement

	Percentage	Number
Friends and colleagues	38.1	16
Books and tapes	19.0	8
Relatives	9.5	4
Combination of the above	26.2	11
Members of the movement	2.4	1
Personal contact with Satya Sai Baba	2.4	1
Self-seeker	2.4	1

to their recruitment into the movement. One respondent, a Tamil man who works as a prison officer, claimed that he became a devotee after *Seva Dal* members conducted *bhajan* at the prison where he worked. Another Tamil respondent, a retired civil servant, became an ardent devotee after he personally met Satya Sai Baba in India. Only one respondent identified himself as a seeker who became interested in Satya Sai Baba after having experimented with assorted religious alternatives both inside and outside the Hindu tradition.

Although these findings indicate that friendship networks are more important in the recruitment process than printed material and kin influences, the relative salience of these three factors cannot conclusively be established given the small size of our sample. Furthermore, the combined influences of these factors, as a somewhat significant response in our survey, suggest that they cannot easily be separated into discrete or independent categories of explanation. Most likely, recruitment occurs through a complex interplay of these three factors —an individual may become a devotee only gradually, learning about different aspects of the movement from various friends, relatives, and books over a period of time. Sources of influence with a low percentage of responses should not be dismissed as insignificant. For example, although only four respondents named their relatives as the agents of recruitment, we found that 37 of them (88 percent of our sample) claimed that they presently have relatives in the movement. This suggests that kin involvement is an important variable in recruitment and maintenance of faith, but its dynamics cannot readily be deduced from the limited survey data. Similarly, the other factors with low responses do not necessarily reflect their diminished importance, since our sample is not truly representative of the population of Sai Baba devotees. As such, these results may at best be treated as a general statement of a range of recruitment techniques that are seemingly effective within the Malaysian environment.

Opposition to the Satya Sai Baba Movement

Like many of the new religious alternatives in Malaysia, the Satya Sai Baba movement is not unified, nor has it received full support from all quarters of the Hindu community. While Satya Sai Baba's following in Malaysia comes almost exclusively from the urban middle classes, not all middle-class Hindus have been drawn to his message and miracles. Members of the Malaysian Hindu Sangam have quietly rejected him as a flamboyant showman with mass appeal. They prefer to maintain ties with the more sedate, established Hindu bodies in South India; for example, the Sankara *math* in Kanchipuram. Some orthodox Brahmins have condemned Satya Sai Baba as a "cheap" *guru,* claiming that genuine *guru* do not exhibit their supernatural powers. However, none of the opposition posed by these groups or individuals has crystallized into an anti-Satya Sai Baba movement. Rather, the backlash against the movement has come from within its own ranks, arising more from disillusionment with the *guru*'s moral standing than from disaffection with the movement's leadership.

The campaign to discredit Satya Sai Baba began in late 1980 and comprised mainly taped revelations by several Malaysian Indian students who claimed that they had been sexually abused by him. Another thrust of this campaign has been the reexamination of the Hindu scriptures to highlight the assumed contradictions in Satya Sai Baba's claim that he is an incarnation of both Siva and Sakti.[18] The Chinese press has also been influenced by this campaign and has published several articles with dire warnings and misgivings about Satya Sai Baba. The campaign has been fairly successful; several devotees have renounced Satya Sai Baba as their savior and some have even withdrawn their children from colleges in India sponsored by Satya Sai Baba. Others have removed from their altars all paraphernalia related to the worship of Satya Sai Baba and have returned to worshipping other deities. However, some have become concerned about the impact of their disillusionment on the mental state of family members who have allegedly been "cured" by Satya Sai Baba. They harbor the fear that defection from the movement may destroy their kin's faith in the healing powers of Satya Sai Baba, thus possibly triggering illnesses that have been "cured" or kept under control. For these individuals, the dissonance created by this dilemma could only be resolved by a forced commitment to the movement.

The drive against Satya Sai Baba originated primarily from a disenchanted Malaysian Indian professional, a former true believer whose devotion was completely shattered by his discovery of the *guru*'s proverbial feet of clay. Like many religious seekers, this man had sampled a variety of religious alternatives since his youth, ranging from Catholicism to Transcendental Meditation, before settling on Satya Sai Baba as his personal *avatar* of the 1970s. He rendered much legal assistance in the formative stages of the movement, and he and his wife organized many trips to India for Malaysian devotees who were eager to receive *darshan* and advice from Satya Sai Baba. Much of his time was also spent on missionary activities among Tamil estate workers. In late 1980, he learned about a case of sexual victimization involving his *guru*. The victim, a Malaysian Indian youth enrolled in a Satya Sai Baba college, reported that he had been seduced by Satya Sai Baba. Unable to reconcile these charges with his beliefs, the Malaysian Indian professional set out for India to conduct further investigations, whereupon he encountered dozens of disaffected devotees who related their experiences of deceit and debauchery within the movement on the subcontinent. With faltering faith and taped evidence, he returned to Kuala Lumpur and almost immediately launched a one-man crusade against Satya Sai Baba and his Malaysian supporters. For several months his home became an open court of inquiry on Satya Sai Baba, visited by a continuous stream of people who were anxious to examine the compiled evidence. Those who were convinced of the authenticity of the evidence not only left the movement but also fanned the flames of disaffection elsewhere.

For a while, the tensions generated by this moral crisis retarded the movement's growth. But gradually the leaders and core members of various Satya Sai Baba organizations rose to defend their *guru*. The campaign against Satya Sai Baba had inadvertently provided a catalyst for the feuding groups to join forces temporarily in the face of a common threat to the movement. Apologetic announcements were made in the hope of checking defections; for example, a prominent leader in the movement beseeched devotees not to waiver in their faith, for all great religious leaders, he argued, often suffered persecutions. In 1981 these defenders of Satya Sai Baba organized a public lecture to salvage their *guru*'s image and to recruit more devotees. They enlisted the services of several Indian and Chinese devotees of high status—among them a former cabinet minister, a psychiatrist, and a trade union leader—in an attempt to draw a large crowd to the lecture. Since that occasion the movement has receded from public view for two reasons. First, recent government attempts to disintegrate a fast-growing Chinese cultic alternative (see chapter 5) have indirectly cowed Satya Sai Baba devotees into adopting a lower profile in public. Second, the movement has entered a phase of internal consolidation with greater stress on group meditation and study than on expansionism. Meanwhile, members of the pan-Malaysian Satya Sai Council, the umbrella body of the movement, have renewed their efforts to obtain formal recognition from the government, especially in the wake of recent proposed amendments to the Societies Act.[19]

Despite the agitations of the anti-Satya Sai Baba faction, the movement continues to retain a following as a result of the determined efforts of a dedicated group of devotees. Moreover, the healing powers of Satya Sai Baba are still in high demand by many individuals in search of thaumaturgy and miracles. Even devotees whose moral revulsions at the sex scandals have embittered them toward the movement still express awe at the alleged siddhic abilities of their former *guru*. The survival of the movement, however, is not a guarantee for its fragile unity: as the crusade against Satya Sai Baba loses its shock appeal and the threat recedes, the movement will gradually resume its decentralized structure with each group returning to its own sphere of activities. It is difficult at this time to determine the integrative role of the Satya Sai Council because its status has yet to be legitimated by the Malaysian government. Until the council is fully operational and tested, the movement continues to be characterized by a loose conglomeration of competing *bhajan* groups run by independent leaders.

The Social Significance of Satya Sai Baba in Malaysian Hinduism

In discussing the social significance of the Satya Sai Baba movement, we need to compare it with the other forms of Hinduism in Malaysia. We suggested earlier that Malaysian Hinduism is a loosely integrated system with beliefs and practices that reflect a multiplicity of religious forms rather than the predominance of a single authoritative tradition. The Satya Sai Baba movement constitutes only one component of this Hindu diversity. Nevertheless, it shares some characteristics with other Hindu alternatives on the peninsula. One common feature is that many local Hindu forms have origins in the Indian subcontinent. The proximity of the peninsula to India has made possible a sustained contact between members of both Hindu communities. Religious ideas imported by returning Indians, itinerant godmen, and ritual technicians from the subcontinent have had a lasting effect on the local Hindu environment. Despite this ideological dependency on religious developments in India, the ultimate determinants of the local Hindu forms are the responses of Malaysian Indians to varying social conditions on the peninsula. One of these conditions is rapid urbanization, which has provided a context for the growth of various Hindu activities initiated by middle-class Indians. It is this context that has brought into prominence the religious leadership of middle-class Indians in contemporary Malaysia. Our comparison will focus on this urban characteristic as the basis for discussing religious change among the Indians in Malaysia.

The two waves of Hindu reformism and revivalism in the first half of the twentieth century were led by middle-class Indians. The Hindu reforms of the 1920s and 1930s were attempts to modernize and purify the practice of Hinduism so that it could be presented as a dignified religion to other ethnic groups in Malaya. In their efforts to abolish various ritual practices and to introduce proper religious instruction, the middle-class leaders were hoping to remold the image of the Indian community according to their values. After the war, many middle-class Indians became concerned about the effects of Westernization on traditional ideals and practices. They feared that the second generation of Indian youth, exposed to Western education and ideas, were gradually losing interest in Hinduism. The susceptibility of Indian youth to proselytization by other religions, particularly in a heterogeneous urban environment, was also perceived as a growing problem. In the face of these threats to communal (especially Tamil) solidarity, many middle-class Indians reacted by organizing classes on Saivism, by inviting religious scholars from South India to deliver lectures, and by encouraging the celebration of major Hindu festivals and participation in various religious activities. Among the Tamil majority, there was a strong emphasis on the revival of Tamil arts and literature and Saiva Siddhanta philosophy. The effects of this revivalism can still be observed today—especially in the myriad cultural and religious activities organized by middle-class Indians, which we will discuss below.

The Satya Sai Baba movement is not, on the other hand, concerned with reforming or reinterpreting Hindu beliefs and practices. Its activities are directed toward the fulfillment of earthly needs and the attainment of salvation through the practice of simple rituals. Also, unlike the earlier reformist and revivalist movements, which confined their activities to the Indian community, the Satya Sai Baba movement seeks to reach out to a wider constituency. In fact, it can be regarded as the first religious movement in the annals of popular Hinduism to have attracted a significantly large number of Chinese devotees. The Satya Sai Baba movement, however, has a class structure similar to the earlier socioreligious movements, suggesting that the sentiments of the middle-class leadership may have shifted over the last fifty years. If we examined the backgrounds of the leaders who were active in the 1930s and 1950s, we would find that they differ significantly from those who lead the Satya Sai Baba movement. There were relatively more vernacular-educated, orthodox Hindus in the leadership of the earlier movements as compared to the distinctly English-educated leaders of the Satya Sai Baba movement. Many of the leaders in the earlier movements had migrated from South India; for example, Ramanathan Cettiyar, who played an important role in the Tamil revivalism of the 1950s, was an Indian national who arrived in Malaya in 1947 (Rajoo n.d.:14). Many of the leaders in the Satya Sai Baba movement are local-born Indians who are comparatively more Westernized than their counterparts in the earlier movements. Unlike the vernacular-educated Indians, these English-educated leaders are less attached to the classical Hindu traditions. As a result of their Western outlook, they are more likely to perceive Hindu rituals that are grounded in the classical traditions as lacking in meaning. But Hinduism remains an important symbol of Indian ethnicity, especially at a time when Indian minority status is keenly felt vis-à-vis increased Malay privileges.[20] A limited background in the Hindu scriptures therefore becomes an obstacle in the consolidation of Indian ethnicity around religious symbols. A knowledge of Hindu scriptures, however, is not an important criterion in the Satya Sai Baba movement, because the rituals in the *bhajan* can be performed by a lay devotee. In other words, the Satya Sai Baba movement provides an acceptable and accessible Hindu symbol among English-educated Indians in their maintenance of Indian ethnic identity. For the leaders of the earlier movements, the question of ethnic identity revolved more around the proper practice and dissemination of Hindu teachings. Since the British colonial government at that time encouraged the segregation of the various ethnic communities, the maintenance of ethnic identity as a response to interethnic competition did not arise as a fundamental issue. Rather, these leaders chose to redefine Indian ethnicity through the manipulations of Hindu doctrines and practices.

The effects of urbanization on the process of Indian identity formation have oscillated between two extremes. On one hand, urbanization has provided a context for the gradual dilution of Hindu beliefs and practices. Exposure to Western secular education and increased contact with other ethnic groups in the urban milieu have predisposed many Indians to accept a lifestyle other than that prescribed by the Hindu tradition. The revivalist movements of the 1950s were partly reactions to the erosion of Indian (especially Tamil) cultural and religious symbols in the urbanization process. On the other hand, as more and more Indians seek opportunities for social mobility in the urban areas, the likelihood of their competing with other ethnic groups for scarce resources increases. Urbanization has sharpened the boundaries of Indian ethnic identity as the Indians confront larger ethnic groups in the competition for material privileges, especially in the context of accelerated sponsored mobility of the Malays since 1969. Contemporary mobilization of Indian ethnicity can be inferred from the increased organization of Indian cultural activities, much of which is based on the groundwork established by the earlier movements. Many Hindu bodies have organized religious classes, lectures, and cultural performances to revive interest in the neglected traditions. In recent years, the number of students attending religious classes arranged by the Malaysian Hindu Sangam and other similar organizations has increased markedly (Rajoo 1975:271). Most of these classes teach the works of the Tamil poet-saints with some emphasis on the Indian epics. We have observed increasing enrollments of middle-class Indian children in classes for classical dance *(bharata nattiyam)* and classical music *(karnataka sangidham)*. There is also a growing interest in various devotional activities, as seen in the spread of urban *bhajan* and *bhakti* programs in the mass media (Rajoo 1975:273, 291).

All of these activities are conducted with the aim of raising Indian consciousness of the higher scriptural tradition in Hinduism and the cultural performances associated with it. If Sanskritization in Malaysian Hinduism is taken to denote a social process underlying Indian identity formation through the sustained promotion of a higher, more uniform code of religious behavior, then these recent developments among middle-class Indians reflect a trend parallel to the endeavor of their lower-class counterparts toward agamic worship. The Sanskritic model therefore provides a contemporary cultural anchor for all classes of Indians seeking a more respectable definition of themselves. The Satya Sai Baba movement must be placed within the context of these recent developments: its popularity can only be considered meaningful in the light of the efforts of Indians to delineate the parameters of their ethnic identity. Although the primary function of the Satya Sai Baba movement is thaumaturgical, it has unwittingly provided a vehicle for the continuity of the Hindu tradition in its promotion of the urban *bhajan*. In the recent diversification of its activities to include the Study Circle, the movement has attempted to steer devotees toward the higher scriptural tradition. It is not a unique movement in this respect, because it shares with other Hindu organizations the tendency to derive inspiration from the Sanskritic paradigm.

Yet the Satya Sai Baba movement is easily distinguished from the other Hindu organizations by its large recruitment of Chinese devotees.[21] The recruitment of Chinese devotees into the movement has been facilitated by the increased interaction between Indians and Chinese as a result of rapid urbanization in Malaysia over the last two decades. The involvement of Chinese in the movement is based largely on their attraction to the thaumaturgical services offered by Satya Sai Baba. Most of the Chinese devotees first learned of Satya Sai Baba's healing powers through their Indian friends and private screenings of Satya Sai Baba films. Some Chinese spirit mediums have even taken advantage of the current mania by claiming that they can perform miraculous healings through possession by Satya Sai Baba's spirit. Because it is not unusual to find many mediums in Malaysia who are often possessed by spirits of different nationalities, this claim is unlikely to evoke any skepticism on the part of the medium's clientele.

A racket has also emerged in which some enterprising Chinese have made money by organizing special charter trips for their sick clients to see Satya Sai Baba in India. On the outskirts of Kuala Lumpur, a Chinese devotee has established a commune dedicated to the worship of Satya Sai Baba and various Chinese deities.

Why are the Chinese so receptive to Satya Sai Baba? This question can only be answered by reference to Chinese folk religious beliefs (see chapter 5). The concept of a religious specialist who has access to supernatural powers that are unavailable to the laity is fundamental to the Chinese folk religious system. Like the concept of the *guru* in Hinduism, the religious specialist in Chinese folk religious beliefs is revered for his ability to provide thaumaturgical and spiritual services for the laity. Some religious specialists (such as spirit mediums, monks, and priests) are considered gods or potential gods by Chinese worshippers. This convergent belief in the special role of a holy person does not imply that there are no differences between Hinduism and Chinese folk religion. Rather, it explains the relative ease with which the devotees have come to accept a Hindu *avatar*. Many Chinese devotees find it easy to accept Satya Sai Baba as their personal deity without rejecting the Chinese folk deities because Satya Sai Baba has repeatedly emphasized the unity of all religions. In the homes of many Chinese devotees framed pictures of Shirdi and Satya Sai Baba are found alongside images or pictures of Chinese folk deities on the family's altar. Since there are no stringent requirements for total commitment in the Satya Sai Baba movement, many Chinese devotees do not feel constrained to maintain ties with other Hindu and non-Hindu alternatives.

The large turnout of Chinese devotees in Satya Sai Baba *bhajan* in recent years implies their acceptance of the Indians as a new reference group in religious worship. Chinese devotees who regularly attend these *bhajan* have mastered devotional songs in Sanskrit and Tamil. It has been reported that some Chinese devotees sing these devotional songs better than their Indian counterparts, although many of them are unfamiliar with the meaning of the songs. The simplicity of *bhakti* rituals as an instrument of salvation also appeals to many Chinese devotees who are ignorant of the classical Hindu scriptures. Although many Chinese devotees have adopted a vegetarian diet and continue to attend *bhajan* regularly, very few actually perceive themselves as pure Hindus. Satya Sai Baba is merely treated as one of the many folk deities that are regularly worshipped for protection and prosperity. For the Chinese devotees, there is no evident realignment of their ethnic identity through their worship of Satya Sai Baba. Rather, their adoption of a Hindu style of worship resembles a superficial pattern of religious assimilation that is related more to their thaumaturgical needs than to a change in ethnic identity. Even many of the innovations introduced by the Chinese devotees in religious worship are highly Chinese in character. For example, at some *bhajan* dominated by Chinese devotees, many of the devotional songs are sung in Chinese; the *prasad* offered by some Chinese devotees do not consist of the traditional Indian sweets, but include large dishes of noodles, rice, and Chinese cakes. These innovations suggest that there is still a strong element of Chinese ethnicity in the approach of the Chinese devotees to Hinduism.

There are two important implications of Chinese participation in the Satya Sai Baba movement in Malaysia. First, most Indian devotees have accepted Chinese participation in the movement without qualification. The Chinese devotees have not been asked to assume Indian-Hindu identity. The Indian devotees have not condemned the various Chinese innovations in Satya Sai Baba *bhajan*. Many Indian devotees have, in fact, begun to place images of Chinese deities on their altars in the belief that this practice is consistent with Satya Sai Baba's teaching of religious universalism. This tolerance of syncretic practices reflects partly the need of the Indian devotees to affirm their ethnic identity. Introducing the Chinese devotees to a Hindu religious figure without attempting full ethnic assimilation suggests the adoption of a strategy by Indian devotees to assert their ethnic identity through their role as "culture donors" for the Chinese who participate in the movement.

Second, Chinese membership in the Satya Sai Baba movement provides a symbolic alliance of two ethnic groups whose political powers are limited. Because all Malays are Muslims by birth, their religious status is almost always perceived by the non-Malays as synonymous with their political dominance. The political and religious exclusiveness of the Malays impose a social distance between them and the non-Malays. On the other hand, the Chinese and Indians share some common religious grounds, such as Christianity and Buddhism. The Satya Sai Baba movement provides one of these meeting grounds. Although it is strictly a religious movement without overt connections to any political group, its non-Malay membership is nevertheless symbolic of a loose alliance between the Indians and Chinese that articulates their separateness from the Malays. This symbolic alliance draws its strength from the thaumaturgical needs of the Chinese and Indians and, at the same time, projects a syncretic religious image that is somewhat distinct from traditional Hinduism.

In sum, the Satya Sai Baba movement in Malaysia is more than just a healing movement. From a historical perspective, it forms a link in the chain of social events dating back to the prewar years when the Indian community was concerned with the question of Hindu reformism. The ideological remnants of Hindu revivalism initiated by middle-class Indians in the 1950s are discernible in current wave of Sanskritic enthusiasm, of which the Satya Sai Baba movement forms a part. Thus developments in the Satya Sai Baba movement mirror to an extent the wider social changes that are occurring in the Indian community. The intense participation of Chinese devotees in the movement also reveals the effects of urbanization on ethnic interaction in the postwar years. The future of Chinese involvement in the Satya Sai Baba movement is not only dependent on the access of Chinese to thaumaturgical services, but also on the demands made upon their ethnic allegiances. As long as total adoption of Hinduism is not stressed, Chinese attraction to the movement will be maintained.

CHAPTER FIVE

The Path of Mystical Dissent: The Baitiangong Alternative in Chinese Religion

LIKE their Indian counterparts, the Chinese immigrants to the Malay Peninsula brought with them their deities and particular styles of worship. Unlike the Indians, the Chinese sojourners gravitated to the tin mines, small towns, and various urban centers where they organized themselves into an assortment of trade guilds and voluntary associations attendant with patron saints and protective deities. As the Chinese became more settled on the peninsula so did their gods, some of whom have over time assumed new forms and names. Urbanization can be considered a major contributor to changes in the repertoire of Chinese religion in Malaysia. Interaction with other ethnic groups and exposure to other cultural ideas have predisposed many urban Chinese to innovate beyond their traditional religious practices. A comparison of the old and new forms of Chinese religion may provide some insight into the changing notions of Chinese ethnic identity in Malaysia; our first task in this chapter is to develop this comparison. We will then describe and analyze a new religious movement—the Baitiangong movement—in relation to sociopolitical developments in the Malaysian Chinese community.

The Chinese Religious Complex in Malaysia

Chinese religion has been recognized by many researchers as a relatively open and flexible system that is not rigidly institutionalized but is coextensive with Chinese culture.[1] Like popular Hinduism, Chinese religion lacks a strong organizational structure but is unified by a belief system that is shared collectively. This system, however, has evolved from many sources because its practitioners have borrowed extensively from other religions and reinterpreted their doctrines within the Chinese cultural mold. This religious eclecticism has resulted in not only a tradition of "interfaith polytheism" (Fleming 1962:75), but also in the flowering of numerous competing groups. The tendency of Chinese religion to absorb readily foreign beliefs is consistent with a cultural pragmatism that emphasizes the preservation and promotion of one's well-being in this world and the hereafter. The readiness of its practitioners to venerate the elements, deceased individuals, and a multitude of religious figures (Chinese and non-Chinese) has earned Chinese religion several epithets such as "shenism" (Elliott 1955),[2] "spiritism" (Kulp 1925), and "animism" (de Groot 1964).

Notwithstanding these epithets, Chinese religion has been conveniently dissected by various writers into its three components of Confucianism, Taoism, and Buddhism. Some researchers consider this division a parsimonious method for tracing the roots of Chinese religion (Soothill 1923), whereas others object to its oversimplification and misleading classification (Tan 1983). On a theoretical level, the former approach may reduce the complexity of empirical analysis, although in actuality many Chinese would explain their religion as a practical blend of the three components. Yet Confucianism cannot be accurately labeled a religion; it is more a system of ethics devised by Confucius and his followers that reinforces various ritual practices (such as ancestor worship and funeral rites) than an independent religious system. Confucianism, however, can be said to have formed "the basis of an official religion of which the rites and beliefs enjoyed a special position in Chinese society" (Freedman and Topley 1961:8). Similarly, Taoism as a religious system must be distinguished from Taoism as a school of philosophy—the former originating from indigenous Chinese beliefs and occult practices and the latter represented by the writings of Laozi, Zhuangzi, and Liezi. By the beginning of the Christian era, however, Taoist religion had developed an organized structure with priests using some of these sages' writings as their scriptures (Welch 1965). Although this structure is no longer a central feature of Taoism, the many beliefs and practices developed by Taoist priests and masters continue to exert a lasting influence on Chinese religion.

Buddhism, on the other hand, was introduced into China from India and Central Asia, probably between the latter part of the first century B.C. and the beginning of the first century A.D. Buddhism made inroads into Chinese society during the early part of the Christian era, competing with the incipient Taoist movement but eventually achieving rapprochement with some Taoist philosophers (Ch'en 1964: 62) and influencing the thoughts of many Confucians (Yang 1961:17).

This brief excursion into the history of Chinese religion highlights the syncretic nature of its development. Considered as a whole, Chinese religion (especially in its popular form) comprises a system distinct from Buddhism, Taoism, and Confucianism, although it has borrowed extensively from all three. As a decentralized belief system, Chinese religion has flourished in varied forms without the organized direction of any religious bureaucracy. Unburdened by ecclesiastical interference, the Chinese masses could freely select their gods from the Buddhist/Taoist pantheon or engage in worship peculiar to particular regions in China. In one case, Chinese immigrants to Malaya arrived accompanied by deities specific to various territorial and occupational groups.[3] These gods, however, comprised a fraction of an expanding pantheon that now includes deities not found in China. Many of the latter are actually deified individuals who had distinguished themselves on the peninsula or are Chinese frontiersmen long remembered for their pioneering endeavors.[4]

As a practical religion par excellence, the gods in the Chinese pantheon are believed to wield considerable powers over affairs in the human world. Although these gods command vast sources of supernatural power, many of them are treated by their devotees as though they possess human characteristics. Most Chinese supplicants understand the psychology of the gods sufficiently to know that few requests are free. Thus they offer sacrifice, food, and drinks to the deities in exchange for the fulfillment of their wishes. Some may engage the services of religious specialists who perform various rituals in the hope that their clients' requests are heard and answered. These specialists (who include Taoist priests, Buddhist monks, spirit mediums, geomancers, and individuals trained in the various branches of divination) form an important intermediary body between the world of men and that of the gods. The organization of much temple worship among Malaysian Chinese today is contingent upon the availability of these experts in satisfying thaumaturgical demands.

Chief among these specialists whose skills are frequently sought is the spirit medium, also known in Hokkien as *dang ki* or divining youth. As the human vehicle of various *shen*, the *dang ki* attracts clients through his ability to deliver advice and perform healing services in an entranced state.[5] Spirit mediums are almost invariably associated with temple worship. They operate in either established temples or private homes. Many temples that are maintained by residential communities, voluntary associations, and clubs employ spirit mediums on a regular basis to answer the needs of the worshippers. Some spirit mediums may even double as temple keepers. Other mediums may turn their homes into store-front temples, filling their living rooms with large altars, images, and other ritual paraphernalia. Most mediums hold other jobs and are only available for consultation at selected times when they become possessed by a *shen* or several deities in succession.[6] Since most mediums are independent entrepreneurs eking out a living in a competitive spiritual market, there is little cooperation and much rivalry among them. Nevertheless, spirit mediumship has become more popular since independence in 1957. According to Choo Chin Tow (1968:48), during the first ten years of independence thirty-five Chinese temples of various sizes were built in Kuala Lumpur, partly as a result of the economic prosperity of this period. The influence of legalized lotteries was another factor stimulating the increased flow of fortune-seekers to these temples. Consequently, spirit mediums specializing in possession by lottery deities, such as *Huang Zhi Guo* and *Huang Kun Shan,* were enjoying a booming business. The ideology and practice of "shenism" is so pervasive that even many staid Mahayana Buddhist temples are not spared its influence. Although spirit mediumship is forbidden in these temples, some permit the practice of divination that is self-administered, such as the throwing of divination sticks. Orthodox Buddhist monks may disdain such practices but maintain tolerance so as not to discourage worshippers who contribute to the upkeep of the temples.

While Chinese religious behavior is concerned to a large extent with tapping *shen* power for mundane purposes, its other practical aspects include the regulation of human relationships within institutional settings. This is most evident in the religious functions of various voluntary associations described by Maurice Freedman and Marjorie Topley (1961) and Topley (1961). Most voluntary associations are not explicitly religious in their structural organization and orientation, but their adherence to various religious rituals and a patron god provides a focal point for strengthening ties among members recruited on the basis of origins, dialect, surname, or occupation.[7] Particularly during the late nineteenth century, many makeshift temples were constructed for communal worship by dialect associations in Kuala Lumpur. Some of these temples have since grown into large, wealthy establishments (Choo 1968:41). Similarly, many Chinese women who migrated to Malaya in the 1930s formed religious sisterhoods for mutual comfort and protection. These sisterhoods were often housed in religious establishments known as vegetarian halls (Topley 1954), some of which are still active today. In other words, these various organizations drew on religious symbols as a means of promoting fellowship and other benefits among immigrants cut loose from their tight kinship networks and lineage systems in China.

By the early part of the twentieth century, several China-based sectarian organizations that preached salvationary goals had reached Malaya, thus introducing ideological alternatives to the more pragmatically oriented spirit medium temples and voluntary associations. These organizations, which Topley (1961) termed universalist, were persecuted in China for their suspected involvement in political rebellions yet were free from interference by the colonial government in Malaya. Some of the organizations were linked initially to various economic functions, but had less prestige than the voluntary associations because they did not restrict membership to specific territorial or kinship groupings. The most prominent of these organizations was the Great Way of Former Heaven *(Xian Tian Da Dao)*, which spread to the peninsula by the late 1800s.[8] According to Freedman and Topley (1961:12), sects of the Great Way in nineteenth-century Singapore were administered through vegetarian halls that were mainly concerned with providing shelter for Chinese immigrants. Later sects of the Great Way such as the Fellowship of Goodness *(Dong Shan She)*, which was established in Singapore in 1928 under the name of Nanyang Sacred Union, were more concerned with spiritual cultivation and salvation. Generally, the Chinese who were involved in these syncretic religions were intellectually traditional and politically conservative. They were uninterested in local political developments and preferred to direct their energies toward reforming Chinese religion (Freedman and Topley 1961:18).

Perhaps the most fervent attempt at reforming Chinese religion on the peninsula occurred between 1899 and 1911. In 1898, Kang Youwei, a Chinese intellectual, made several efforts to introduce Confucianism as a state religion in China. Although his campaigns ended in failure his ideas spread to the peninsula the following year, where they seized the imagination of several Malayan Chinese, particularly a straits Chinese doctor by the name of Lim Boon Keng. Lim and his colleagues embarked on an intensive campaign to preach the establishment of Confucian temples and modern schools. Much of this enthusiasm for religious and social reform can be said to have been fired by a rising Chinese nationalism that developed during the transition in China from imperial to republican power. The first phase of the Confucian movement in Singapore and Malaya was led by scholars and merchants who were ideologically inclined. After 1902, the Qing government in China established political patronage with the Chinese merchants on the peninsula through the government's support of the movement. The ideological elements of the movement were gradually eroded as the merchants turned the movement into a vehicle for enhancing their personal prestige (Yen 1976). Even though the movement declined after 1911, its remnants are still visible today in the two languishing Confucian Associations of Penang and Singapore (Tan 1983:226).[9]

Since the recession of the Confucian movement after 1911 no other Chinese religious organization or sect has taken its place in advocating religious and social reforms. Chinese religious sects in contemporary Malaysia are largely introverted organizations that shy away from political involvement. Most of these organizations are highly syncretic in their teachings and compete for members with the spirit medium temples. For instance, the *Dejiao Hui* (also known as the Moral Uplifting Society) instructs its members to worship all the deities in the Chinese pantheon with the addition of Jesus Christ and the Prophet Mohammad (Tan 1983:241). The *Dejiao Hui* has established branches all over Malaysia and Singapore. Another sect that we recently discovered, known as the Sinru Temple, propagates syncretic ideologies and specializes in divinatory practices. The Sinru Temple disseminates some rather esoteric teachings—based on the revelations of its leader (a Chinese prophet cum businessman)—that combine popular ideas from Western marginal science (such as the writings of Erich von Daniken) and traditional Chinese occultism. Its members don long robes and mitres for ceremonial occasions. The leader and some of his close disciples conduct special divination sessions for troubled members who are prepared to pay a small fee. Unlike *Dejiao Hui*, Sinru Temple is based only in Petaling Jaya although the leader is awaiting the right moment to expand his sect (see Lee 1986a). These examples illustrate the wide range of religious alternatives that are available at present to the Chinese in Malaysia. Membership in these sectarian alternatives is strongly associated with the cultivation of spiritual power, even though the neophytes and seasoned practitioners may not manifest ecstatic behaviors as in the spirit medium trances.

In summarizing the sociohistorical pattern of Chinese religion on the peninsula, we find that it is dominated by a this-worldly orientation quite similar to that of folk Hinduism practiced by Indian immigrants. This orientation is a consequence of lower-class Chinese immigration where "few or none of the Confucianist gentry [were] involved and none sufficiently educated to understand the philosophical aspects of Taoism or the doctrinal content of Buddhism" (Nyce 1971:84). Generally speaking, the pattern of worship among the Chinese immigrants was not greatly different from that of their village kinsmen in southeastern China. Except for various modifications that developed over the years, traditional worship has continued in homes, temples, and voluntary organizations. Social reform within Chinese society in Malaysia has been largely devoid of religious content, except for the brief period of Confucianist revivalism in the early 1900s. Unlike the tradition of reform in Hinduism first established by the Tamil nationalists and perpetuated by the Hindu Sangam and its rivals, no strong leaders have emerged to formalize an ideology that centralizes the beliefs and practices of Chinese religion. Even the relatively better-organized Buddhist bodies, such as the Singapore Federation of Buddhists, were more interested in building their public images than in advancing serious reforms (Freedman and Topley 1961:17).

Despite its fragmented nature, Chinese religion has continued to provide a source of cultural identity for the Chinese of Malaysia. The various traditional forms of worship have always been taken for granted by the Chinese as a familiar part of their daily lives. Even the innovative groups described above have retained many traditional elements of worship, thus giving them a distinct Chinese character. With the exception of the Confucianist movement, no other group has attempted to launch a large-scale renewal of Chinese identity through the reformulation of religious ideas and symbols. In the mid 1970s, however, a religious movement arose in the Chinese community of Kuala Lumpur that attempted to spread new definitions of Chinese identity. This was the Baitiangong movement, which we will now describe.

The Emergence of the Baitiangong Movement

The Baitiangong movement (which literally means "pray to the heavenly father") originated in a middle-class suburb of Kuala Lumpur. This suburb was until recently a predominantly Chinese working-class residential area. Recent housing development and city expansion have turned it into a middle-class suburb although large parts are still occupied by squatters and working-class Chinese. This suburb has over the years attained notoriety as a haven for Chinese criminals and secret society elements. In recent years it has been the scene of various flourishing religious movements, among them the Satya Sai Baba and Charismatic Renewal movements.

The origins of the Baitiangong movement can be traced to the claims of its leader-founder, Zhao Chongming,[10] who believes that he is an enforcer of divine laws, reborn on earth to rescue the Chinese in Malaysia from the diabolical influences of polytheism and to introduce them to monotheistic worship. In 1976 Zhao experienced a vision that he later interpreted as a divine instruction for his mission on earth. In this vision he was standing by the sea and heard a voice commanding him to destroy temples. When he protested that he lacked the powers, the voice instructed him to examine his wrists. Zhao saw rays of light emanating from his wrists. He was then transported on a pilotless airplane to a place with Indian and Chinese temples that he promptly destroyed with his laser beams. When his mission was completed, he heard the voice say, "I am pleased. You are a disciple of God. You are the deliverer of all unclean spirits." This vision made a profound impact on his life, at a time when he was experiencing employment frustrations. Other visions occurred that provided a new frame of reference for his role as God's messenger in Malaysia.

As an initial effort in organizing his movement, Zhao attempted to unite various Chinese spirit mediums and occult groups in his neighborhood. His tactic was to demonstrate the superiority of his powers over them. He invited the neighborhood groups to attend meditation sessions in the grounds of an unused Chinese temple, yet none attended the sessions. Undaunted, he proselytized a group of elderly Chinese women known as the Baiqijie (Seven Praying Sisters)[11] who met regularly at the temple to chant and go into trance. Zhao awed them with his alleged supernatural powers and taught them to meditate. Soon crowds of Chinese curiosity-seekers flocked to the meetings to listen to his message, learn meditation, and witness miraculous healings. But Zhao still had not consolidated his powers over the Chinese spirit mediums who were potential threats to his inchoate movement. Challenges from these mediums led to several spiritual duels in which Zhao claimed to have paralyzed them in their trances. These mediums later apologized and acknowledged Zhao's superiority over them. News of these events spread rapidly throughout the Chinese community, thus establishing Zhao's reputation as a spiritual master to be treated seriously and with deference. He later adopted the title *Xiansheng* (teacher).

With the defeat of the spirit mediums, Zhao could now divert all his energies to building up his movement. He began to experience more visions. In one vision, he saw his previous two incarnations (a warrior and a magistrate in ancient China) and his present self dressed completely in white with five buttons of different colors sewn to his coat, each button representing a different element (metal, wood, fire, water, earth). This vision convinced him of his eternal role as a celestial enforcer. Whenever Zhao goes preaching and healing, he dresses in his white costume as a symbol of his purity and power. After his vision involving the white clothing, Zhao had a series of visions in which he received the verses for the movement's prayer as well as instructions on the style of meditation. The verses of the prayer are often recited in the Cantonese dialect that praises God and his creations. Meditation comprises a simple technique of sitting crosslegged with eyes closed, arms resting on the abdomen, and palms facing upward. Before adopting this posture, the acolyte kneels with his hands clasped and, facing skyward, surrenders himself to God. As Zhao's reputation spread, he began to cultivate a unique image of himself through the public narration of his visions as well as the acquisition of various power objects such as a stick and several ballbearings (which he rolls in his palms) that are allegedly magical in nature.

In the early days of the movement, the thrust of recruitment was toward the Buddhists, Taoists, and occultists in the Chinese community. As the movement progressed, Zhao and his followers attempted to win converts from Chinese Christians. Zhao has even claimed that on one of his astral journeys he struck a compromise with the spirit of Jesus Christ in converting Christians to Baitiangong. He envisions the expansion of his movement to embrace people of different religions. The Baitiangong movement now boasts of more than two thousand members throughout peninsular Malaysia. In addition, a branch has been established in Singapore, and several Chinese residents in Denmark, Taiwan, and the United States have become converts. Until 1983 the mainstay of the movement was composed largely of working-class Chinese, while a small group of English-educated, middle-class Chinese occupied its upper echelons. In early 1978, Zhao designated two deputies as "button-holders." Each deputy wore a gold button representing the metal element and symbolizing knowledge. The button-holders were appointed to manage spiritual matters in the movement, while a working committee was established to oversee financial and other organizational affairs.

In late 1978, conflicts arose over the interpretation of Zhao's visions and his moral conduct. The dispute over Zhao's visions was initiated by a Chinese truck driver, an early convert who charged that Zhao's interpretive ability was marred by his low competence in the Chinese language. The truck driver claimed that since Zhao was not Chinese-educated, he had misunderstood the movement's prayer. This disagreement over scriptural interpretation extended into the movement's monotheistic ideology. The truck driver interpreted a vision of a smiling face in the sun as indicating the divinity of all the planets in the universe. Zhao rebuked him, fearing that such an interpretation would lead to idol worship. As a result of this dispute, the truck driver formed a faction comprising his kin and friends to oppose Zhao.

Further seeds of dissension were sown when a number of incidents involving Zhao's moral conduct were publicized by some followers. In one incident, two members charged that Zhao had neglected the safety of their kin when he held a meditation session on a hill, exposing his followers to rain and sun for several days. A tense confrontation followed in which verbal abuse was exchanged between Zhao and his accusers, leading almost to blows between the two parties. A more serious incident concerned charges of rape against Zhao who claimed that the woman involved was being used by her kin (her sister and the truck driver) to defame him. Zhao did not deny having had affairs with this woman and other female followers but argued that they had not resisted his advances. This scandal caused considerable consternation among the more conservative members, many of whom began to doubt Zhao's claim that he was God-sent. Many reinterpreted Zhao's powers as evil and departed hastily to seek salvation elsewhere, among them a gold button-holder. The more loyal followers, however, who interpreted Zhao's sexual prowess as concomitant with his supernatural privileges, rationalized the whole scandal as a test of their faith in their leader.

Incessant denouncements of Zhao by his rivals in the local Chinese press, as well as the departure of many of the movement's members, prompted Zhao to reorganize the movement to prevent the dissolution of his authority. Zhao appointed two more button-holders in 1979, one with the rank of gold button and the other the rank of water button (symbolizing tranquility). The three button-holders were recognized as Zhao's spiritual disciples. The movement also comprises several elders appointed by Zhao to handle administrative matters. Each elder was given a specific task, such as finance, publications, and so forth. In addition, each elder was responsible for instructing and supervising a group of counselors in the area under his charge. One of these elders was given the rank of cochairman, the duties of which were to work closely with one of the button-holders in supervising the other elders. The counselors functioned as middlemen between the decisionmakers and the ordinary followers. They recruited members and reported their activities to the elders. These records of members' activities were filed in an elder's house and reviewed regularly at committee meetings. Ordinary members were encouraged to apply annually for the position of counselor. After screening their applications, Zhao would send the successful applicants to a three-day training camp. There the counselors were exposed to all types of religious teachings and trained to do missionary work.

Despite the structural reorganization of the movement between 1979 and 1980, defections continued to occur. Zhao attributed the high rate of turnover to spies and rumormongers in the movement. In 1982 he was preparing new strategies to meet this problem when another crisis developed that involved the government. Between 1977 and 1979 Zhao gave weekly sermons, performed healings, and conducted mass trances at an unused Chinese temple. In 1980 he acquired a piece of land near a Chinese new village in Kuala Lumpur.[12] The land was actually a disused mining pool that was filled in and claimed by Zhao as his property, although he had sought no legal transactions to protect this claim. For two years, Zhao preached on his reclaimed land without realizing that a secret deal had been made between an elder and an influential Chinese businessman. The latter had eyed the Baitiangong grounds as an ideal location for his industrial expansion and had paid the elder (who lived near the grounds) a hefty sum as part of the land sale. He was confident that an eventual legal land transfer in his name would constitute a strong reason for evicting the Baitiangong members from their prayer grounds. By the time Zhao discovered this conspiracy he was placed at a disadvantage, having insufficient time and resources to resist the rapid advances of the businessman. In a last-ditch effort to save the prayer grounds Zhao requested that City Hall halt the movement of industrial equipment on his land, but he received no concrete response from them. His stubborn resistance further incurred the wrath of members of the Chinese business community, many of whom had already felt threatened by his ideological attacks on traditional Chinese mores.

These tensions came to a head on the night of October 2, 1982, when the members of Baitiangong celebrated their sixth anniversary at the prayer grounds. Zhao had originally planned to hold the anniversary dinner in a large hall owned by members of the Chinese business community in Kuala Lumpur. Although he had paid a deposit on the hall a year in advance, his reservation was abruptly cancelled shortly before the anniversary celebrations, forcing him to use the prayer grounds as a substitute. He threatened to sue the businessmen concerned and refused their overtures to settle out of court. Hardly had the celebrations begun on that wet, rainy night when a large contingent of riot police surrounded the prayer grounds, arrested two hundred Baitiangong members (including Zhao and his close disciples), and dispersed the gathering of about one thousand people. Zhao later claimed that his enemies in the Chinese business community had alerted the police.[13] The events of October 2 marked the beginning of a protracted legal confrontation between Baitiangong and the government. After a month of much-publicized court proceedings. Zhao and ninety-five members were found guilty of unlawful assembly and fined. In late January 1983, Zhao was rearrested and detained in jail on three charges of swindling, seduction, and street fighting. He was released twelve days later because of the lack of incriminating evidence, but he was immediately placed under restricted residence for almost seven months.[14] In March 1983, Zhao and several close disciples who held government jobs received suspension orders from their employers on the grounds that they had participated in illegal activities. This punitive action by the government proved to be effectively intimidating, since it caused several elders and two button-holders to defect from the movement. In October 1983, Zhao and several high-ranking members were charged with holding office in an unregistered movement. The movement's previous three attempts to obtain legal endorsement from the Registrar of Societies had been unsuccessful.[15]

The present growth of the movement has been arrested by a seemingly unending series of legal assaults from the government. Legal harrassment and continuous defection have severely taxed the movement's resources. Yet Zhao has demonstrated his resilience in preventing a total disintegration of the movement: although unemployed and persecuted, he is supported by a strong core of working-class Chinese and he continues his missionary activities throughout Malaysia. In 1983, Zhao organized several luncheons to raise morale and funds for the legal battles to come. At these luncheons, which were usually attended by three hundred or more people, group consciousness was heightened through songs and lectures while the loyalty of the high-ranking deserters was impugned. Zhao has expressed optimism in the resolution of his legal problems, which have been rationalized as an acid test of his followers' commitment to Baitiangong. He envisages a stronger movement and more-dedicated members emerging from the current crisis, but until he meets his legal challenges successfully the reorganization of Baitiangong will prove to be a long, arduous task.

The Leader of the Baitiangong Movement

Zhao is a garrulous, English-educated Chinese in his late forties. He received his education at a teachers' college and university in peninsular Malaysia, and is a secondary school teacher by profession. He is married and has two children. Zhao is illiterate in Chinese but speaks the Cantonese dialect. In the last few years, he has endeavored to read and speak Mandarin because of his missionary activities among Chinese who are illiterate in English.

Zhao was born on August 6, 1936, in the northern Malaysian city of Ipoh. He lost his mother during the Japanese invasion of Singapore in 1942. After his father remarried, he was passed around like a football—to use Zhao's words—among his relatives. Young Zhao grew up on his own without developing strong attachments to his family. He saw very little of his father. He claims that he had a tough childhood and endured much ill treatment from his relatives: there were only a few people in his early life who were kind to him. One person who befriended him was his school principal's wife, a European woman, who brought him presents and invited him to attend church. She was not the only person, however, who introduced him to Christian teachings—Zhao was brought up by his aunt, a Methodist. Despite his feelings of alienation from his relatives, he still likes to believe that he is a descendant of a Sung emperor. He has an old Chinese manuscript given to him by his great-uncle that allegedly contains evidence of his royal genealogy.

Zhao's familiarity with the spirit world dates back to his childhood. His grandmother was a spirit medium who specialized in blessing water and talismans. As a youth he experienced several visions and miracles. He remembers that when he was six years old he saw a huge figure surrounded by angels. When he was eighteen years old, he was saved from an accident by a mysterious voice. While traveling home in a bus, he suddenly heard a voice instructing him to move to the rear. A few seconds later, the bus crashed into a ravine. Zhao speculated that had he not followed the voice's advice, he surely would have been killed. Five years later he experienced an unforgettable vision. As he was lying in bed he looked up at the sky through an open window and saw that a bright star was approaching him. The star turned into a beautiful woman dressed completely in white who stooped down and kissed him on his forehead. Then she opened the bedroom door and left. Zhao was so overwhelmed by the vision that he was paralyzed for several minutes. In recollecting this vision, Zhao claims that the woman was actually an angel sent to appoint and prepare him for his role as God's messenger.

In later years, Zhao's contacts with the spirit world diminished as he became deeply involved in the mundane world of teachers' union politics and business. Between 1960 and 1970, he was a school teacher in Kuala Lumpur while holding important portfolios in two teachers' unions. He was also active in several voluntary associations.

In 1969 his career as a teacher was interrupted when he enrolled in a local university to study public administration. After graduation he lost his teaching job but found a job as a management consultant in a local firm. His brief stint in the business world ended a year later, following disagreements with his employers. He returned to teaching but was gravely disappointed by his failure to obtain a position as a school principal. Around this time, he participated in the activities of the Malaysian Chinese Association (MCA), the major Chinese party in the coalition government of Malaysia. He established an MCA branch in his neighborhood and became closely associated with several young Turks who were involved in organizing the Chinese Unity Movement within the MCA.[16] His disagreements with this faction over the matter of political strategies finally led to his departure from the MCA.

During this ten-year period, Zhao was never fully successful in his quest for power and recognition. He failed to unite various ethnic factions in the teachers' unions and thereby failed to gain prominence as a renowned unionist. As a minor politician, he was unsuccessful in influencing the course of Chinese politics in Malaysia. During his brief career as a management consultant, his colleagues thwarted his grandiose plans for business expansion. Even as a teacher he was unable to attain his ambition of becoming a school principal, despite his qualifications and long years of experience in education. His vision of temple destruction symbolized for him what he could achieve in the spiritual world, and formed a resolution to his failures as a leader in the mundane world. Other dreams and visions followed. He dreamed that a lion, a white elephant, and a white horse took him up a mountain to meditate.[17] He also claimed that he had visited heaven and hell in his astral sojourns, whereupon he discovered his origins in the "plane of nothing." While meditating one evening, he saw a huge tablet descend from the sky and felt it enter his body. He interpreted this vision as the beginning of his new spiritual self, a tabula rasa on which his future actions were to be recorded. His previous visions and miracles were recalled and fitted into a scheme of events now defined as spiritually significant.[18]

In the classic Weberian sense, Zhao acquired charismatic status through his claims of supernatural endowment. It must be noted, however, that his charisma is meaningless unless it can evoke a sense of awe or enthusiasm among his followers. Zhao was able to inspire awe among his followers through his demonstrations of mastery over

The Baitiangong Alternative in Chinese Religion

events, and able to generate enthusiasm through his representation of his followers' ideals (Spencer 1973).

The reverential posture of many members toward Zhao is a clear indication of their belief in his powers. Even members who have left as a result of disagreements speak slightingly of Zhao as a person yet do not doubt his powers. The charisma of Zhao derives from his alleged powers to control objects and people. He claims to possess the ability to extract power from idols and other physical objects of worship. This ability has been verified by some followers who claim that the shapes of these objects change whenever Zhao meditates before them. Zhao displays in his house the idols and objects of worship surrendered to him by followers as "trophies" and as a reminder of his powers. Aside from his powers to heal, exorcise, and win supernatural duels, Zhao also claims to have guided the souls of his followers to heaven and hell where they communicated with their deceased relatives. On one occasion, he even delivered to heaven the soul of a follower who committed suicide. This event was confirmed by some followers who witnessed it in their dreams. Accounts of Zhao's mastery over events in the spiritual realm are narrated at public meetings and confirmed by followers who have witnessed or experienced them. In addition to these accounts, which are designed to inspire awe and reverence among his followers, Zhao also reveals his forceful and aggressive character to demonstrate his mastery over mundane events. In addition to showing the scars he received from violent encounters with his enemies, Zhao verbally abuses and antagonizes his followers at public meetings. He does this with great relish as a strategy to convince his followers that he is fearless and unreproachable. Part of this image is maintained by his status as a lieutenant in the reserve army, which he joined in early 1981. He proudly displays in his home color photographs of himself in uniform and carrying weapons.

The question of a charismatic leader representing his followers' ideals must be discussed in terms of his role as a producer of social fantasy (Schwartz 1976:185). This means that he becomes audience-oriented in his performances, engaging in behaviors that conform to the fantasies and ideals of his followers. In the case of Zhao, the plausibility of his heroic image is sustained by a milieu that thrives on mystical martial arts fantasies as depicted in popular Chinese movies and fiction.[19] Zhao's awareness of the proper image required to fulfill his followers' fantasies is evidenced by his selection of a particular costume and various power objects as the identifying characteristics of a spiritual master normally seen on the movie screen. His explanation to his followers of his choice of paraphernalia through visions and other supernatural events reinforces his image as a master of the mystic arts. The production of social fantasy is also contingent upon the growth of a legend centering on Zhao's acquisition of supernatural powers and their use in combatting spirits, diseases, and other malignant forces. His victory over spirit mediums and other challengers has become the nucleus of a legend perpetuated through countless tales of exorcism, healing, and astral travel. As a model of martial arts fantasy, Zhao has thus far succeeded in generating and maintaining his followers' enthusiasm by his self-aggrandizing performances.

The charismatic image that Zhao has carefully cultivated over the years is now being challenged by the government. In subjecting Baitiangong to the pressures of the legal machinery, the government has attempted directly to undermine Zhao's reputation as an infallible wielder of power. To a certain extent this campaign has been successful; many followers have left the movement feeling that Zhao cannot provide them with adequate protection from government harrassment. Zhao has expressed more disappointment with the defection of his button-holders than with his legal problems. He considers betrayal by his closest disciples a serious affront to his credibility as a charismatic leader, whereas governmental persecution has brought him all the publicity he has craved. But within this limelight, spiritual endeavors have receded into the background as Zhao's leadership is tested in the courts of Kuala Lumpur where several of his cases are pending—cases that range from appeals against job suspension to suits against his detractors. At this stage of his career, Zhao has to demonstrate his skills in legal maneuvers rather than in spiritual combat.[20] Until he achieves a minimal level of success in the courtroom, his reputation as a religious leader in the Chinese community will be stunted.

The Followers of the Baitiangong Movement

From its formation in 1976 until late 1982, the Baitiangong movement was organized as a three-tiered, male-dominated structure. The most powerful positions were held by Zhao and his button-holders, the middle-managerial levels were filled mainly by English-educated, middle-class Chinese, and the grassroots comprised mainly Chinese-educated, working-class Chinese. Although there were some Indian followers involved in Baitiangong, none of them rose to high ranks in the movement. The control of the movement along class lines reflects to a large extent Zhao's class background and preferences. Zhao handpicked button-holders who were relatively well educated and at the same time receptive to his teachings. All four individuals who were button-holders in the movement were English-educated, worked as teachers or civil servants, ranged in age from the mid-thirties to the mid-forties, and shared with Zhao similar interests in the attainment of mystical powers.

The first button-holder was Zhang, a secondary school teacher in Ipoh who heard about Baitiangong from his friends. During a missionary trip to Ipoh, Zhao met Zhang, and was impressed with Zhang's knowledge of Chinese martial arts. Zhang had been an avid practitioner of Chinese martial arts for many years and was a member of Self-Realization Fellowship (SRF)[21] long before he met Zhao. Both men developed a mutual respect: Zhao often referred to Zhang as a "master of meditation," while Zhang was convinced of Zhao's powers, especially on one occasion when Zhao allegedly absorbed strange forces emanating from Zhang's SRF altar. About two years ago, Zhang became interested in Subud (a mystical Javanese movement), yet continued his activities in Baitiangong. He remained loyal to Zhao during the sexual morals crisis, but in 1983 he left the movement after he was suspended from his job for participating in the sixth anniversary celebrations.

Not long after Zhang's appointment Li was named the second button-holder. Li, who works as a civil servant in a government department in Kuala Lumpur and lives in the same neighborhood as Zhao, claimed to be a seeker of mystical knowledge, having read many books dealing with religion and the occult. He naturally became attracted to Zhao's teachings and miracles when the movement was gaining momentum in his neighborhood. Ironically, he was the harbinger of Zhao's teachings in Ipoh, having first acquainted Zhang with his master's name yet receiving his button after Zhang. He worked very closely with Zhao, proselytizing in different parts of the country and supervising various activities in the movement. In late 1978, Li was forced out of the movement because he disagreed with Zhao over the latter's sexual conduct. His wife was displeased with some harsh remarks that Zhao made about women and pressured Li to leave the movement. After his departure from Baitiangong, he wandered into the Charismatic Renewal.

Not long after Li's ouster, Huang was appointed to take his place. Among the button-holders Huang has the highest formal qualifications; he holds a university degree in geography and teaches in a government college near Kuala Lumpur. Like the others, Huang experimented with several religious alternatives—including Taoism, Buddhism, and Christianity—before turning to Zhao's teachings. He first heard about Zhao's powers from his brother-in-law, but was skeptical. Later, Huang and his wife became convinced of Zhao's powers after they had witnessed several healing performances. One of his brothers was appointed as an elder in the movement and was responsible for keeping records on the members. Like Zhang, Huang did not desert the movement when Zhao was accused of sexual licentiousness but left only after he was suspended from his job for taking part in the sixth anniversary celebrations.

We do not know much about the fourth button-holder, except that he is a senior civil servant based in the east coast state of Terengganu. Although he was present at the disastrous celebrations in 1982, he was not suspended from his job. He is presently the sole remaining button-holder in the movement.

The middle-ranking members of the movement were mainly English-speaking Chinese who held white-collar jobs in the government and private sector. Among the fifteen members with administrative duties, only two were female (although the vice-chairman of the Singapore branch is also a female). The ages of middle-ranking members ranged from the mid-thirties to the fifties. Most of these members first heard about Zhao from their friends and relatives. They joined the movement after Zhao awed them with his healing performances. Only a small number remained firm in their beliefs after the recent upheavals in the movement. One such individual is Yeh, an art teacher in a government college in Klang, a port city about thirty kilometers from Kuala Lumpur. Yeh lost his job after his arrest along with the others on the night of October 2, but he refused to withdraw his appeal against the charge of illegal assembly. He has since found a new job as a draughtsman in his brother-in-law's company. As one of the few remaining loyal elders in the movement, Yeh is a likely candidate for the position of button-holder. Most of his colleagues in the upper echelons of the movement have left because of government persecution.

The ordinary members of Baitiangong are mainly working-class Chinese from the squatter settlements in Zhao's neighborhood and other parts of Kuala Lumpur. There is also a sizable following in various Chinese new villages, particularly in the states of Pahang and Perak where Zhao established missionary bases. Most of these low-ranking members work as petty traders, vendors, taxi drivers, mechanics, and a variety of other skilled and unskilled occupations. While the middle-managers outwardly maintain a rather businesslike relationship with Zhao, the grassroots members tend to display more reverence toward their leader. Many offer gifts and services to Zhao; they deliver free foods, offer free haircuts, and some have even volunteered to renovate part of Zhao's house without labor costs. However, mobility from the lower to the middle level is greatly limited. Although ordinary members are given the opportunity to apply for the position of counselor, the competition is stiff and those who succeed rarely move beyond that level. The case of Wu clearly illustrates the problems faced by the rank and file in ascending the social hierarchy of the movement. Wu, a printer in his late thirties, came from a poor Chinese family in Melaka. He attended Chinese primary school for only three years before he began working at the age of fifteen. By the time he was eighteen, he was a committee member in a workers' union. In the late 1950s, he was a member of the now-defunct Labor Party. In the early 1970s, during a period of intense political mobilization among the Chinese, Wu drifted into PEKEMAS (the now-defunct Social Justice Party) and was active as its organizing secretary. Like Zhao, Wu became disillusioned with union and party politics. He entered the printing business but was swindled by his partner. At the height of his desperation, he turned to spirit mediums for help. It was at this time that he met Zhao and became one of his close disciples. He soon became a troubleshooter for Zhao who sent him on various missions to exorcize victims of spirit possession. Zhao was aware that Wu was harboring intentions of becoming a button-holder, but he refused to fulfill Wu's ambitions on the grounds that Wu had little formal education. Frustrated, Wu left the movement after three years.

Most people join Baitiangong because they are attracted by Zhao's healing abilities. At every public meeting followers bring their sick and maimed relatives to be healed, believing that the prayers and touches of Zhao and his close disciples are charged with curative properties. Many bring bottles of water to be blessed by Zhao. Because many followers are interested mainly in thaumaturgy, their commitment to the movement is contingent upon their state of health. Once "cured," their interest in the movement quickly wanes. To prevent high turnover, Zhao no longer performs instant healing. Now he claims to heal the sick and stricken over a relatively longer period of time, thereby indirectly forcing them to return to listen to his teachings. Similarly, he reserves the right to turn down requests for healing if he suspects the supplicant to be impervious to his teachings. Many followers are also eager to derive power from meditation with Zhao for improving their skills in the martial arts. At public meditation sessions, many such followers are seen performing various combat techniques—supposedly in a state of trance. Others believe that only Zhao has the ability during meditation to guide their souls on astral journeys or to heaven and hell. In fact, Zhao has warned all his followers to meditate only in his presence. Without his guidance, each person in meditation is vulnerable to spirit possession and other supernatural dangers.

These motives, however, are not very obvious in the responses of fifty-one Baitiangong members we surveyed (forty-eight Chinese and three Indians). The data in Table 3 show that a large proportion of the respondents listed ideological reasons for joining Baitiangong. Many of the respondents voiced their agreement with Zhao's teachings as the most effective path to salvation. Curiously enough, there seems to be a uniform pattern to the responses given by these respondents: "I believe that Xiansheng's teachings are right and true" is the typical response to the question "Why did you join Baitiangong?" There are two possible interpretations of these results. First, many Baitiangong members may not see any clear separations between the teachings espoused by Zhao and his supernatural powers. To claim belief in his teachings as the

Table 3. Reasons for Joining Baitiangong

	Percentage	Number
Ideological (pertaining to Zhao's teachings)	86.3	44
Healing	11.8	6
No response	1.9	1

central motive for joining the movement may be another way of saying that access to supernatural power is contingent upon ideological commitment. Second, many Baitiangong members may be embarrassed by their thaumaturgical motives, since Zhao has reprimanded them on many occasions for their short-sightedness in seeking cures without understanding his teachings. The response quoted above may therefore represent a discreet way of circumventing their embarrassment. What leads us to suspect that our respondents are just as interested in obtaining supernatural power as the average religious seeker in Malaysia is the fact that 96 percent of our sample (or 49 respondents) reported that they have experienced a variety of visionary and healing events. This suggests that regardless of their ideological motives most respondents expect to derive some form of supernatural experience from their association with Baitiangong. Those who do not eventually leave the movement.

When we compared mystical experiences across class lines, we discovered that the middle-class members, especially those in administrative positions, tend to report fewer spiritual encounters than the working-class members. None of the button-holders reported having experienced intense spiritual events, such as traveling to various astral planes or meeting deceased relatives. Li, for example, told us that the most "mystifying" experience he had during his two years in the movement was a sudden, uncontrollable jerking of his left arm at a meditation session. We have also observed that few elders and counselors participate in meditation at mass gatherings. Instead, they move among the crowds, supervising and attending to meditators who have entered a deep trance, or controlling those who become violent in their martial arts performances under trance. Despite the lack of supernatural experiences among the members of the upper echelon, they are committed to the movement because of the leadership roles that Zhao has assigned them. Broadly speaking, reports of supernatural experiences, particularly at the grassroots level, occur more frequently among members whose chances of attaining leadership positions in the movement are limited.

Our survey data show that a large percentage of the respondents first heard about Zhao and Baitiangong through friends and through members of the movement. Table 4 gives the breakdown of the initial contact of the respondents with Baitiangong. The data suggest that recruitment is effected more by word-of-mouth techniques and per-

Table 4. First Contact with Baitiangong

	Percentage	Number
Friends and colleagues	33.4	17
Members of movement	35.3	18
Relatives	19.6	10
Pamphlets, tapes, and newspapers	5.9	3
Stranger	1.9	1
No response	3.9	2

sonal networks than by printed material and tape recordings. To a certain extent, this finding is not surprising since Zhao has carved Kuala Lumpur, Petaling Jaya, and other towns in Malaysia into distinct areas for proselytization through the movement's counselors. These counselors in turn use their personal connections to disseminate Zhao's teachings. What is surprising, however, is the relatively low incidence of printed material as a source of influence. Since the formation of the movement, numerous accounts of the healing and mystical experiences of members have been printed and distributed in English and Chinese. Similarly, tape recordings of Zhao's harangues and speeches form an important component of the movement's archives. These materials, however, are probably circulated mainly among members and therefore have not made an impact on outsiders.

Two major crises over the last four years have seriously affected the membership structure of the movement. In 1978, the scandal over Zhao's sexual activities caused the more puritanical members, especially those among the middle-class, to leave the movement. Although the scandal originated from the ranks of the working-class members (Zhao's accusers were from the grassroots level), its effect was more profound on the upper levels of the movement. Zhao was able to prevent a total disintegration of the movement by codifying his promiscuity into a set of moral principles (see next section), but he could not effectively recoup his losses from among the middle-class members. The arrest of Zhao and his subordinates in 1982 precipitated even more radical changes in the movement. Many middle-ranking members left for fear of government persecution, thereby causing a large vacuum in the administrative machinery of the movement. Unlike their middle-class counterparts (many of whom are government employees), the working-class members are mainly self-employed and therefore are less intimidated by the governmental threat of job suspension. These members are more willing to weather the current legal crisis and their loyalty to Zhao may prove to be a passport to future upward mobility in the movement. In other words, both crises have alienated many middle-class members from Zhao but have consolidated strong working-class support for him. Government pressure on the movement ironically has promoted the rise of its working-class members rather than suppress them.

Ideological Developments in Baitiangong

Like many religious movements, the eschatological and ethical systems of Baitiangong are still in their formative stages. Zhao is still struggling to establish a coherent system of thought that will form the basis of the movement's theology and soteriology. Nevertheless, at this juncture of the movement's development, several core ideas have evolved that center on the problems of salvation and morality.

Zhao defines salvation in terms of blissful existence in heaven after physical death. He often exhorts his followers to set their minds on heaven rather than on a limited earthly life, although he does not emphasize a total renunciation of the world. A phrase that he had coined—"we die to live"—is frequently repeated in his speeches to stress the rewards of paradise that await the true believer. But a person has to accept five spiritual principles before he can even begin his search for salvation. These principles are: Realization of Consciousness, Realization of Self, Realization of the Soul, Realization of Heaven and Hell, and Realization of the Creator. An understanding of these five principles is said to enhance a person's spiritual awareness and prepare him for the higher planes of existence after death. The direct experience of the spiritual world in meditation is believed to open new vistas in a person's life, thereby accelerating the maturity of his thoughts in the direction of the five principles. Zhao encourages his followers to meditate in order to travel in the astral dimension, to witness sufferings in hell and tranquility in heaven, and to experience contact with other spiritual beings. Many followers who allegedly have accomplished these sojourns affirm the importance of meditation as a channel of communication with the spiritual realm. Zhao teaches, however, that even with this achievement man can never truly understand the nature of God. In short, salvation is something that can be worked for but it does not necessarily imply divine enlightenment.

According to Zhao, the Divine Will requires man to respect and fear God, but deviations from the Divine Will have continued to occur despite the warnings of various prophets throughout the ages. Zhao sees himself as merely refulfilling the role that other prophets had assumed earlier to help man regain his bearings on the path to righteous actions and pass what he calls the "Examination of Life." He teaches that the self consists of the body and the soul. The body is the vehicle for the soul to undergo the "Examination of Life," which essentially comprises the moral bases of a person's actions and their consequences after death. It is quite similar to the Christian concept of "you reap what you sow." After death the soul continues to exist in one of four spiritual dimensions: heaven, hell, limbo, and the earth plane. Heaven refers to planes of tranquility and ecstasy that can be further graded from low to high heaven. In heaven all ties with the human world are severed because the "Examination of Life" is no longer applicable. Pleasure in heaven is so profound that it is beyond human imagination. In the upper strata of heaven, individual souls are sustained eternally by overwhelming bliss as they continue to pray to God. Once the soul qualifies to ascend to heaven there is no more reincarnation unless it is returned to earth by God's will. Hell is where sinful souls are punished. People who have lied, cheated, murdered, stolen, and so forth will descend into hell after death to experience agonizing punishments commensurate with their crimes. Limbo is reserved for agnostics who have committed few sins and many good deeds in life. These souls are neither exposed to sufferings nor bliss but are given another opportunity to realize the existence of God. The earth plane is inhabited by roaming souls or ghosts who, during their lifetime, committed suicide or very serious sins. Souls on the earth plane are subjected to extreme loneliness before being cast into hell for further punishments. Souls in hell, limbo, and the earth plane will eventually be reincarnated on earth to repeat the "Examination of Life."

In Zhao's efforts to correct the moral conduct of man, he has alerted his followers to two actions that he considers cardinal sins. Those who once accepted and prayed to God but reverted to worshipping idols are said to have committed an unpardonable sin. Similarly, those who commit suicide are merely seeking an easy way out of the "Examination of Life" and have therefore contravened the divine law of nature that all individuals are bound to on earth. The first type of sinner is condemned to the earth plane for thousands of years before descending into hell for further punishments. The second type of sinner also expects the same fate, but Zhao reserves the right to forgive them and send them to the lower levels of heaven. Despite the codification of these sins, Zhao does not subscribe to the idea of the original sin. He believes that all reincarnated souls begin life as humans on a clean slate, having already paid for their sins in hell or the earth plane. However, he has warned his followers that man has become so sinful and incorrigible that it is only a matter of time before he incurs the wrath of God, which will result in global destruction. He has not predicted when doomsday will occur but has revealed that only the faithful on earth and enlightened souls in heaven will be saved. All other forms of existence, including the dimensions of hell and limbo, will be destroyed.

Zhao has assured his followers a direct passage to heaven if they adhere to a list of rules for prayers and various life-cycle rites. He advises them to remove all idols from their homes and to place on their family altars a brass urn with four joss sticks in it. This in fact is the movement's logo: the largest joss stick representing God and the three smaller ones representing Christianity, Islam, and Baitiangong. They are instructed to pray to God at least twice a day, once upon waking and once before sleeping. They must kneel facing skyward with their hands clasping a joss stick and recite one of three prayers or all three prayers; that is, the Lord's Prayer, some verses from Al-Fatihah (the opening chapter of the Quran),[22] and the Baitiangong Prayer. Recently Zhao instructed his followers to replace the urn with a plaque of the movement's logo, on the assumption that many of them were treating the urn as an idol. He believes that idol worship is spiritually deleterious because a person unconsciously transfers his energy to the idol while praying to it, a phenomenon that he has termed "spiritual vampirism." According to Zhao's teachings, a person in meditation or prayer projects life-force energies onto the object of his worship. These energy vibrations are easily absorbed by the idols, turning them into animated objects that can influence the unwary worshipper. Unless the worshipper is aware of these dire osmotic effects, he will unwittingly become enslaved by the idols. Zhao claims that only he has the power to neutralize the influences of animated idols and other objects of worship.

Zhao insists that life-cycle rites should be conducted without pomp and ceremony. At funerals the deceased and mourners are required to be dressed in white. Cremation is preferred to burial, with the ashes of the deceased scattered on a river or the sea. All family members are advised to pray for the soul of the deceased but not to him. Zhao prohibits his followers to make offerings to the dead. Similarly, marriages are performed by Zhao and his button-holders according to the following rules: the minimal age limit for brides is eighteen years and that for grooms is twenty-one years; both the bride and bridegroom are required to wear white for the ceremony, which simply entails kneeling and praying to God for his blessings; and, at the end of the ceremony, the couple and the witnesses sign their names in the Baitiangong record of marriages. Zhao also conducts blessings for newborn babies by anointing their foreheads, solar plexus, shoulders, palms, and soles with ashes from an urn while reciting the Baitiangong Prayer. He claims that this ritual enhances the child's consciousness and wards off evil spirits.

In addition to these practices, Zhao introduced in 1979 a set of rules for sexual conduct in response to accusations of moral vagaries following his scandal with some female members. Baitiangong members are permitted to practice fornication (defined as sexual relations between unmarried couples or between married men and unmarried women) and bigamy,[23] but must refrain from homosexuality, prostitution, incest, adultery, and rape. The more conservative members rejected Zhao's permissive ideology, arguing that he had introduced these rules to justify his immoral behavior. The more loyal members accepted these rules without question. Zhao has interpreted the ideological enshrinement of sexual permissiveness in his movement as an assault on traditional Chinese morality. Similarly, his repudiation of Chinese ancestor worship, elaborate funerals and marriages, and the use of idols in worship comprises part of his efforts in forging an ideology of desinification to differentiate Baitiangong from other Chinese religious groups. Yet Zhao does not dare to alienate too many Chinese from his movement, particularly those at the grassroots level who are Chinese educated. Thus he has formed a lion dance troupe as well as promoted the use of Mandarin to project the movement's Chinese identity.

Zhao's emphasis on monotheistic worship and particular Chinese religious and cultural practices represents his attempts to redefine Chinese identity through a synthesis of Protestant Christian themes and

Chinese cultural symbols. The core elements of Baitiangong ideology —anti-idolatry, strict monotheism, and promotion of simplicity in funerals and marriages—are derived from Zhao's encounter with Protestant Christianity during his school days. On the other hand, his selection of the brass urn with joss sticks as the movement's logo, and the promotion of such cultural activities as martial arts, playing traditional musical instruments, lion dance performances, and use of the Mandarin dialect, underscore the Chinese character of the movement. Furthermore, he has drawn upon a wide range of Taoist and Buddhist concepts—such as the five elements *(wu xing)*, meridian points, heaven and hell, reincarnation, and "plane of nothing" (or the void)— to construct his incipient ideological system. Yet he continues to deride Confucianism, Taoism, and Buddhism, which he facetiously calls "Conto-Buddhism," as sources of religious backwardness in Chinese society. These ideological contradictions are not apparent to Zhao and his followers; rather, they suggest the high degree of opportunism in ideological innovations in the early stages of the movement's growth, as is also reflected in Zhao's political alignments.

Zhao has never been explicitly antigovernment. Rather, he has made strenuous efforts to demonstrate his loyalty to Malaysia. He has publicly defended himself against accusations of antinationalism by asserting that patriotism runs in his family. He claims that his grandfather sought refuge in China because the British suspected his involvement in the murder of James Birch, the colonial resident of Perak, and that his two brothers are now employed in the government service, one in the military and the other in the police force. He has urged his followers to donate blood en masse, especially during the Muslim fasting month of Ramadan when there is a shortage of blood donors, and to visit political dignitaries on all major festive occasions. He has recently emphasized the use of the national language, Bahasa Malaysia, in public speeches and the movement's publications. All of these activities suggest Zhao's efforts to project an image of Baitiangong as an altruistic, progovernment movement. Despite government harrassment of Baitiangong, Zhao has not turned militant but continues with the above activities in the hope that he will make a good impression on the government and thereby gain legal recognition for his movement. In other words, increasing government interference has facilitated a certain degree of political consciousness in a movement that is founded on dissent against Chinese traditionalism rather than against the political establishment. To what extent this political consciousness will be maintained in favor of the government depends on the outcome of Zhao's upcoming court cases.

The Relevance of Baitiangong in Chinese Politics and Religion

Baitiangong may be considered the first Chinese religious movement in postindependence Malaysia to have received widespread publicity in its conflict with members of the Chinese community and the government. That the movement has resorted to legal means in its confrontation with the government raises interesting questions on the problem of religious legitimacy in a plural society. Similarly, the movement's dissension with various segments of the Chinese community suggests the problem of legitimacy of reform in Chinese religion. Before we can discuss these questions at length, it is necessary to examine the sociopolitical context from which Baitiangong has emerged. It is within this context that the question of legitimacy can be most fruitfully studied as an issue in power relations.

Baitiangong was founded seven years after the 1969 race riots, in a period of relative political stability following the reestablishment of parliamentary democracy in 1971.[24] This was also a period of relative political quiet in the Chinese community following the failed efforts by the MCA between 1971 and 1973 to foster Chinese unity. Intense political agitation concerning Chinese rights on the eve of the 1969 national elections had not only aroused mass support for the Chinese-based opposition parties but also, tragically, triggered the race riots. In the aftermath of the riots, in which many Chinese lost their lives and property, there was generally a mood of frustration and despair in the Chinese community. Even though the MCA continued to represent Chinese interests in the government, the organization was regarded by a large section of the Chinese community to be ineffective. The gains made by the Chinese opposition parties came to nought when emergency rule was declared in the wake of the race riots. As political gloom settled over the Chinese community, the MCA desperately attempted to revive its image by organizing a series of campaigns that were supposedly reformist in design. The leaders recruited young professional Chinese to direct these campaigns in the hope that their enthusiasm and respectability would recover lost ground and thereby regain public confidence in the party. No sooner had the campaigns been launched in 1971 when the MCA leaders discovered that they had unleashed political elements that threatened their interests and those of the Malay community. The young Turks in the MCA felt that it was necessary to challenge the old guards before reforms could be effectively implemented. By that time they had already achieved large-scale grassroots support with their pro-Chinese reforms. Government support, however, for the MCA leaders meant defeat for the young Turks. Thus the MCA crisis came to an end in 1973—the promised reforms stalled and Chinese unity barely accomplished (see Loh 1982).

Chinese political activities in the early 1970s to a large extent reflected the perennial tensions between the pro-Malay MCA leaders and the communally oriented Chinese majority. That the latter had felt betrayed by the MCA was incontrovertibly evidenced by the former's losses in the 1969 elections. But the Chinese masses quickly rallied behind the young Turks whom they had hoped would remold the MCA in their interests. The fiasco of the MCA reform movement not only dashed these hopes but also left the Chinese masses without strong leadership. The crossover of many young Turks into the opposition parties provided alternative sources of political allegiance for the Chinese masses, although these parties lacked sufficient resources to pursue radical reforms. Chinese politics in this period was characterized by a heightened awareness of ethnic rights and grievances, yet an awareness that was constrained by the bloody events of May 13, 1969. Baitiangong was founded at a time when Chinese political differences remained unresolved and more Chinese began turning to opposition parties for political satisfaction. Although the movement is not explicitly political in its policies and activities, the timing of its establishment and popularity suggests a symbolic alternative within the context of Chinese political impotence.

Ironically, Zhao had been an active but marginal member of the MCA young Turks. In spite of this association, he felt that the young Turks had failed to appreciate his contribution to their cause and had even rebuked his suggestions for resolving the crisis.[25] This bitter experience with the MCA reform movement left him disillusioned with party politics and he gradually turned to religion to fulfill his political needs. Out of his multiple visions and astral travels emerged an answer to the problem of Chinese disunity in Malaysia—the subordinate political position of the Chinese community was attributed to divine punishment for idolatry and failure to worship God. The Baitiangong ideology of salvation has been advanced as a solution to what Zhao perceives as the political and spiritual damnation of the Chinese community in Malaysia. The political strength of the Malays, according to him, is derived from their spiritual integrity as Muslims, who do not worship idols. In reducing the complex political history of the peninsula to a question of piety, Zhao codified political dissatisfactions into a religious message. The Baitiangong movement, although not outwardly political, represents not only Zhao's political failures but also his search for other power alternatives in the Chinese community. Various symbols of political prestige similar to those of the MCA —such as the white outfits worn by Baitiangong members, as well as an active youth corps—suggest the movement's identification with the sources of political power in the Chinese community. The religious reforms advocated by Zhao are in a way substitutes for the political reforms of the MCA young Turks in their quest for Chinese unity. In a sense, Baitiangong can be considered a religious ramification of the Chinese political crises of the early seventies.

The basis, however, of reform legitimacy in Baitiangong differs radically from that of the MCA reform movement. The pro-Chinese reforms advocated by the MCA young Turks were tacitly approved by their superiors. Until this support was withdrawn, the reforms remained politically viable. But Zhao did not rely on any secular body to legitimate his antitraditionalist reforms. He believes that as God's representative on earth his reforms are sacralized by the mandate of heaven, the jurisdiction of which extends beyond all secular authority. The basis of this claim lies in Zhao's enactment of a shamanistic role that appeals to many members of the Chinese community. He styles himself as a mediator between heaven and earth, and commands prestige as a powerful shaman able to exteriorize his soul and travel to supernatural realms, to perform miraculous healings, to exorcise evil spirits, and to subdue his rivals in spiritual duels. The institution of shamanism flourished in China as early as 109 B.C. (de Groot, 1964): Zhao has merely drawn on an established cultural style to win support from the Chinese community. Despite his shamanistic performances, Zhao has not been able fully to establish legitimate claims to his other role as religious reformer, for two reasons. First, Baitiangong's drive to suppress Chinese traditionalism appears to be antithetical to the pro-Chinese reforms of the MCA young Turks. At a time when political events were defined by many Chinese as detrimental to their cultural well-being, Zhao's reformist strategy was bound to irritate already frayed nerves and therefore alienate many people from his movement. For this reason, he was willing to back down on his antitraditionalism rhetoric and even play up various Chinese themes in the movement's activities. Second, there is a distinct separation between political and supernatural sanctions in a secular state such as Malaysia where communal reforms become meaningful only when they are endorsed by recognized political bodies. Thus the reforms advocated by the MCA young Turks were legitimate as long as they had powerful political patronage; in the case of Baitiangong, however, such patronage was nonexistent. The supernatural basis of Zhao's reforms was only relevant to the followers who believed in him, and its legitimacy did not extend beyond their circle of interaction. Given the limitations of Baitiangong's reform legitimacy, Zhao could not effectively broaden his role beyond that of a shaman. On the contrary, the absence of political support for Baitiangong's reforms has made Zhao highly vulnerable to charges of fraud and charlatanry by his rivals.

The government, on the other hand, has not been greatly concerned with Zhao's calls for cultural and religious reforms in Chinese society; such issues pose no immediate threat to the government's rule. Unlike the MCA young Turks whose reforms directly challenged the party leadership—and hence the established networks in the government coalition (Loh 1982:73)—Baitiangong's attempts at reform hardly affected the political structure of the Chinese community. Both the MCA young Turks and Zhao had similar aims in reaching the Chinese masses, but the impact of their reforms differed in content and consequences. Nevertheless, the government intervened to disrupt Baitiangong's activities for at least two reasons. First, Baitiangong's rapid growth occurred during a period of religious unrest among the Muslims. Fearing that its campaign to control Muslim dissidence might affect the Islamic image of the country, the government calculatingly diverted its attention to other religious groups in order to generalize the problem. In late 1982, the deputy prime minister openly voiced his concern that "deviationist teachings" were not confined to Islam alone. He cited Baitiangong as an example of "Buddhist deviation." Baitiangong had become a prime target of government censure of "deviant" non-Islamic groups because it was one of the more-publicized new religions in Malaysia. Second, the government was influenced by powerful elements in the Chinese business community who desired restraint on Zhao's activities. As described earlier, the contest over Baitiangong's prayer grounds precipitated a chain of events that eventually culminated in legal proceedings against Zhao and his followers. On the surface, it appears that the present conflict revolves around the government's charge of security violations and Zhao's invocation of constitutional rights concerning religious matters. Yet in actuality, the question of Baitiangong's legitimacy is meaningful only if we examine the movement's position in the framework of national and local events.

Within the context of Chinese religion in Malaysia, Baitiangong cannot be considered a unique movement because it shares with many groups a tendency toward ideological syncretism. Baitiangong, like the sects of the Great Way, Sinru Temple, and *Dejiao Hui*, has borrowed extensively from various religious traditions, but it differs from the others in ideology and style of leadership. Baitiangong is explicitly reformist in its orientation, using the rhetoric of antitraditionalism in its attempts to refashion the parameters of Chinese identity, whereas the other groups make no such claims. One exception is the Confucianist movement, which was organized in the early 1900s to revive traditional Chinese values; its motive, however, is antithetical to that of Baitiangong. Moreover, the growth of the Confucianist movement was influenced by events in China, whereas Baitiangong is a local phenomenon. In comparing leadership style, Zhao tends to be more aggressive and ostentatious than the leaders of the other groups. Zhao perceives himself to be an indispensable mediator between heaven and earth, a powerful individual who can guide his followers' souls in astral travel, perform healings and exorcisms, and paralyze his rivals in trances. Zhao's style resembles, to a certain extent, that of the spirit mediums. Yet unlike them he is never possessed by deities temporarily manifesting supernatural powers through a medium's body. Furthermore, his shamanic performances, unlike those displayed by spirit mediums, are not characterized by ecstasy or frenzy—he is always in control of himself. Despite these differences, Baitiangong cannot be strictly defined as a schismatic movement in Chinese religion. It has not come into open conflict with any Chinese religious group and its ideologies have not been publicly repudiated by Buddhist or Taoist priests. On the other hand, Baitiangong continues to borrow freely from the Chinese religious system for enhancing its Chinese image. The question of religious schism becomes appropriate if Baitiangong's antitraditionalist rhetoric and activities are perceived as threats by an organized body of religious officials. Since Chinese religion in Malaysia is not centrally administered, Zhao has no religious bureaucracy to dissent against. Instead, he uses the diffused notion of Chinese traditionalism as a convenient foil for advancing his interests.

Given these conditions, the question of Baitiangong's legitimacy does not fall precisely within the confines of Chinese religion. Rather, it is a problem related to governmental recognition of the movement's existence. In this respect, Baitiangong is no more religiously deviant than the Great Way sects, Sinru Temple, or *Dejiao Hui*. The major difference is that the latter groups are registered bodies while Baitiangong has yet to attain such status. Until it receives legal endorsement from the government, Baitiangong is best identified as a cultic alternative that is competing with various formal Chinese religious organizations for membership and ideological supremacy. But the future of Baitiangong as a cultic alternative is uncertain because it is no longer in a position to conduct its activities without government consent. Without strong political patronage and communal support, Baitiangong has only limited resources in its struggle to win formal recognition from the government. The implication of this discussion on religious legitimacy is that Chinese religion in Malaysia is subordinate to the overall political system. The determination of this legitimacy among Chinese religious groups in Malaysia reflects more government than communal control. This is most evident when we consider that Baitiangong's deviant status was imposed by a high-ranking government official rather than by other Chinese religious groups.

CHAPTER SIX

Searching for New Heavens: Secularization and Ethnic Identity in the New Movements

WHAT are the wider implications of Baitiangong, the Charismatic Renewal, and the Satya Sai Baba movement for Malaysian society? This question must be considered in relation to the problem of secularization raised earlier. Broadly considered as a macro-social process, secularization is predominantly characterized by the decline of religion as a political ideology and as an obligatory institution with strong influence in the main spheres of public life. In societies experiencing secularization, religion becomes a voluntary and private pursuit that generates increased demand for alternative beliefs. Religious experimentation as a response to secularization has been observed in various urban centers throughout the world (e.g., Davis 1980; De Craemer 1977; Pressel 1974; Zaretsky and Leone 1974). Much of this experimentation has taken the form of individualistic movements offering immediate access to mystical power and practical solutions in everyday life. The search for salvation through experimentation with a variety of new heavens is by no means a preoccupation peculiar to the uneducated and economically deprived. Many middle-class urbanites, disillusioned with the promises of technological advancement, endeavor to seek personal fulfillment among the burgeoning religious innovations that flourish in secular societies.

The proliferation of new religious movements also characterizes the process of secularization in Malaysia. But this process occurs within the context of an asymmetrical relationship between the Muslim and non-Muslim religious fields. In other words, the consequences of secularization in Malaysia must be examined on two levels: as a general response to a rapidly urbanizing and industrializing environment and as a specific response to the changing political circumstances. The first level of analysis focuses on the social boundaries of religious experimentation in Malaysia and the impact of the three new movements on the non-Muslim religious field. The second level of analysis is concerned with the state's promotion of ethnic politics through a religious idiom and the significance of the three movements as vehicles of non-Malay ethnic identity. Together these two levels of analysis provide an understanding of the particular historical course taken by secularization in Malaysia. We will now examine these two levels of analysis separately.

The Process of Salvation in the New Movements

As described in chapter 2, participation in the Muslim religious field is obligatory for all Malays. On the other hand, non-Malays are not constrained by similar legal requirements in the non-Muslim religious field. As a result, the non-Muslim religious field is highly fluid and more open in structure. Participation in non-Muslim religions in Malaysia is generally a voluntary activity that does not necessarily impinge on the seeker's performance of his social roles. The diversity of non-Muslim options, especially those with thaumaturgical appeal, promotes highly personalized forms of salvation with no significance as legitimations of the social order. This pattern of salvationary expectations, reinforced by the increasingly individualistic character of urban life in Malaysia, underlies the trend of innovation and experimentation observed in the new non-Muslim movements.

Experimentation in the non-Muslim religious field is primarily concerned with meeting worldly needs through direct and personal experience of a charismatic presence and thaumaturgical efficacy. Miracles in the mundane world legitimate the transcendental claims of the various non-Muslim options. As practical religions, the new non-Muslim movements demonstrate their concern for man's welfare through therapeutic routines focused on healing. As seen in the previous chapters, healing comprises a central activity in the three new movements. Most participants in these movements treat the transcendental aspects of their leaders' objectives as abstract ideologies that are secondary to their need for thaumaturgical services. Thus direct contact with the Holy Spirit, Satya Sai Baba, or the Baitiangong prophet is the means of entering a new heaven in which individual suffering in the here-and-now is alleviated, and a community with others devoted to the same goals is formed. These communities are by no means highly exclusive but are open to individuals seeking concrete experiences of salvation. Participation in the apostolic prayer groups of the Charismatic Renewal, the *bhajan* of the Satya Sai Baba movement, or the meditation sessions conducted by the Baitiangong prophet forms the basis of community-building in the new movements.

The emphasis on community-building, however, has not eroded the individualism of the movements' membership, since none of these movements subscribe to the principles of communal living and total commitment. The three new movements vary in the degrees of commitment required of their members. Baitiangong's concept of commitment is somewhat more exclusive and demanding than that of the Satya Sai Baba and charismatic movements. The Baitiangong prophet discourages his followers from forming attachments to other religious alternatives, and attempts to engage as much of his followers' time and energy as possible in an expanding number of activities. Commitment to the charismatic movement, in contrast, is compatible with concurrent participation in a broad range of formal religious organizations and cultic alternatives within the Christian tradition. The Satya Sai Baba movement, relative to the other two movements, is based on the most flexible concept of commitment. Satya Sai Baba devotees are free to participate in religious groups associated with any tradition and to maintain attachments to other sources of religious inspiration.

The differing concepts of commitment underlying the three new movements entail particular patterns of competition with other formal religious organizations and cultic alternatives. The Baitiangong prophet's attempt at forging exclusive commitment to the movement has led him to assume an aggressive stance toward other groups within the non-Muslim religious field. As the majority of Baitiangong's membership is drawn from the clientele of Chinese cultic alternatives, the prophet's most immediate competitors are spirit mediums and occultists who ply their trade in commercialized temples set up in their homes and, occasionally, in public places. Since the role of the Baitiangong prophet as shaman and thaumaturge is continuous with Chinese folk beliefs concerning supernatural abilities, he appeals to the Chinese community on the same basis as the other religious entrepreneurs. Thus contests of power between Baitiangong and the Chinese cultic alternatives are not strictly pursued as doctrinal issues but as mystical and physical duels to determine control over sources of recruitment and revenue.

Unlike Baitiangong, involvement in the Satya Sai Baba movement is compatible with multiple religious affiliations. But this liberal approach to seeking salvation has not prevented antagonism between the movement's organizers and traditional Hindu leaders who are concerned about the declining interest in temple worship among Hindu devotees of Satya Sai Baba. Competition between the Satya Sai Baba movement and other Hindu alternatives mainly involves formal religious organizations (e.g., registered Hindu temples, or the Malaysian Hindu Sangam) rather than cultic alternatives, such as unregistered Hindu temples and shrines. Registered Hindu temples tend to operate more elaborate and expensive establishments. Loss of supporters usually results in greater financial hardship for a registered temple with Brahmin priests in residence and high maintenance costs than for an unregistered temple or shrine housed in a wooden hut with little or no overhead costs. Concretely, then, the Satya Sai Baba movement has tended to deprive registered temples of badly needed financial support, while unregistered temples and shrines are relatively unaffected by fluctuations in donations. As in the case of Baitiangong, competition between the Satya Sai Baba movement and other Hindu alternatives is centered around economic rather than doctrinal issues.

The Charismatic Renewal movement's relationship to other religious alternatives within the non-Muslim religious field is less antagonistic than that of Baitiangong, but also less flexible than that of the Satya Sai Baba movement. Participants in the charismatic movement are free to maintain multiple affiliations but only within the Christian tradition. Typically, participants are members of the Roman Catholic church or various Protestant denominations, and are involved in church-controlled lay groups or in interdenominational groups independent of any particular church. They may also concurrently attend more than one charismatic prayer group. Nevertheless, competition has arisen between the charismatic movement and other Christian alternatives, revolving around various doctrinal issues that comprise an implied threat to church authority. The gifts of the Holy Spirit, for example, shift the locus of authority from the clergy to the laity, while also disrupting the order and routine of conventional worship services. The mainline Protestant denominations emphatically reject the central charismatic doctrine of Pentecost as a continuing Christian experience, while the Roman Catholic church affirms the validity of the New Pentecost and spiritual gifts but opposes such Protestant charismatic doctrinal "deviations" as the imminent Second Coming of Christ and glossolalia as a sign of salvation.

The patterns of commitment and conflict outlined above show that the new movements tend to compete directly with other groups within the same parent tradition and only indirectly among themselves. This suggests that the new movements do not yet have the potential to transcend the fragmented nature of the non-Muslim religious field. Furthermore, no non-Muslim religious group enjoys legal sanctions to enforce its worldviews among followers. Both new and traditional non-Muslim religions are on an equal footing, from a legal standpoint, in competition among themselves. Registration with the government does not necessarily enhance the ability of a non-Muslim religious group to attract and hold a following. Unregistered groups, such as Baitiangong, can win popularity as easily as registered groups. Government recognition through registration simply affords protection from police harrassment but does not significantly alter the credibility, prestige, or attractiveness of a group's path to salvation.

The inability of any of the new movements to dominate the non-Muslim religious field and to establish a world-defining monopoly precludes authoritative claims of building a new heaven valid for all non-Muslims. The multiple forms of salvation offered within the non-Muslim religious field constitute highly specific new heavens directed toward limited clienteles. In that the new heavens have at best only partial jurisdiction over the non-Muslim sector of Malaysian society, commitment to the realities that they attempt to create is always tenuous. The constant introduction of new models of salvation, imported and indigenous, to the non-Muslim religious field heightens the awareness of the inherently pluralistic situation with which non-Muslim groups must eventually come to terms. In short, the unrestricted choice among non-Muslim paths to salvation in a secularizing context has generated a sense of heaven as a transitional state of well-being.

The Politics of Salvation in Malaysian Society

Although the search for new heavens among non-Muslim seekers is an open-ended enterprise, its direction is also influenced to a large extent by a situation of religious asymmetry promoted by the postcolonial state. The institutionalization of Islam as an official component of Malay identity has not only introduced ethnic factors into religious experiences, but also produced uneven trends of secularization between the Malay and non-Malay communities. The ramifications of this aspect of state development are most evident in the recruitment patterns of the new movements and their legal position in Malaysian society.

Given the legal restrictions on non-Muslim proselytization of Muslims, the new movements can only recruit members from the non-Malay, non-Muslim population. Even then, the three movements have shown sharply differing capacities in attracting multiethnic followings. Baitiangong is the most definitively ethnic movement in its recruitment patterns. Its strongholds are based in several Chinese sections of Kuala Lumpur and, in recent years, it has attracted mainly working-class, Chinese-educated followers. On the other hand, the interethnic potential of the Satya Sai Baba movement has not been fully realized. Although the movement appeals to many Indians and Chinese, the most influential leaders are Indians and Sri Lankans. Moreover, there is a tendency toward the formation of Chinese enclaves within the Indian-dominated movement. Compared with the Satya Sai Baba movement and Baitiangong, ethnic boundaries are least rigid in the charismatic movement. The latter is not associated with a specific ethnic constituency, and its leadership, as well as its rank and file, is genuinely multiethnic in composition. In terms of class characteristics, the charismatic and Satya Sai Baba movements tend to be more middle-class and English-oriented than Baitiangong. Despite the complex ethnic and class dimensions of the new movements, none have consciously established a definitive tie between religious affiliation and ethnic identity. This can be attributed to the historical circumstances of the postcolonial era, where non-Malay ethnic identities are articulated and organized in explicit political categories without religious connotations. Unlike the Malays, religious affiliation is at best a partial ethnic marker among the Chinese and Indians.

Furthermore, the lack of political motives in the new movements has inhibited the emergence of salvationary ideologies with strong ethnic overtones.

The potential of these movements as vehicles of ethnic expression, however, may become more marked as a result of recent changes in state religious policies. The plausibility of this development must be considered in the context of the state's management of Muslim and non-Muslim affairs. While the precolonial Malay states relied on religious ideologies and elaborate court rituals to legitimate dynastic interests, the postcolonial state adopted secular ideologies of economic development and promotion of Malay ethnic interests to enhance centralization of political authority and to justify the power of the new administrative elites. At the same time, Islam was legitimated as an ethnic religion to strengthen Malay identity. The close articulation of Islam with the modern state has given rise to strong ambivalence toward secularism among many Malays. Pressures on the state to assume an explicitly religious character are uneasily juxtaposed with demands for accelerated economic growth. The adoption by the modern Malaysian state of secular ideologies, accompanied by the strategic use of religious symbols, has ironically imposed limits on its control of the Muslim religious field. In upholding its Islamic credentials vis-à-vis the Malay electorate and the wider Muslim world, the state cannot easily suppress dissident groups that claim to be acting in accordance with the true principles of Islam. The state's attempts to discredit Muslim opposition groups are hindered furthermore by the decentralized nature of Islamic administration in Malaysia. The federal government cannot openly issue authoritative pronouncements concerning the orthodoxy of the doctrinal stances of particular Muslim groups, because such determinations are subject to the jurisdiction of the state-level religious bureaucracies and the sultans. The non-Muslim religious field, in contrast, presents the state with a clear-cut situation regarding regulation and control. As non-Muslim religions have no ideological point of articulation with the state, their secular status is less problematic than in the case of Islam. Contending non-Muslim groups, within the same religious tradition or between different traditions, are similarly endorsed by the Malaysian government through registration under various legal statutes without evaluation of doctrinal orthodoxy or deviance.

The uneven relationship of the state to Islam and the non-Muslim religions has presented problems concerning the centralization of political power. In an attempt to overcome these problems, the state recently adopted an explicitly secular approach to the control of the Muslim religious field, consistent with principles previously applied only to the non-Muslim religious field. The state's definition of Islamic orthodoxy is now directed along civil rather than specifically religious lines. New amendments to the Penal and Criminal Codes, passed by the Malaysian Parliament in late 1982, empower the federal government to act against any religious group deemed to endanger public order. The control of Muslim and non-Muslim religious groups alike has been formally defined in terms of "security" without reference to doctrinal issues. Although the new legislation is primarily directed toward dissident Muslim groups, it has nevertheless strengthened the state's hand in dealing with non-Muslim groups. In extending legal controls to Muslim groups, the federal government has avoided formally challenging the religious prerogatives of the sultans and state-level bureaucracies, and at the same time has consolidated central authority. Although the Malaysian state has begun to impose uniform legal controls over both the Muslim and non-Muslim religious fields, it is unlikely to encourage a similar extension of voluntarism to Muslims. The state's commitment to promotion of Malay ethnic interests precludes freedom of movement between the Muslim and non-Muslim religious fields.

As state policy toward Islam began to infringe upon the activities of non-Muslims, formal organizations within the latter field reacted by mobilizing their resources to meet the perceived threat. The formation of a non-Muslim interreligious council in late 1983 has provided a public forum for the expression of non-Muslim grievances (see Lee 1986b). For the first time since independence, a registered non-Muslim pressure group has raised several issues concerning the impact of state authority on non-Muslim religious freedom. The mobilization of non-Muslims of various religious traditions under the auspices of this council thus far includes only long-established formal religious organizations, such as the Catholic church, the mainline Protestant churches, and recognized Hindu, Sikh, and Buddhist bodies. The new religious movements, both registered and unregistered, animistic tribal religions, and traditional Chinese folk religion are not represented on the council. The exclusiveness of the council can be traced to the original appointment of its members on the National Unity

Board, a government body established after the 1969 race riots to promote harmonious interethnic relations. The experience of meeting together at the National Unity Board for more than a decade has made possible closer non-Muslim cooperation in the form of the interreligious council. In contrast, decentralized cultic alternatives and new movements that are marginal to their parent traditions lack the experience in direct consultation with the government and are less able to mobilize non-Muslims for concerted action.

The exclusion of the new movements from the interreligious council does not imply that their role in harnessing ethnic resources is limited. While it is possible that the new movements may eventually be drawn into an alliance with the council, their independence allows them to operate as an unorganized front for consolidating ethnic sentiments. Unlike the interreligious council whose objectives are largely secular, the new movements are not bound by any formal rules of interaction with the state. As informal, non-Malay organizations, the new movements possess much flexibility in alternating between the promotion of secular and spiritual ideologies. Some leaders of the Satya Sai Baba movement, for example, have recently begun campaigning for the introduction of universal religious education—as a counterweight to compulsory Islamic instruction for Muslims—in the local school curriculum. In short, the new movements originated from the diverse choices available in the non-Muslim religious field, but growing perceptions of the state as an adversary have increased the movements' potential as ethnic interest groups.

Conclusion

THE phenomenon of secularization must be understood as both a social and political process, as our study of the new religious movements in Malaysia has demonstrated. As a social process, secularization individualizes participation in religious activities. The new religious movements reflect this process in the sense that they attract followers on a voluntaristic basis, offering concrete methods both of problem-solving and of meeting personal needs in everyday life. The rapid turnover of membership in these movements suggests a market-like situation where commitment is not fixed but dependent on the availability of diverse religious ideologies. This highly fluid body of seekers, however, is restricted to the non-Muslim religious field, attesting to the unevenness of secularization that reflects the political conditions in Malaysia. The legal establishment of Islam as a necessary component of Malay ethnic identity and interests sets a limiting condition to secularization of the Muslim religious field. Incomplete secularization of the Muslim religious field has weakened the state's authority by retarding its ability fully to control dissident Muslim groups. But the recent changes in penal laws that affect religion imply an attempt at the gradual establishment of symmetry between the non-Muslim and Muslim religious fields with respect to state regulation and control. Secularization at the political level has increased state power in the management of religious affairs, but without a proportional increase in voluntarism in the Muslim religious field.

Following the theoretical model described in chapter 2, the differences between the two religious fields can be conceptualized in terms of the various levels of religious competition. Within the non-Muslim field, the highly fluid nature of religious affiliation suggests that competition occurs on all three levels; that is, among organizational alternatives, among cultic alternatives, and between organizational and cultic alternatives. On the other hand, political and legal restrictions in the Muslim field tend to limit competition to two levels: among cultic alternatives, and between organizational and cultic alternatives. Even if competition occurs among Muslim organizational alternatives, it is kept to a minimum level or shielded from public attention to preserve the image of Muslim unity. In the case of Muslim cultic alternatives, especially *tarekat,* there is relatively more freedom for individualistic pursuits since they are not bound by formal religious or legal rules of operation. Accordingly, each cult will be more concerned with its level of growth and attractiveness vis-à-vis other cults than with the question of maintaining Muslim unity. These cults are therefore a threat to formal Muslim organizations, as they comprise a potential source of heretical teachings and practices that may accentuate divisiveness in the Malay-Muslim world.

In attempting to reduce this threat, state intervention in the Muslim field constitutes an effort to eliminate competition between Muslim organizational and cultic alternatives. Competition among Muslim cultic alternatives is also controlled in the process, because government proscription of these cults is likely to drive them underground or terminate their existence gradually. However, competition at all three levels in the non-Muslim field is not similarly affected by state regulation of religious activities, because the government has not defined the scope of religious dissidence to include issues of doctrinal orthodoxy in the non-Muslim field. Uneven secularization with respect to state control of religion implies an increasingly tighter boundary around the Muslim field in contrast to the laissez-faire conditions surrounding the non-Muslim field. The continuation of intense competition in the non-Muslim field suggests that the integration of any non-Malay ethnic identity through religious symbols remains problematic. Thus the expression of ethnicity in religious participation in the non-Muslim field is less sharply focused than in the Muslim field where the narrowing of religious competition enhances political sensitivity to changes in the religious component of Malay ethnicity.

Conclusion

Our study of non-Muslim religious movements in Malaysia provides another perspective on secularization in terms of religious competition and control in a plural society with no dominant model of the sacred. It shifts the focus from the church-sect paradigm of secularization to the problem of state authority in a situation of religious diversity. By conceptualizing religious diversity as religious fields and the relationships therein, we show secularization to comprise a series of microsocial processes rather than an encompassing monolithic process. A development of this approach to secularization requires further in-depth ethnographic studies of religious movements in similarly complex plural societies. Results from these studies will further understanding of the nature of state authority and its relationship to the growth of movements in various religious fields.

Notes

INTRODUCTION

1. Malaysia during the colonial period was known as Malaya. After World War II it was renamed the Federation of Malaya. In 1963 it merged with two Borneo states (Sabah and Sarawak) and Singapore to form Malaysia. Singapore left the union in 1965. Today, the peninsula is known as West Malaysia while Sabah and Sarawak are known collectively as East Malaysia. Our study focuses only on West Malaysia.

2. According to the 1980 census, the Malays form 55.3 percent of the population in West Malaysia, the Chinese 33.8 percent, the Indians 10.2 percent, and the remaining 0.7 percent is classified as "Others"—pockets of aborigines, Eurasians, Europeans, and various individuals with unclear or marginal identities.

3. Malays who wish to discard their Muslim identity are required to make a statutory statement to a *kadi* (a Muslim religious official) so that they are free of various Islamic obligations. Most Malays are reluctant to convert to other religions for fear of losing their social and political privileges. But in recent years, there have been rumored reports of increased Malay conversion to Christianity as a result of proselytization by Indonesian Christian immigrants. Some government officials have expressed concern about the threat these conversions pose to the integrity of Malay-Muslim identity.

4. Islamic fundamentalism *(dakwah)* in Malaysia became the focus of much political and scholarly concern in the 1970s. A comprehensive statement on this phenomenon has been published by Nagata (1984). However, developments in the non-Muslim religions were obscured by excessive atten-

tion to *dakwah* activities. Our purpose in writing this book is to correct the imbalance and provide a complementary perspective to Nagata's book (see also Muzaffar 1987).

CHAPTER ONE

1. British colonial rule in Malaya combined both direct and indirect forms of administration. The Straits Settlements that included Penang, Singapore, and Melaka became a Crown Colony under the direct rule of a British governor. Penang was taken over in 1786, Melaka wrested from the Dutch in 1795, and Singapore acquired in 1819; all served as bases from which the British gradually extended their influence throughout the peninsula, a development known as the "British Forward Movement." The nine Malay sultanates on the peninsula became protected states. Unlike the Straits Settlements, they were not legally British territories. British protection was extended over to Perak, Selangor, Negri Sembilan, and Pahang during the period from 1874 to 1888, and in 1895 these states were joined together as the Federated Malay States (FMS) to centralize their administration to a greater degree. In 1909 the British gained control over four Malay states formerly under Siamese influence—Kedah, Perlis, Kelantan, and Terengganu. The last of the Malay states to retain its nominal sovereignty, Johor, became a British protectorate in 1914 after a century of de facto British control. The five most recent British protected states became known as the Unfederated Malay States (UMS), as they were allowed a semblance of political separateness and administrative autonomy. A British official, known as an advisor in the UMS and as a resident in the FMS, was assigned to the rulers of the Malay states who were required to follow British advice on all matters with the exception of Malay custom and religion. This patchwork of administrative structures masked the strong central authority exercised through the high commisioner for the Malay states who was also at the same time governor of the Straits Settlements (Emerson 1964).

2. Some of the *orang asli* groups in the southern region of the peninsula, the Proto-Malays in particular, are actually recent migrants from Sumatra. Some *orang asli* have become Christians, Muslims, or Baha'is, although the majority have remained animists (Carey 1976:23).

3. Although the maritime Malays probably had been in contact with India for at least several centuries before the Christian era, Indians did not arrive in large numbers until around the first centuries A.D. Coedès (1968:19–20) has hypothesized that the intensification of Indian contact with Southeast Asia occurred in response to India's loss of access to gold from Siberia and the Roman Empire. The desire to find another source of gold, according to this

hypothesis, motivated Indian merchants to turn their attention toward the Golden Khersonese.

4. The term "Malay" is used here in a broad, inclusive sense to refer to the maritime peoples settled along the coasts of Sumatra and the Malay Peninsula.

5. Sinhalese exponents of Mahayana Buddhism and tantric cults played an often-overlooked role in propagating these forms of Buddhism among the Buddhists of Srivijaya and other Malay kingdoms located along the sea route to China. Mahayana Buddhism, the predominant form of the religion in most parts of India during the early centuries of the Christian era, was introduced to Ceylon (Sri Lanka) by Indian Mahayana teachers enroute to Southeast Asia and China. Although Ceylon continued for the most part to adhere to the Theravada school of Buddhism, Mahayana and tantric doctrines gained a considerable number of followers there by the eighth century, particularly among the monks at the Abayagiri Vihara (Paranavitana 1966:183).

6. The Sumatran empire of Srivijaya flourished from the seventh until the twelfth centuries during which period it exercised effective control over the strategic shipping lanes of the Straits of Melaka. Srivijaya exercised hegemony over the southeastern coast of Sumatra up to the isthmus of Kra. After the twelfth century, Srivijaya began to retreat in the face of increasing Siamese power in the north and Javanese strength in the south. Srivijaya disintegrated completely by the fifteenth century.

7. Indian cultural influence was not, as Coedès (1968:32) emphasizes, "clearly delimited in time and space." As a gradual process of diffusion taking place over a span of several centuries, Indianization involved successive phases of contact with both the northern and southern regions of India. The first Indianized kingdoms of the Malay Peninsula, having the earliest and most direct relations with Indian traders and missionaries, became "relay stations" for the transmission of Indian culture throughout the rest of the Southeast Asian region (Wales 1976).

8. Seventh-century Srivijayan inscriptions indicate that Mahayana Buddhism flourished in Sumatra at this time, although the Theravada school predominated. A century later, Mahayana had eclipsed Theravada. Wales (1976:85) points out that although Bengal was the ultimate source of Mahayanism, this school reached Srivijaya "wholly via south India," speculating that Dharmapala of Kanchi actually introduced it to Southeast Asia in the seventh century.

9. Tantrism involved the worship of feminine deities conceived of as the consorts and active creative power of the Buddhas and bodhisattvas of the Mahayanist pantheon and of the Hindu deities Siva and Vishnu. Tantric doctrines and ritual practices that infused both Mahayana Buddhism and Hinduism contributed much to minimizing the distinctions between these religions in Southeast Asia. The Chinese traveler, Wang Ta-yuan, vividly described the

tantric practices prevalent in the peninsular states of Terengganu and Pahang in the thirteenth century (Wheatley 1964:113, 202).

10. Popular knowledge of tantric court ritual is reflected in a Kelantanese folk curing seance known as *main puteri* in which the village magician-healer *(bomoh)* takes the part of Siva's Sakti. Winstedt (1961:27) has described *main puteri* as a survival of tantric rites "where union with the divine was effected through a nude woman worshipped as a goddess."

11. Arab traders en route to Canton (Guangzhou) obtained many of the commodities in demand in the Chinese, Indian, Arab, and European markets during their visits to Southeast Asian ports. As Arab trade with China increased during the eighth century they began to found settlements in Canton. The closing of Chinese ports to foreign merchants after a rebellion in the last quarter of the eighth century encouraged greater interest on the part of the Arabs in trade and settlement in Southeast Asia (Di Meglio 1970:108–109).

12. An Arabic inscription dated A.D. 1082 or A.D. 1101–1102 found at Leran indicates that Islamic influence first penetrated the coastal areas of Java. Islam consolidated its foothold on the northern coast of the island with the conversion of the prince of Tuban in the mid-thirteenth century and was subsequently adopted as the official religion of the state (Di Meglio 1970:116).

13. The commercial and political motives that led Melaka to adopt Islam were less obvious in the Islamization of the Indonesian archipelago. Wandering Sufi mystics, as Johns (1961a) has argued, played a central role in the transmission of Islam at both the levels of the village and royal court. Johns (1961a:145) rejects the view that people converted to Islam merely in acquiescence to their rulers. Sufi missionaries teaching a syncretic doctrine complementary to animism and Mahayana Buddhist mysticism presented Islam within a context that preserved a degree of continuity with earlier religious traditions, which had broad appeal throughout Indonesian society. The wandering Sufi fakir who converts the local ruler to Islam through miraculous means is a familiar figure in Malay and Javanese chronicles (Johns 1961b:15, 16, 17). This tradition was incorporated into the *Hikayat Raja-Raja Pasai* and the *Sejarah Melayu,* which suggests that the influence of Sufi missionaries should not be underestimated, even on the peninsula.

14. An Islamic fundamentalist reform movement known to the Dutch as the Padri movement, from the Portuguese pidgin term for cleric, swept through the Minangkabau area of Sumatra early in the nineteenth century after the return of three pilgrims from Mecca who had been influenced by the Wahhabis in Arabia (Roff 1970:165). The leaders of the Padri movement were mainly *tarekat* teachers associated with orthodox mystical orders strongly emphasizing *Shari'ah* law. The disturbed conditions in Minangkabau that created constant uncertainty of life and property for merchants aroused

the concern of the reform-minded *tarekat* teachers (Dobbin 1974:329). Their crusade to purge Minangkabau society of non-Islamic practices and to establish peace and order through uncompromising adherence to *Shari'ah* law pitted them against the traditional *adat*-oriented (customary law) elites. The Padri reformers resorted to violent coercion to impose their vision of a purified, orderly community. The conflict between the Padris and the *adat*-oriented elites took the form of a protracted civil war lasting from 1821 until 1837, with Dutch intervention on the side of the *adat* chiefs.

15. The Malay proponents of Egyptian modernism were known as *Kaum Muda* (the young group). They attacked the Muslim traditionalists called *Kaum Tua* (the old group), particularly the old fashioned rural *ulama*, from whose ranks the Malay rulers recruited officials to staff the burgeoning religious bureaucracies established during the last decades of the nineteenth century. In their insistence that religious truth must be determined by the use of man's reason *(akal)* rather than by unquestioning acceptance of intermediate authority, the *Kaum Muda* threatened the foundation of traditional authority in the Malay states. Not surprisingly, *Kaum Muda* religious scholars were often banned from the Malay states (see Roff 1967:56–91).

16. The *madrasah* provided instruction in both purified Islam and modern secular knowledge. Emphasis was given to the study of Arabic and English as international languages of learning (Roff 1967:58, 66). The *madrasah* sought to produce students with sound, rational religious understanding and with the ability to compete in the contemporary secular world.

17. This discussion of the Islamic modernist movement among the Malays is drawn largely from Roff (1967).

18. Although the missionaries devoted most of their efforts to working among Chinese and Indian immigrants, some Christian evangelism was carried out among aborigines *(orang asli)*. Catholic missionaries during the nineteenth century established small missions for aborigines in fringe jungle areas surrounding Melaka and Ipoh, and in towns in Negri Sembilan and Johor (Williams 1976). The Methodists began a mission to the Sengoi people in Perak and Pahang in the 1930s. Christian evangelization of aborigines was politically sensitive throughout the colonial period and continues to remain so. British administrators discouraged such missionary activity but did not outright prohibit it (Means and Means 1981). In its attempt to Islamize the aborigines, the Malaysian government has continued and strengthened the British policy toward missionaries.

19. Malaysian leaders of two major Protestant denominations related this information in personal interviews.

20. Little published work exists on Chinese and Indian folk religion in Malaya during the colonial period. The paucity of historical documentation

CHAPTER TWO

1. Not much is known about Buddhist and Taoist activities during this period. The dearth of literature reflects either a paucity of significant events in Malaysian Buddhism and Taoism, or the neglect and unconcern of previous researchers with developments in this area, or both.

2. This includes the animistic religions of the politically impotent *orang asli* (aborigines) of the Malay Peninsula.

3. The Malayan Union plan proposed by the returning British authorities sought to give equal rights to the non-Malays, reduce the power of the sultans (sovereign heads of individual Malay states), and thus implicitly introduce direct British rule. The plan fell through as a result of nation-wide protests by the Malays. The resulting compromise was the Federation of Malaya Agreement (see Allen 1967).

4. UMNO was the first secular Malay national party organized in 1946 to oppose the Malayan Union plan. Its first president was Datuk Onn Jaafar, a Johor aristocrat. The UMNO leadership has always been associated with the Malay traditional elite. For the background of UMNO and its conflicts with the Islamic party, see Stockwell (1979) and Funston (1980).

5. PAS soon established its strongholds in the northern Malaysian states of Kelantan, Terengganu, Kedah, and Perlis. In 1973 it joined the coalition *Barisan Nasional* (National Front) government but left it in 1977. In 1978 a political crisis in Kelantan resulted in the ouster of PAS from the state government under the emergency regulations declared by the federal government. Since then, PAS has been wracked by several internal crises resulting in the removal in 1983 of its long-standing president, Datuk Asri Muda. For an interesting study of the career of PAS in Kelantan, see Kessler (1978).

6. For a more detailed account of this case, see Hughes (1980) and the Report of Singapore Riots Inquiry Commission of 1951.

7. Among members of this committee was Burhanuddin Al-Helmy, a Malay radical who had been closely associated with the MNP and later became the president of PAS. Another active member of this committee was Karim Ghani, a Tamil Muslim from India, who ran a chain of newspapers in Singapore.

8. The Malays are by no means a homogeneous group of people. Many of them are recent immigrants or descendants of recent immigrants from various

Notes to Pages 40–44

parts of the Indonesian archipelago. They include the Minangkabau and Batak from Sumatra, Bugis from Sulawesi, Javanese and Sundanese from Java, and so on.

9. Although Islam is the state religion of Malaysia, the country is by no means a theocracy. The Malaysian Constitution also guarantees the rights of non-Muslims to practice their own religions.

10. Before the war there was no such thing as Malayan citizenship. Those born in the Straits Settlements were automatically British subjects. Those resident in the Malay states were subjects of the Malay rulers.

11. Ratnam (1965) provides a detailed account of the politics in determining citizenship rights between the period 1946 to 1957.

12. The Federated Malay States included the states of Negri Sembilan, Pahang, Perak, and Selangor, which jointly came under the control of the British Residential System in 1895 (see Chai 1967).

13. For instance, the entire country was paralyzed during the race riots of May 1969, which only occurred in certain sections of Kuala Lumpur.

14. Petaling Jaya was created in 1952 to ease the population explosion in Kuala Lumpur. Located five miles from the capital city, it has developed from a rubber estate into a sprawling, middle-class township of over 100,000 residents.

15. McGee uses the term "orthogenetic" to discuss the possible role that Kuala Lumpur will play as the center for the dissemination of a new Malayan culture.

16. A term that has been used to describe Chinese followers of the syncretic combination of Buddhism, Taoism, and Confucianism. Sidhu and Jones (1981:246) argue that few Chinese are exclusively Buddhists and it is more realistic to categorize them as adherents of the Chinese religious complex.

17. Refers to the constitutional monarch who is chosen from among the nine Malay sultans at the Conference of Rulers to serve for a five-year term as titular head of the country.

18. The Federal Territory was officially established in February 1974, creating a distinct sphere of influence and control for federal administrators and officials. It includes the city of Kuala Lumpur and its surrounding areas.

19. It must be noted that neither the Federal Constitution nor the State Constitution has stipulated that Islam is the state religion of Melaka, Penang, or Sarawak (Ahmad Ibrahim 1978:50). This constitutional anomaly has not yet been resolved and provides an interesting case of legal contradictions in nation-building.

20. Federal attempts to standardize astronomical calculations for the beginning and end of Ramadan (the month of fasting) have been met with opposition from various states (Baker 1973:175). In 1982 the Sultan of Johor

refused to authorize the *Maulud* procession marking the prophet Muhammad's birthday, claiming that it was unnecessary, thus openly demonstrating to the federal authorities his autonomy in making religious decisions.

21. Other mosques in the city are run by committees appointed by the Federal Territory Religious Council.

22. These denominations include the Anglican church, Assemblies of God, Baptists, Christian Brethren Assemblies, Evangelical Free Church, Tamil Evangelical Lutheran church, Lutheran church, Mar Thoma Syrian Church of Malabar, Methodist church, Presbyterian church, Roman Catholic church, and the Salvation Army. Among these denominations, only the Christian Brethren (and several independent churches) has no common organization and each Brethren church is completely autonomous. Other denominations in Malaysia not mentioned by Vierow and Shelby include the Jehovah's Witnesses, the Pentecostal church, and the Seventh Day Adventists.

23. The more significant deities of the Saivite tradition are Siva, Ganesh, and Subrahmanyam. Those of the Vaisnavite tradition are Vishnu, Rama, and Krishna. For a further discussion of these two divisions in Hinduism, see Weber (1958). At the popular level of worship in Malaysia, however, these distinctions are not greatly emphasized.

24. Sanskritization, according to Srinivas (1968:5), is the process by which a low Hindu caste or other group changes its customs, rituals, ideologies and way of life in the direction of a higher caste. In the case of this temple, the status of Mariyamman was raised to that of the scriptural deities; i.e., deities that are sanctioned in scriptural texts written largely in Sanskrit. The term "Sanskritization" is often used interchangeably with "Brahmanization" and "Agamization."

25. The *Devastanam* has formed its own Council of Hindu Temples in Malaysia as a rival body to the Hindu Sangam (personal communication with R. Rajoo, February 1983).

26. Most of the data reported here were provided by Mr. T. C. Teh, president of the Buddhist Missionary Society, in an interview conducted on April 3, 1983. Published sources on the sociology of Buddhism in Malaysia are limited. The most relevant sources to date are a short monograph by Blofeld (1971) and a longer one by Lester (1973).

27. The church-sect typology was first introduced by Weber (1930) and later elaborated by Troelstch (1931). It was used mainly as an ideal type to analyze the major religious bodies in pre-nineteenth century Christian Europe. The church was treated as the dominant religious institution that was almost synonymous with the larger society and the sect as a schismatic organization within the prevailing religious tradition. Sects were thought to be evolving organizations that underwent changes over time to eventually become a church. This issue has continued to stimulate discussion and criticism over the

years (Hill 1973). We do not wish to become embroiled in this issue, but we agree with many critics that it is almost impossible to fit many religious groups into either of these categories.

28. Many definitions of cult have been offered but scholars in the sociological tradition seem to agree that it represents an independent religious system that may be in conflict with its surrounding sociocultural environment. Several types of cults have been identified and discussed by Nelson (1968) and Stark and Bainbridge (1979). We take an opposite stance and argue that cults need not represent a fundamental break with a religious tradition. Cults may, in fact, form the primary structure of various religions, such as the cult of Murugan in Hinduism, the cult of the Virgin Mary in Catholicism, and so on. In other words, in cults there is a strong attachment to a figure (or figures), whether living, dead, or deified. Charisma and ecstasy may be treated as important but not necessarily the sole characteristics of a cult. Because of the slipperiness of the term "cult," we prefer to use "religious alternatives." Nevertheless, we use "cult" as a convenient term to mean self-contained religious groups that lack complex organizational structures and stress intense emotional participation.

29. Many religious organizations are registered under the Societies Act and their activities are monitored by the Registrar of Societies, an arm of the Ministry of Home Affairs. Some, however, are registered under the Companies Act and are treated formally as business organizations. This strategy is sometimes used to circumvent the more stringent conditions of the Societies Act. Some churches and temples had been established under various government ordinances and legal acts since the colonial period. We are using the Malaysian government as our main point of reference because it is the central decisionmaking body in the country that is invested with much power in granting legitimacy to or withholding it from any religious (or nonreligious) group. Our choice of the government as a frame of reference will become clearer in later chapters.

30. The most renowned case in recent years is the visit of a high-ranking Malay politician to the *ashram* of Satya Sai Baba in southern India for consultation of his political future.

31. A classic example is the case of a retired Sikh civil servant whom we met in 1981. He had experimented with Theosophy, Transcendental Meditation, the teachings of Sri Bhagwan Rajneesh, and other religions before focusing his energies on the Subud Brotherhood and the teachings of Edgar Cayce. He continues to preside over Sikh Bhog ceremonies at private homes where he chants the *Guru Granth Sahib* (the Sikh holy book) and introduces Subud-style worship among the Sikh participants. He also performs exorcisms and gives spiritual advice to various supplicants. One of his followers, a Chinese man in his late thirties, attends his Edgar Cayce Study Group regularly and is

also involved with the Inner Peace Movement, Subud, and Silva Mind Control.

32. The short-lived attempt in 1982 to introduce the morals law was also aimed partly at solving the problem of *khalwat* (close proximity) between a Muslim and a non-Muslim. Muslims are prosecuted under the *Shari'ah* law if caught in *khalwat*, but a non-Muslim partner cannot be charged under *Shari'ah* or civil law. Had the morals law been successfully incorporated as part of the civil law, non-Muslims arrested for *khalwat* would be equally liable to prosecution.

33. The word *dakwah* is derived from the Arabic *da'wa*, which literally means an invitation to become a Muslim. In Malaysia, however, *dakwah* has lost its missionary connotations because many people have associated the movement with religious fanaticism and extremism. For more detailed analyses of the *dakwah* movement, see Lyon (1979), Kessler (1980), Nagata (1980, 1984), Funston (1981), and Mohammad Abu Bakar (1981).

34. ABIM has faded into obscurity since its leader, Anwar Ibrahim, was coopted into UMNO in 1982. In the same year, following the general elections, Anwar was made a deputy minister in the Prime Minister's Department with special functions in the Religious Division. He was appointed Minister of Agriculture in 1984 and Minister of Education in 1986.

35. This incident occurred in October 1980 when a group of armed Muslim extremists, led by a Kampuchean refugee who had declared himself the Mahdi (a charismatic Islamic leader preaching millennialism), attacked the police station in Batu Pahat, wounding many people there. Eight of the assailants were subsequently killed by the police and seven were arrested.

36. One reason for this action is that the haphazard growth of shrines and temples has become a problem for public works officials engaged in urban renewal projects. Ironically, the Hindu Sangam has been partly instrumental in politicizing this issue. The Sangam has always associated the random construction of Hindu shrines and temples with the lower forms of Hinduism, which it hopes to reform.

37. The violence erupted when temple guards discovered five Muslim fundamentalists breaking into a Hindu temple in Kerling, Selangor to wreck idols. A fight ensued and four of the five iconoclasts were killed. Eight of the temple guards involved in the fight were subsequently charged with culpable homicide and sentenced to imprisonment for several years.

38. Many researchers have regarded the events of May 1969 as an important watershed in Malaysian political history. The race riots that occurred in that year not only caused many deaths and substantial loss of property but also changes in the perception of power relations between the Malays and non-Malays. The riots were precipitated mainly by the enormous gains made by the non-Malay opposition parties in the 1969 elections. Many Malays

feared a shift in political power to the Chinese was imminent. The racial violence of May 13 marked the beginning of the rise of a Malay leadership dedicated to the transformation of Malay constitutional privileges into actual policies (see von Vorys 1975).

CHAPTER THREE

1. The Christian communities of Sarawak and Sabah in North Borneo, an examination of which is beyond the scope of this chapter, are far larger and more diverse than that of peninsular Malaysia. Significant proportions of Christians are found among at least five of the indigenous Borneo ethnic groups—Sea Dayaks, Land Dayaks, Kadazans, Melanaus, and Muruts—as well as among people of Chinese origin. Christians in the Borneo states, unlike those on the peninsula, are strongly represented in the rural areas (Vierow and Shelby 1979). During the colonial period, these states were administered separately from the peninsula under structures of government that did not include the maintenance of indigenous rulers. Islam had not yet attained an officially recognized relationship with the state in North Borneo at that time. For this reason, colonial policy toward Christian evangelism was more encouraging in the Borneo states.

2. The 1980 census showed that Christians comprised 3.8 percent of the urban population.

3. These figures are from the 1980 census. In terms of the proportion of Christians in each ethnic group, Chinese Christians are only 3.3 percent of their ethnic community while Indian Christians are 7.5 percent of their ethnic group.

4. The idea of the CCM took shape during the Japanese occupation of Malaya and Singapore. While interned in Singapore's Changi Prison by the Japanese, foreign missionaries representing the Anglican, Methodist, Presbyterian, and Lutheran churches vowed to promote Christian unity after the war through the establishment of an interdenominational Christian council and theological seminary. After the war the clergymen who survived internment cooperated to form the Malayan Christian Council, which later became the CCM. The member denominations of the CCM include the Anglicans, Methodists, Lutherans (Chinese), Evangelical Lutherans (Indians), Protestant Church of Sabah (Rungus Dusun), Basil Church of Sabah (Chinese), Salvation Army, Mar Thoma Church, and the Syrian Orthodox Church. The Methodists, the largest and wealthiest Protestant denomination, dominate the CCM. Nonchurch Christian bodies, such as the YMCA, YWCA, Malaysian Care, and the Christian Students' Movement, are associate members. The Presbyterians have unofficially left the CCM as a result of theological differences.

Compared with the other CCM members, the Presbyterians are more oriented toward fundamentalist theology, as well as lay rather than clerical control of the church.

5. For an account of the formation of the World Council of Churches and its present role in the ecumenical movement, see Till (1972:223–290).

6. Among the eighteenth-century revivalist Protestant movements were the Great Awakening, which began in 1734, and millennial Shakerism, derived from the Quaker and Camisard traditions. The latter was brought to America from England by Ann Lee Stanley in 1774. Nineteenth-century revivalism took the form of camp meetings where thousands of people gathered to participate in mass conversions, often leading to splits within the established churches and thereby producing new denominations. The Holiness Movement of the mid to late nineteenth century, the direct predecessor of Pentecostalism, was an interdenominational mass revival emphasizing emotional preaching, Spirit Baptism, miracles, and the Second Coming of Christ. The history of these movements is presented in detail in Bloch-Hoell (1964), Williams and Waldvogel (1975), and Knox (1950).

7. Glossolalia refers to a broad range of ecstatic speech regarded in particular religious contexts as divinely inspired. Spontaneous speaking in authentic languages or dialects generally unknown to the group present, or uttering sounds in "heavenly" languages known only to God and the angels are included in the category of glossolalia. The scriptural basis of Pentecostal teachings on glossolalia embraces both the Old and New Testaments. In Joel (2:28, 29) ecstatic speech is closely associated with prophesy, while in Acts of the Apostles it is a demonstration of reception of the Holy Spirit. Corinthians identifies glossolalia as one of the gifts of the Spirit (Williams and Waldvogel 1975:61–63). For linguistic studies of glossolalia, see Goodman (1972) and Samarin (1976, 1979). The ritual significance of glossolalia is examined in Hutch (1980).

8. As Christianity became institutionalized through the centuries and allied itself with the political establishments of the day, protest reactions taking the form of mass movements with characteristics similar to those of Pentecostalism developed. These movements, among which Montanism in the second century A.D. was one of the earliest, sought a return to the spontaneity and spiritual intensity of the earliest days of the church. In their striving for direct experience, the adherents of these movements rejected the rigid, formalized worship and scholastic theology of the established churches. The vicissitudes of the Montanists, Donatists, Waldenses, Albigenses, Anabaptists, Quakers, Jansenists, and other ecstatic Christian movements are considered in historical perspective in Knox (1950).

9. Gatherings were racially mixed in the early phase of Pentecostalism. Later, as the Azusa Street mission dissolved and evangelists went forth to pro-

mote the new movement by forming local Pentecostal congregations, black and white participants went their separate ways (Bloch-Hoell 1964:54–56).

10. Small sectarian Pentecostal bodies insistent on strict discipline to shun worldly temptations proliferated in the southeastern part of the United States. Other Pentecostal sects cater to ethnic and racial minorities. Black, Hispanic, and Italian Pentecostals formed their own local groups. Pentecostal sects also include groups centered around certain charismatic leaders or "deviant" practices such as fire and snake handling. The influence of sectarian Pentecostalism is eclipsed by the large denominations and international organizations that have become the mainstream of the movement. The Assemblies of God, the largest Pentecostal denomination in America, has played an important role in the shift of the Pentecostal movement from lower- to middle-class orientation. In cooperation with Oral Roberts' revival ministries, the Assemblies of God have attained remarkable success in extending Pentecostalism into traditional Christian churches. The varieties of Pentecostal organizations are described in Nichol (1966:94–157).

11. Shakarian, whose family migrated to Los Angeles from Armenia in the early twentieth century, represents a long-standing family tradition of ecstatic religious experience. For over one hundred years, members of Shakarian's family were involved in prophetic revelations, glossolalia, spiritual healing, and visions. The family participated in the Azusa Street revival and, in 1905, founded one of the first Pentecostal churches in America in their home. FGBMFI has published an account of the Shakarian family's role in the Pentecostal movement (see Nickel 1964).

12. Several studies of middle-class Protestant and Catholic Pentecostal groups have been published—see McGuire (1974, 1975, 1977), Westley (1977), and McGaw (1980).

13. The Cursillo de Cristiandad or "The Little Course in Christianity," a Roman Catholic movement originating in Spain in the late 1950s, popularized the encounter group as a mode of religious expression among the middle-class laity. The Cursillo was an intense weekend retreat where laymen shared their personal feelings and renewal of faith in a supportive group setting. This was a departure from the traditional practice on religious retreats of maintaining silence for the purpose of individual meditation and limiting discussion to private consultations with the priest in charge. The Cursillo was the most prominent of the series of lay-centered movements preceding the Catholic Charismatic Renewal (Lane 1976:174–175).

14. A recent Assemblies of God newsletter noted with satisfaction that the Charismatic movement among Roman Catholics and members of traditional Protestant denominations in the United States had "helped the Assemblies of God gain a wider beachhead in Middle America," attracting a large influx of converts from the mainline churches (Plowman 1982).

15. Several participants in CCR groups privately admitted to attending prayer meetings organized by the Assemblies of God and claimed that these meetings were more inspiring than those of the CCR.

16. Reported in a local English language newspaper, *The Star,* November 11, 1983.

17. Malaysians, including Malaysian Christians, frequently view problems of everyday life—such as illness, accidents, financial difficulties, interpersonal conflicts, loss of property, and other misfortunes—to be the result of supernatural forces.

18. Pseudonyms are used to refer to all Charismatic prayer groups described in this chapter.

19. Although the CCR leaders had an understanding with their Protestant Charismatic associates not to raise the issue of Marian devotion, it nevertheless surfaced.

20. This account of Charismatic doctrine is drawn from the "Life in the Spirit Seminars Team Manual," Word of Life (Ann Arbor, Michigan 1973) and CCR pamphlets and lectures.

CHAPTER FOUR

1. Ideally speaking, Sanskritic Hinduism is characterized by a large body of sacred literature, such as the Veda, Upanishad, Itihasa, and the Purana. Sanskritic rituals are normally prescribed and performed by Brahmin priests, whereas popular Hinduism is more akin to the religious practices of villagers who do not subscribe to a scriptural tradition. Many of these beliefs and practices are passed on through an oral tradition. Furthermore, non-Sanskritic rituals are invariably performed by non-Brahmin priests.

2. Smarta Brahmins are a subcaste of Brahmins who adhere to the teachings of Sankaracarya who espoused a monistic theology known as *Advaita-vedanta.* In Malaysia, these Brahmin priests are not initiated *kurukkal* but generally serve as domestic priests *(purohita).* In India, *purohita* are professionally distinct from *kurukkal,* especially in terms of Vedic learning (Singer 1972:84), but in Malaysia the interchangeability of these two roles suggests a vacuum in the Sanskritic tradition that has yet to be appropriately filled. Smarta Brahmins have been accepted in assuming these fluid roles because many Hindus in Malaysia believe that a Brahmin is by definition a potential priest.

3. In a sense, the term "Sanskritization" is meaningless unless used as a diachronic concept. This is because Sanskritic Hinduism is actually a composite of many traditions that have undergone changes over time. As Staal (1963:266–267) argues, "The oldest and apparently most pivotal forms of the

great tradition are often of a type which many anthropologists would tend to describe as 'non-Sanskritic' and which are in fact based upon little traditions. The origins of the great tradition lie in numerous little traditions, widespread throughout Indian history and geography." Nevertheless, we still maintain that Sanskritization is an important heuristic concept, provided that we keep in mind the necessity for modification according to varying empirical situations. For some recent critiques of Sanskritization, see Sharma (1970) and Carroll (1977).

4. Munisvaran is a male guardian deity that is widely worshipped by South Indian villagers. Munisvaran shrines are normally found in temples dedicated to the goddess Kali. It is popularly believed that Munisvaran travels on horseback at midnight to ward off evil spirits. In return for his services, devotees are required periodically to sacrifice animals to him. The mode of worship at Munisvaran temples or shrines is usually non-agamic, performed by a *pujari* who may also function as a part-time medium. Occasionally, high-caste Hindus have been observed to visit Munisvaran shrines to request supernatural help.

5. Mariyamman is a South Indian village goddess who has been most commonly associated with outbreaks of smallpox and cholera (Elmore 1925). This goddess is often identified with Sakti, the consort of Siva (Whitehead 1976:29). In Malaysia, Mariyamman is the most popular female deity worshipped by Tamils living in estate settlements and urban areas.

6. The appointment of Brahmin priests to a temple of a lower deity is not exceptional to Malaysia. Whitehead (1976:19) has reported on a Mariyamman temple near Tanjore (Tamilnadu) served by Brahmin priests.

7. *Taipusam* is celebrated mainly by Saivite devotees of the deity Subrahmanyam (otherwise known as Murugan or Skanda). This festival is considered a major event by many Malaysian Hindus, especially those who have taken vows to carry *kavadi* for the deity. A traditional *kavadi* is a decorated wooden arch with a pole connecting the two ends and carried on the shoulders by the devotee. In recent years, *kavadi*-bearing in Malaysia has become more ostentatious as penitents compete with each other in displaying larger and heavier *kavadi*s (some complete with electric lights), or in inserting needles, hooks, and skewers into their bodies. The attendance of these celebrations at the Subrahmanyam shrine in Batu Caves near Kuala Lumpur by various Malaysian ministers and politicians attests to the importance of the occasion as an ethnic event. In 1983, a record number of 70,000 people observed the celebrations at Batu Caves, while at least 2,000 *kavadi* carriers (some of whom were non-Indians) participated in the event. The grandeur of this festival has not been reported elsewhere, except at the Kataragama shrine (also dedicated to Subrahmanyam) in Sri Lanka and at Palani in Tamilnadu.

8. We do not imply, however, that caste consciousness no longer persists

among Malaysian Indians. We merely wish to emphasize that the transposition of an age-old institution to a new environment may result in a modified system that has little resemblance to its original form. Caste is not a dead institution in Malaysia but it has little significance when framed against the national political context. Ethnic factors are more important determinants of social mobility than caste in contemporary Malaysia. Nevertheless, caste continues to influence the attitudes and behavior of Malaysian Indians, but this line of inquiry will not be pursued here (see Rajakrishnan 1979).

9. Some evidence for this observation has been provided by Aveling (1978), who reports on the growth of mixed-caste congregations around low-caste ritual specialists whose practices are currently undergoing agamization. She argues that members of these congregations worship at shrines and temples as individuals rather than as representatives of a corporate caste.

10. Because Tamils form the majority of Indians in Malaysia they are politically dominant in the Indian community.

11. For example, the president of the Malaysian Hindu Sangam is also a member of the National Unity Board (a division of the Prime Minister's Department). The Malaysian Hindu Youth Council is affiliated with the Malaysian Youth Council, which is controlled by the Ministry of Culture, Youth, and Sports.

12. Not all these movements, however, are of Tamil origin. Many are international Hindu organizations—such as the Ramkrishna Mission, the Divine Life Society, International Society for Krishna Consciousness, the Divine Light Mission, and Self-Realization Fellowship—which admit Indian and non-Indian members.

13. Perhaps it was the publication in 1971 of a popular book on Satya Sai Baba by Howard Murphet, an Australian devotee, that accelerated Satya Sai Baba's fame abroad, particularly in Western countries. Strangely enough, Satya Sai Baba has not traveled outside of India except for a brief trip to visit Gujerati devotees residing in East Africa.

14. It has been argued (e.g., White 1972) that Shirdi Sai Baba may have been influenced by the syncretic style of Kabir, the medieval poet-saint of North India who was a prominent figure in the second phase of the *bhaki* movement, a phase that was heavily influenced by Sufi ideas (Nabi 1977). Indeed, there is some evidence suggesting that Shirdi Sai Baba's acceptance of Hinduism and Islam may have been related to his belief that he was a reincarnation of Kabir (Osborne 1957:50).

15. Most of the Sri Lankan Tamils and Malayalis (from Kerala in South India) who migrated to the Malay Peninsula were better educated than the South Indian Tamil emigrants, who were largely illiterate laborers. Many Sri Lankan Tamils and Malayalis worked as white-collar professionals in the colonial administration. Even today, members of these two communities are

socioeconomically more advanced than their South Indian Tamil counterparts (see Arasaratnam 1970).

16. The feet of Hindu saints are always regarded as sacred. Devotees who wish to be blessed by a saint usually kneel and kiss his feet *(padanamaskaram)*. Other devotees may massage and oil the saint's feet.

17. One hundred and eight is considered a holy number because the addition of each successive digit amounts to nine (1 + 0 + 8 = 9). Nine is a sacred number in Hindu astrology because there are supposed to be nine major planets that influence the lives and destinies of human beings.

18. Because there is little *avatar* doctrine in Saivism, some members of the campaign have capitalized on this to press charges of fraud against his claim. As an aside, Parrinder (1970:87) argues that Siva is a complex character and is believed to make occasional appearances as a personal god, *guru,* or in some human form.

19. In April 1981, the government introduced stringent laws to restrict the activities of local organizations ranging from business guilds to religious groups. By increasing the powers of the Registrar of Societies through specific amendments of the Societies Act, the government was able effectively to monitor and control the activities of every registered organization in the country. The Malaysian public raised a storm of protest against these amendments. Two years later, the government responded to the organized protest by agreeing to consider removing the offending clauses. More liberal amendments to the Societies Act were tabled in the Malaysian Parliament in March 1983 and await final endorsement.

20. At the official level, the New Economic Policy aims to eradicate poverty and identification of race with occupations, but in practice its implementation favors the Malays in all areas of social development (jobs, education, housing, and so forth). According to this policy, the target of 30 percent Malay participation in all areas of social development must be achieved by the year 1990.

21. Many Chinese have also been observed participating in various Hindu events, such as carrying *kavadi* at the *Taipusam* festival. Some Chinese have also contributed money to the building of Hindu temples. Compared with the Satya Sai Baba movement, however, other Hindu organizations attract fewer Chinese followers.

CHAPTER FIVE

1. We do not intend to provide an exhaustive review of the literature on the history of Chinese religion. Our aim is to sketch the major characteristics of Chinese religion and to relate them to its practice in Malaysia. For more

detailed treatments of Chinese religion, see Chan (1953), de Groot (1964), Freedman (1974), Granet (1977), Maspero (1981), Smith (1968), Weber (1951), and Yang (1961).

2. "Shenism" as used by Elliott is derived from the Chinese word *shen,* which loosely translated means spirit (not soul) manifestations of powerful beings that exist in another dimension but have the ability to influence events in the material world. *Shen* is also considered the positive component of the soul *(ling hun)* while *guei* represents its negative aspect (Elliott 1955:28; Harrell 1979).

3. Some of them include *Wugu Laoyeh* for farmers, *Jiaosheng Laoyeh* for carpenters, *Guandi* for tradesmen, *Tianhou Shengmu* (or *Mazu*) for fishermen and sailors, and *Shuixin Laoyeh* for incense stick makers (Purcell 1967:124).

4. The deified spirit of Cheng Ho, the famous enunch-admiral of the Ming Dynasty who visited Melaka in 1408 and 1414, is worshipped as *Sanbao Taishen,* especially in Penang and Melaka (Purcell 1967:123). Yap Ah Loy, the Kapitan China and leader of the Hai San Society in mid-nineteenth century Kuala Lumpur, is worshipped by many Chinese today. A temple dedicated to his spirit is found in Kuala Lumpur (Choo 1968:137). Another Chinese deity unique to Malaysia is *Dabogong* (most commonly known by its Hokkien designation, *Tuapehkong*) whom Purcell (1967:123) argues is derived from *Tudigong,* the earth god, but is treated by many Chinese immigrants as the personification of the pioneer spirit (for further notes on *Dabogong,* see Han 1940, and Sakai 1981).

5. The spirit medium is known mainly for his ability to become possessed by a *shen.* While in a possessed state, his soul *(hun)* is assumed to be cared for by other *shen.* This supernatural ability must be distinguished from that of the soul-raiser *(mansengpoh* in Cantonese) who allegedly can at will direct her soul into the realm of the dead. Soul-raisers, most of whom are widows, are usually engaged by individuals who wish to communicate with their deceased relatives. For further descriptions of soul-raising, see Elliott (1955:134ff), Potter (1974), and de Groot (1964: 1330ff).

6. Under possession, the medium's behavior changes radically. He assumes the characteristics of the possessing *shen* as if he were the *shen.* In most cases the mediums are possessed by Chinese deities, although there are some who specialize in possession by the spirits of Malay warriors and dignitaries (see Elliott 1955:113, and Lee 1983).

7. Like the voluntary associations, secret societies belonging to the Heaven and Earth League (also known as the Triad Society) were brought into the peninsula by the Chinese immigrants. These societies were not explicitly attached to any formal religious system but their rituals contained many Taoist elements. Religious rituals in these societies were incidental to their

more secular activities that ranged from political brokerage to criminal involvements (see Blyth 1969, and Comber 1961).

8. The Great Way of Former Heaven is a syncretic religion that has as its supreme object of worship a female deity known as the Venerable Mother. The religion is thought to have had close connections with the White Lotus millennarian movement in China. Its origins can be traced to Szechuan in China. Sects of the Great Way did not reach the southeastern provinces of Fujien and Guangdong until the 1860s. Branches of these sects began to move overseas around 1868. For further information on the Great Way, see Topley (1957, 1963).

9. On the other hand, the Confucianist movement in neighboring Indonesia has been relatively more successful. The beginnings of the Confucianist movement there can be traced to the formation of the Batavia Chinese Association in 1900. Between 1923 and 1942, there were several attempts by some Indonesian Chinese to centralize various local bodies known as Khong Kauw Hwee (Confucian Religion Society). Today, Confucianism as represented by the Supreme Council for the Confucian Religion in Indonesia is a legally recognized religion (see Suryadinata 1974, and Coppel 1981).

10. We are not using a pseudonym for the leader because he has received much publicity in the press since late 1982. We will, however, use pseudonyms for his followers because many of them have already left the movement.

11. The Seven Praying Sisters is probably related to one of several *Guanyin* (Goddess of Mercy) sisterhoods that are popular among many old Cantonese spinsters (Topley 1961:306).

12. Chinese new villages in Malaysia were originally Chinese squatter settlements that were relocated, under the Briggs' Plan, from fringe jungle areas to well-guarded centers in various parts of the country. The purpose of this plan was to deprive communist guerrillas access to sources of food supply and manpower during the Malayan Emergency of 1948–1960.

13. The movement has been under police surveillance since its formation. It is routine for police officers from the Special Branch division to gather intelligence on any social or religious movement in the country. Zhao has told us that he is able to recognize Special Branch officers at his public meetings. Ironically, one of Zhao's brothers is a high-ranking police officer.

14. Under the Restricted Residence Enactment (1948), the Minister of Home Affairs is empowered, without recourse to a court order, to restrict a person's movements to a specific area in the country. These regulations are normally used against secret society members. In Zhao's case, he was restricted to a certain area within the boundaries of Kuala Lumpur. He was not allowed to leave his house from 9 P.M. to 6 A.M., and he had to report regularly to the police. During this period of confinement Zhao held meditation

sessions in his house, but after these restrictions were lifted in September 1983 he resumed his missionary activities in other towns and villages.

15. Ironically, the Baitiangong branch in Singapore is a legally registered organization. The Singapore branch has only about one hundred members.

16. The Chinese Unity Movement was established in 1971 by several reform-minded politicians who were concerned with the faltering image of the MCA. We will discuss the implications of this movement later in this chapter.

17. Zhao's ascent to a mountain with the aid of various animals is a familiar motif in Chinese shamanism, especially his reference to a horse which is an important vehicle in the shaman's magical flight (see Eliade 1964:451, 467).

18. There is a striking similarity between Zhao and Hung Xiuchuan, the leader of the Taiping Rebellion in China. Both men experienced visions that suggested their spiritual importance at a time when they were depressed by failures. Unlike Zhao, Hung had failed the civil examinations many times. His hopes for becoming a government official were dashed. Both men were also influenced by Christianity. Unlike Zhao, however, Hung was introduced to Christian teachings as an adult. For a succinct biography of Hung Xiuchuan, see McAleavy (1967); some of Hung's spiritual experiences have been discussed by Shih (1967).

19. Grenfell (1979) has shown that more Chinese than Indians or Malays attend Chinese movies in Malaysia. Most of these movies are of the martial arts genre, which not only provides escapist entertainment but also is a source of enthusiasm for attaining physical powers, as seen in the popularity of martial arts clubs throughout the country.

20. Zhao was able to argue somewhat convincingly in court that meetings on Baitiangong grounds do not constitute a breach of Malaysian security regulations that forbid large public gatherings without police permits. He explained that the movement had spent M$10,000 to fill the disused mining pool and, because soil is "movable property," he was standing on his own land. This argument comprises a fine technical point in the distinction between private and public property on which the necessity of police permits rests. Zhao's training in constitutional law during his university days provided an advantage in his defense preparations. Despite the technical plausibility of his arguments, the judge ruled against his case.

21. Self-Realization Fellowship is a neo-Hindu organization based in the United States and founded by an Indian *swami*, Paramahansa Yogananda, in 1925. It has established branches all over the world. Its sister organization in India is the Yogoda Satsanga Society. In Malaysia, SRF is a relatively unknown organization and there is only a handful of followers of this *swami*.

22. Zhao selected verses from Al-Fatihah because of his admiration for Islam, which renounces idol worship. He has not attempted to convert Mus-

lims to Baitiangong because proselytization of Muslims in Malaysia is regarded as a serious offense.

23. Zhao's ideas on fornication and bigamy are derived from his belief that women outnumber men by two to one. According to this belief, it is only natural for men to be promiscuous. Fornication and bigamy are therefore not moral violations in Zhao's thinking.

24. Parliament was suspended for two years following the 1969 race riots. The country was ruled by an interim body known as the National Operations Council, which was headed by the Prime Minister and wielded absolute power in all matters pertaining to national security.

25. Many MCA young Turks demanded the resignation of Tun Tan Siew Sin, the party president at that time. But Zhao was against this move and urged his colleagues to wait patiently for Tun Tan's imminent retirement. Zhao's suggestion, however, was rejected.

Bibliography

Ahmad Ibrahim. 1978. "The Position of Islam in the Constitution of Malaysia." In Tun Mohd. Suffian, H. P. Lee, and F. A. Trindade (eds.), *The Constitution of Malaysia, Its Development: 1957–1977*, 41–68. Kuala Lumpur: Oxford University Press.
al-Attas, Syed Naguib. 1963. *Some Aspects of Sufism As Understood and Practised Among the Malays*. Singapore: Malaysian Sociological Research Institute.
Allen, James D. 1967. *The Malayan Union*. New Haven: Yale University Southeast Asian Studies Monograph No. 10.
Amarjit Kaur. 1973. "North Indians in Malaya: A Study of Their Economic, Social and Political Activities, with Special Reference to Selangor, 1870s–1940s." M.A. thesis, University of Malaya.
Arasaratnam, S. 1970. *Indians in Malaysia and Singapore*. London: Oxford University Press.
Aveling, Marian. 1978. "Ritual Change in the Hindu Temples of Penang." *Contributions to Indian Sociology* 12, 173–193.
Babb, Lawrence. 1974. "Hindu Mediumship in Singapore." *Southeast Asian Journal of Social Science* 2, 29–43.
Bainbridge, W. S. and R. Stark. 1980. "Sectarian Tensions." *Review of Religious Research* 22, 105–124.
Baker, David J. 1973. "Local Muslim Organizations and National Politics in Malaysia." Ph.D. dissertation, University of California, Berkeley.
Benda, Harry. 1970. "Southeast Asian Islam in the Twentieth Century." In P. M. Holt et al. (eds.), *The Cambridge History of Islam*, vol. 2, 182–209. Cambridge: Cambridge University Press.
Berger, Peter L. 1969. *The Sacred Canopy*. New York: Anchor Books.

Bloch-Hoell, Nils. 1964. *The Pentecostal Movement.* New York: Humanities Press.
Blofeld, John. 1971. *Mahayana Buddhism in Southeast Asia.* Singapore: Asia Pacific Press.
Blythe, Wilfred. 1969. *The Impact of Chinese Secret Societies in Malaya.* London: Oxford University Press.
Brown, C. C. 1970. *Sejarah Melayu or Malay Annals.* Kuala Lumpur: Oxford University Press.
Burridge, K. O. L. 1957. "Racial Relations in Johore." *Australian Journal of Politics and History* 2, 151–168.
Carey, Iskander. 1976. *Orang Asli: The Aboriginal Tribes of Peninsular Malaysia.* Kuala Lumpur: Oxford University Press.
Carroll, Lucy. 1977. " 'Sanskritization,' 'Westernization,' and 'Social Mobility': A Reappraisal of the Relevance of Anthropological Concepts to the Social Historian of Modern India." *Journal of Anthropological Research* 33, 355–371.
Chai Hon Chan. 1967. *The Development of British Malaya, 1896–1909.* Kuala Lumpur: Oxford University Press.
Chan Wing Tsit. 1953. *Religious Trends in Modern China.* New York: Columbia University Press.
Cheah Boon Kheng. 1981. "Sino-Malay Conflicts in Malaya, 1945–1946: Communist Vendetta and Islamic Resistance." *Journal of Southeast Asian Studies* 12, 108–117.
Ch'en, Kenneth. 1964. *Buddhism in China: A Historical Survey.* Princeton: Princeton University Press.
Choo Chin Tow. 1968. "Some Sociological Aspects of Chinese Temples in Kuala Lumpur." M.A. thesis (in Chinese), University of Malaya.
Coedès, George. 1968. *The Indianized States of Southeast Asia.* Honolulu: University of Hawaii Press.
Comber, Leon. 1961. *The Traditional Mysteries of Chinese Secret Societies in Malaya.* Singapore: Eastern Universities Press.
Coppel, Charles A. 1981. "The Origins of Confucianism as an Organised Religion in Java, 1900–1923." *Journal of Southeast Asian Studies* 12, 179–195.
Cortesão, A. 1944. *The Suma Oriental of Tomé Pires,* vol. 2. London: Hakluyt Society.
Das, K. 1983. "An Eye on the Imams." *Far Eastern Economic Review,* Jan. 13, 9–10.
Dasgupta, S. B. 1976. *Obscure Religious Cults.* Calcutta: K. L. Mukhopadyay.
Davis, Winston. 1980. *Dojo: Magic and Exorcism in Modern Japan.* Stanford: Stanford University Press.

De Craemer, Willy. 1977. *Jamaa and the Church*. Oxford: Clarendon Press.
De Graaf, H. J. 1970. "Southeast Asian Islam to the Eighteenth Century." In P. M. Holt et al. (eds.), *The Cambridge History of Islam*, vol. 2, 123–155. Cambridge: Cambridge University Press.
deGroot, J. J. M. 1964. *The Religious System of China*, vols. 1–6. Taipei: Literature House Ltd.
Devine, George. 1975. *American Catholicism*. Englewood Cliffs: Prentice-Hall.
Di Meglio, R. 1970. "Arab Trade with Indonesia and the Malay Peninsula." In D. S. Richards (ed.), *Islam and the Trade of Asia*, 105–136. Oxford: Bruno Cassirer.
Dobbin, Christine. 1974. "Islamic Revivalism in Minangkabau at the Turn of the Nineteenth Century." *Modern Asian Studies* 8, 319–345.
Eliade, Mircea. 1964. *Shamanism: Archaic Techniques of Ecstasy*. Princeton: Princeton University Press.
Elliott, A. J. A. 1955. *Chinese Spirit-Medium Cults in Singapore*. London: Athlone Press.
Elmore, Wilbur T. 1925. *Dravidian Gods in Modern Hinduism*. Madras: Christian Literature Society for India.
Emerson, Rupert. 1964. *Malaysia: A Study of Direct and Indirect Rule*. Kuala Lumpur: University of Malaya Press.
Endicott, Kirk M. 1970. *An Analysis of Malay Magic*. Kuala Lumpur: Oxford University Press.
———. 1979. "The Batek Negrito Thunder God: The Personification of a Natural Force." In A. L. Becker and A. Yengoyam (eds.), *The Imagination of Reality*, 29–42. Norwood: Ablex Publishing Corporation.
Fichter, Joseph. 1975. *The Catholic Cult of the Paraclete*. New York: Sheed and Ward.
Fleming, J. R. 1962. "The Growth of the Chinese Church in the New Villages of the State of Johore, Malaya, 1950–1960." Th.D. dissertation, Union Theological Seminary, New York.
Freedman, Maurice. 1974. "On the Sociological Study of Chinese Religion." In A. P. Wolf (ed.), *Religion and Ritual in Chinese Society*, 19–41. Stanford: Stanford University Press.
Freedman, Maurice and Marjorie Topley. 1961. "Religion and Social Realignment Among the Chinese in Singapore." *Journal of Asian Studies* 21, 3–23.
Funston, John. 1980. *Malay Politics in Malaysia*. Kuala Lumpur: Heinemann.
———. 1981. "Malaysia." In Mohamad Ayoob (ed.), *The Politics of Islamic Reassertion*, 165–189. London: Croom Helm.
Glock, C. Y. and R. Stark. 1965. *Religion and Society in Tension*. Chicago: Rand-McNally.

Goodman, Felicitas. 1972. *Speaking in Tongues: A Cross-Cultural Study of Glossolalia.* Chicago: University of Chicago Press.
Granet, Marcel. 1977. *The Religion of the Chinese People.* New York: Harper and Row.
Grenfell, Newell. 1979. *Switch On, Switch Off: Mass Media Audience in West Malaysia.* Kuala Lumpur: Oxford University Press.
Gromacki, Robert G. 1967. *The Modern Tongues Movement.* Phillipsburg: Presbyterian and Reformed Publishing Co.
Haines, Joseph H. 1962. "A History of Protestant Missions in Malaya During the 19th Century, 1815-1881." Th.D. dissertation, Princeton Theological Seminary.
Hall, D. G. E. 1964. *A History of Southeast Asia.* London: MacMillan.
Hall, Kenneth R. 1981. "The Expansion of Maritime Trade in the Indian Ocean and its Impact Upon Early State Development in the Malay World." *Review of Indonesian and Malayan Studies* 15, 108-135.
Han Wai Toon. 1940. "Research on 'Tuapekkong.'" *Journal of the South Seas Society* 1, 18-26 (in Chinese).
Harper, Edward. 1957. "Shamanism in South India." *Southwestern Journal of Anthropology* 13, 267-287.
Harrell, Stevan. 1979. "The Concept of Soul in Chinese Folk Religion." *Journal of Asian Studies* 38, 519-528.
Hill, Michael. 1973. *A Sociology of Religion.* London: Heinemann.
Hughes, T. E. 1980. *Tangled Worlds: The Story of Maria Hertogh.* Singapore: Institute of Southeast Asian Studies.
Hutch, Richard A. 1980. "The Personal Ritual of Glossolalia." In V. C. Hayes (ed.), *Religious Experience in World Religions,* 78-93. South Australia: Australian Association for the Study of Religions.
Johns, A. H. 1961(a). "The Role of Sufism in the Spread of Islam to Malaya and Indonesia." *Pakistan Historical Society Journal* 9, 142-161.
———. 1961(b). "Sufism as a Category in Indonesian Literature and History." *Journal of Southeast Asian History* 2, 10-23.
———. 1975. "Islam in Southeast Asia: Reflections and New Directions." *Indonesia,* no. 19, 33-35.
Kasturi, N. 1973-1975. *Sathyam, Sivam, Sundram—Bhagavan Sri Sathya Sai Baba,* vols. 1-3. Prasanthanilayam, A. P.: Sri Sathya Sai Publications.
Kessler, Clive S. 1978. *Islam and Politics in a Malay State, Kelantan 1838-1969.* Ithaca: Cornell University Press.
———. 1980. "Malaysia: Islamic Revivalism and Political Disaffection in a Divided Society." *Southeast Asian Chronicle,* No. 75, 3-11.
Knox, R. A. 1950. *Enthusiasm: A Chapter in the History of Religion.* Oxford: Clarendon Press.

Bibliography

Kulp, Daniel H, II. 1925. *Country Life in South China.* New York: Columbia University Press.
Lane, Ralph, Jr. 1976. "Catholic Charismatic Renewal." In C. Y. Glock and R. N. Bellah (eds.), *The New Religious Consciousness,* 162–179. Berkeley: University of California Press.
Lee, Felix G. 1963. *The Catholic Church in Malaya.* Singapore: Eastern Universities Press.
Lee, Raymond L. M. 1983. "Dancing With the Gods: A Spirit Medium Festival in Urban Malaysia." *Anthropos* 78, 355–368.
———. 1986a. "Continuity and Change in Chinese Spirit Mediumship in Urban Malaysia." *Bijdragen Tot de Taal-, Land- en Volkenkunde* 142, 198–214.
———. 1986b. "The Ethnic Implications of Contemporary Religious Movements and Organizations in Malaysia." *Contemporary Southeast Asia* 8, 70–87.
Lester, Robert C. 1973. *Theravada Buddhism in Southeast Asia.* Ann Arbor: University of Michigan Press.
Lim Heng Kow. 1978. *The Evolution of the Urban System in Malaya.* Kuala Lumpur: University of Malaya Press.
Loh, F. S. Philip. 1975. *Seeds of Separatism: Education Policy in Malaya, 1874–1940.* Kuala Lumpur: Oxford University Press.
Loh Kok Wah. 1982. *The Politics of Chinese Unity in Malaysia.* Singapore: Institute of Southeast Asian Studies Occasional Paper No. 70.
Lyon, M. L. 1979. "The Dakwah Movement in Malaysia." *Review of Indonesian and Malayan Affairs* 13, 34–45.
McAleavy, Henry. 1967. *The Modern History of China.* New York: Praeger.
McGaw, Douglas B. 1980. "Meaning and Belonging in a Charismatic Congregation: An Investigation into Sources of Neo-Pentecostal Success." *Review of Religious Research* 21, 284–301.
McGee, Terence G. 1963. "The Cultural Role of Cities: A Case Study of Kuala Lumpur." *Journal of Tropical Geography* 17, 178–196.
McGuire, Meredith. 1974. "An Interpretive Comparison of Elements of the Pentecostal and Underground Church Movements in American Catholicism." *Sociological Analysis* 35, 57–65.
———. 1975. "Toward a Sociological Interpretation of the 'Catholic Pentecostal' Movement." *Review of Religious Research* 16, 94–104.
———. 1977. "The Social Context of Prophecy: 'Word-Gifts' of the Spirit Among Catholic Pentecostals." *Review of Religious Research* 18, 134–147.
Mackeen, A. M. M. 1969. *Contemporary Islamic Legal Organization in Malaya.* New Haven: Yale University Southeast Asian Studies Monograph No. 13.

Malhi, Ranjit Singh. 1976. "The Punjabi Newspapers and Sikh Organisations of Kuala Lumpur." B.A. thesis, University of Malaya.
Mandelbaum, David G. 1966. "Transcendental and Pragmatic Aspects of Religion." *American Anthropologist* 68, 1174–1191.
Maspero, Henri. 1981. *Taoism and Chinese Religion*. Amherst: University of Massachusetts Press.
Means, Gordon P. 1969. "The Role of Islam in the Political Development of Malaysia." *Comparative Politics* 1, 264–284.
———. 1978. "Public Policy Toward Religion in Malaysia." *Pacific Affairs* 51, 384–405.
Means, Paul and Nathalie Means. 1981. *And The Seed Grew*. Kuala Lumpur: Methodist Council of Missions.
Meilink-Roelofsz, M. A. P. 1970. "Trade and Islam in the Malay-Indonesian Archipelago Prior to the Arrival of the Europeans." In D. S. Richards (ed.), *Islam and the Trade of Asia*, 137–159. Oxford: Bruno Cassirer.
Milner, A. C. 1981. "Islam and Malay Kingship." *Journal of the Royal Asiatic Society of Great Britain and Ireland*, No. 1, 46–70.
Mlecko, Joel D. 1982. "The Guru in Hindu Tradition." *NUMEN* 29, 33–61.
Mohammad Abu Bakar. 1981. "Islamic Revivalism and the Political Process in Malaysia." *Asian Survey* 21, 1040–1059.
Murphet, Howard. 1972. *Sai Baba: Man of Miracles*. Madras: MacMillan.
Murthi, R. Ganesa. 1969. "The Growth of the Baha'i Faith in Malaysia." B.A. thesis, University of Malaya.
Muzaffar, Chandra. 1987. *Islamic Resurgence in Malaysia*. Petaling Jaya: Fajar Bakti.
Nabi, M. N. 1977. "The Impact of Sufism on Bhakti Movement in India." *Indian Journal of Politics* 11, 123–129.
Nagata, Judith A. 1978. "The Chinese Muslims of Malaysia: New Malays or New Associates? A Problem of Religion and Ethnicity." In G. P. Means (ed.), *The Past in Southeast Asia's Present*, 102–114. Ottawa: Canadian Council for Southeast Asian Studies.
———. 1980. "Religious Ideology and Social Change: The Islamic Revival in Malaysia." *Pacific Affairs* 53, 405–439.
———. 1984. *The Reflowering of Malaysian Islam: Religious Radicals and Their Roots*. Vancouver: University of British Columbia Press.
Nelson, Geoffrey. 1968. "The Concept of Cult." *The Sociological Review* 16, 351–362.
Nichol, John T. 1966. *Pentecostalism*. New York: Harper and Row.
Nickel, Thomas R. 1964. *The Shakarian Story*. Los Angeles: Full Gospel Businessmen's Fellowship International.
Nyce, Ray. 1971. "Chinese Folk Religion in Malaysia and Singapore." *Southeast Asia Journal of Theology* 12, 81–91.
Osborne, Arthur. 1957. *The Incredible Sai Baba*. Bombay: Orient Longmans.

Bibliography

Paranavitana, S. 1966. *Ceylon and Malaysia.* Colombo: Lake House Publishers.
Parrinder, Geoffrey. 1970. *Avatar and Incarnation.* London: Faber and Faber.
Plowman, Edward E. 1982. "Assemblies of God: On the Way Up." *The Assemblies of God of Malaysia Newsletter,* Petaling Jaya, December.
Potter, Jack M. 1974. "Cantonese Shamanism." In A. P. Wolf (ed.), *Religion and Ritual in Chinese Society,* 207–231. Stanford: Stanford University Press.
Pressel, Esther. 1974. "Umbanda Trance and Possession in São Paulo, Brazil." In F. D. Goodman et al. (eds.), *Trance, Healing, and Hallucination: Three Field Studies in Religious Experience,* 113–226. New York: John Wiley.
Purcell, Victor. 1967. *The Chinese in Malaya.* Kuala Lumpur: Oxford University Press.
Rajakrishnan, R. 1979. "Caste Consciousness Among the Indian Tamils in Malaysia: A Case Study of Four Rural and Three Urban Settlements." M.A. thesis, University of Malaya.
Rajeswary, A. 1969. "Social and Political Developments in the Indian Community of Malaya, 1920–1941." M.A. thesis, University of Malaya.
Rajoo, R. 1975. "Patterns of Hindu Religious Beliefs and Practices Among the People of Tamil Origin in West Malaysia." M.A. thesis, University of Malaya.
——. 1981. "Caste, Religion and Ritual Change Among the Tamil-Speaking Hindus in Urban Malaysia." Madurai: 5th International Conference of Tamil Studies.
——. n.d. "Religious Movements Among the Urban Hindus in Malaysia." Unpublished manuscript.
Ratnam, K. J. 1965. *Communalism and the Political Process in Malaya.* Kuala Lumpur: University of Malaya Press.
Roff, William R. 1967. *The Origins of Malay Nationalism.* New Haven: Yale University Press.
——. 1970. "Southeast Asian Islam in the Nineteenth Century." In P. M. Holt et al. (eds.), *The Cambridge History of Islam,* vol. 2, 155–182. Cambridge: Cambridge University Press.
Sakai, Tadao. 1981. "Some Aspects of Chinese Religious Practices and Customs in Singapore and Malaysia." *Journal of Southeast Asian Studies* 12, 133–141.
Samarin, William. 1976. "The Functions of Glossolalic Discourse." In P. R. Leon and H. Mitterand (eds.), *Discourse Analysis,* 37–47. Montreal: Centre Educatif et Culturel Inc.
——. 1979. "Making Sense of Glossolalic Nonsense." *Social Research* 46, 88–105.

Schrieke, B. 1957. *Indonesian Sociological Studies, Part II*. The Hague: W. van Hoeve.
Schwartz, Theodore. 1976. "The Cargo Cult: A Melanesian Type-Response to Change." In George DeVos (ed.), *Responses To Change*, 157–206. New York: Van Nostrand.
Sharma, Ursula M. 1970. "The Problem of Village Hinduism: 'Fragmentation' and Integration." *Contributions to Indian Sociology* 4, 1–21.
Shih, Vincent Y. C. 1967. *The Taiping Ideology*. Seattle: University of Washington Press.
Sidhu, M. S. and Gavin W. Jones. 1981. *Population Dynamics in a Plural Society: Peninsular Malaysia*. Kuala Lumpur: University of Malaya Cooperative Bookshop.
Singer, Milton. 1972. *When a Great Tradition Modernizes: An Anthropological Approach to Indian Civilization*. London: Pall Mall Press.
Skeat, Walter W. 1967. *Malay Magic*. New York: Dover Publications.
Smith, D. H. 1968. *Chinese Religions*. New York: Holt Rinehart Winston.
Soothill, W. E. 1923. *The Three Religions of China*. London: Oxford University Press.
Spencer, Martin E. 1973. "What is Charisma?" *British Journal of Sociology* 24, 341–354.
Srinivas, M. N. 1968. *Social Change in Modern India*. Berkeley: University of California Press.
Staal, J. F. 1963. "Sanskrit and Sanskritization." *Journal of Asian Studies* 22, 261–275.
Stark, Rodney and W. S. Bainbridge. 1979. "Of Churches, Sects, and Cults: Preliminary Concepts for a Theory of Religious Movements." *Journal for the Scientific Study of Religion* 18, 117–133.
Stockwell, A. J. 1979. *British Policy and Malay Politics During the Malayan Union Experiment, 1942–1948*. Kuala Lumpur: Malaysian Branch of the Royal Asiatic Society Monograph No. 8.
Suryadinata, Leo. 1974. "Confucianism in Indonesia: Past and Present." *Southeast Asia* 3, 881–903.
Swallow, D. A. 1982. "Ashes and Powers: Myth, Rite and Miracle in an Indian God-Man's Cult." *Modern Asian Studies* 16, 123–158.
Taib Osman. 1967. "Indigenous, Hindu and Islamic Elements in Malay Folk Beliefs." Ph.D. dissertation, Indiana University.
Tan Chee Beng. 1983. "Chinese Religion in Malaysia: A General View." *Asian Folklore Studies* 42, 217–252.
Teixeira, Manuel. 1961. *The Portuguese Missions in Malacca and Singapore (1511–1958)*, vol. 1. Lisbon: Agencia Geral do Ultramar.
Thomas, Chris D. 1978. *Diaspora Indians: Church Growth Among Indians in West Malaysia*. Penang: Malaysian Indian Evangelism Council.

Till, Barry. 1972. *The Churches Search for Unity.* Harmondsworth: Penguin Books.
Topley, Marjorie. 1954. "Chinese Women's Vegetarian House in Singapore." *Journal of the Malaysian Branch of the Royal Asiatic Society* 27, 51–67.
———. 1957. "The Great Way of Former Heaven: A Chinese Semi-Secret Religion in Malaya." *The New Malayan* 2, 13–23.
———. 1961. "The Emergence of Social Functions of Chinese Religious Associations in Singapore." *Comparative Studies in Society and History* 3, 289–314.
———. 1963. "The Great Way of Former Heaven: A Group of Chinese Secret Religious Sects." *Bulletin of the School of Oriental and African Studies* 26, 362–392.
Troelstch, Ernst. 1931. *The Social Teachings of the Christian Churches.* New York: MacMillan.
Van Leur, J. C. 1955. *Indonesian Trade and Society.* Amsterdam: Royal Tropical Institute.
Vierow, Duain and Jack M. Shelby. 1979. *Malaysian Christian Handbook.* Petaling Jaya: Gladsounds.
von Der Mehden, F. R. 1963. *Religion and Nationalism in Southeast Asia: Burma, Indonesia, The Philippines.* Madison: University of Wisconsin Press.
von Vorys, Karl. 1975. *Democracy Without Consensus: Communalism and Political Stability in Malaysia.* Princeton: Princeton University Press.
Wales, H. G. Q. 1957. *Prehistory and Religion in Southeast Asia.* London: Bernard Quaritch Ltd.
———. 1976. *The Malay Peninsula in Hindu Times.* London: Bernard Quaritch Ltd.
Weber, Max. 1930. *The Protestant Ethic and the Spirit of Capitalism.* New York: Charles Scribner.
———. 1951. *The Religion of China.* New York: Free Press.
———. 1958. *The Religion of India.* New York: Free Press.
Welch, Holmes. 1965. *Taoism: The Parting of the Way.* Boston: Beacon Press.
Westley, Frances R. 1977. "Searching for Surrender: A Catholic Charismatic Renewal Group's Attempt to Become Glossolalic." *American Behavioral Scientist* 20, 925–940.
Wheatley, Paul. 1964. *Impressions of the Malay Peninsula in Ancient Times.* Singapore: Eastern Universities Press.
———. 1975. "Satyānṛta in Suvarṇadvīpa: From Reciprocity to Redistribution in Ancient Southeast Asia." In J. A. Sabloff and C. C. Lamberg-Karlovsky (eds.), *Ancient Civilization and Trade,* 227–283. Albuquerque: University of New Mexico Press.

White, Charles S. J. 1972. "The Sai Baba Movement: Approaches to the Study of Indian Saints." *Journal of Asian Studies* 31, 863–878.
Whitehead, Henry. 1976. *The Village Gods of South India.* Delhi: Sumit Publications.
Williams, George H. and Edith Waldvogel. 1975. "A History of Speaking in Tongues and Related Gifts." In M. P. Hamilton (ed.), *The Charismatic Movement*, 61–113. Grand Rapids: W. B. Eerdmans.
Williams, Kenneth M. 1976. "The Church in West Malaysia and Singapore: A Study of the Catholic Church in West Malaysia and Singapore Regarding Her Situation as an Indigenous Church." Ph.D. dissertation, Catholic University of Leuven, Belgium.
Wilson, Bryan. 1976. *Contemporary Transformations of Religion.* Oxford: Clarendon Press.
Winstedt, R. O. 1951. *The Malay Magician.* London: Routledge Kegan Paul.
———. 1961. *The Malays: A Cultural History.* London: Routledge Kegan Paul.
Wolters, O. W. 1970. *The Fall of Srivijaya.* Kuala Lumpur: Oxford University Press.
Yang, C. K. 1961. *Religion in Chinese Society.* Berkeley: University of California Press.
Yen Ching Hwang. 1976. "The Confucian Revival Movement in Singapore and Malaya, 1899–1911." *Journal of Southeast Asian Studies* 7, 33–57.
Zaretsky, Irving I. and Mark P. Leone (eds.). 1974. *Religious Movements in Contemporary America.* Princeton: Princeton University Press.

Index

ABIM (Muslim Youth Movement of Malaysia), 57; Anwar Ibrahim, leader of, 176n.34
Aceh, 26
Agama, 92, 182n.9
Anglicans, 31, 32, 65, 66, 174n.22
Animism, 11–14
Avalokitesvara, 17–18
Avatar, 98, 111, 117, 183n.18
Azusa Street revival, 67, 178n.9

Baha'i in Malaysia, 50, 55
Baitiangong movement: Chinese politics and, 148–151; development of, 127–132; followers of, 136–143; ideology of, 143–148; leader of, 132–136
Barisan Nasional, 172n.5
Bhajan, 97, 102–107, 115–118, 156
Bhakti, 97, 98, 101, 182n.14
Bomoh (pawang), 13
"British Forward Movement," 24, 30, 168n.1
British Residential System. *See* Federated Malay States
Buddhism in Malaysia: early development of, 14–19; present-day, 47–49. *See also* Chinese popular religion

Caste in Malaysia, 91, 95, 180n.2, 181n.8, 182n.9
Cettiyar, Ramanathan, 114
Charismatic Renewal: ideology of, 80–83; in Malaysia, 6, 72–80, 84–89; in the United States, 66–72

Cheng Ho, Admiral, 184n.4
Chinese popular religion: definition of, 120–122; in Malaysia, 123–127; spirit mediumship in, 50, 122, 123, 184n.5
Christian Federation of Malaysia, 45, 65
Christianity in Malaysia, 11, 26–32, 45–46, 62–66; education and, 29–31
Church-sect model, problem of, 51–53
College General (Penang), 28
Companies Act, 175n.29
Confucianism, 121, 122, 125; in Indonesia, 185n.9
Council of Churches of Malaysia, 64–65, 177n.4
Covenant Communities, 76

Dakwah, 57–59, 176n.33
D'Albuquerque, Alfonso, 26
Darul Arqam, 57
Dejiao Hui, 125–126
Dong-So'n, 12
Dravidian nationalism, 34, 96–97
Dutch East India Company, 27
Dutch Reformed Church, 28
Duquesne Weekend, 70

Ethnicity in Malaysia, 4–5
Eurasians, 6, 26, 27, 62, 78, 85, 167n.2
Exorcism, 74, 83, 86, 87, 135, 136, 139

Federal Territory, 43, 56, 173n.18
Federated Malay States, 41, 168n.1, 173n.12
Federation of Malaya Agreement, 41

199

Full Gospel Businessmen's Fellowship International, 69, 72

Gifts of the Spirit. See Pentecostalism
Glossolalia, 67, 82, 85, 158, 178n.7
Goa, 26, 27
Great Way of Former Heaven, 124, 152, 185n.8

Healing Wings Revival Ministry, 69
Heaven and Earth League, 184n.7
Hertogh, Maria, 38
Hinduism in Malaysia, 46–47, 90–98; Saiva Siddhanta school of, 97, 114. See also Buddhism in Malaysia, early development of
Hindu priests, 91, 180n.2
Hizbul Muslimin, 37
Holy Spirit, Baptism of the, 67, 69

Indonesian archipelago, 17, 172n.8
Islam in Malaysia, 10–11, 19–26, 40, 43–45; apostasy in relation to, 40; political violence and, 35–38, 176nn.35, 37; revivalism of, 55–60; as state religion, 40, 173n.9

Japanese occupation of Malaya, 35
Johor Lama, 26

Kabir, 182n.14
Kang Youwei, 125
Kaum Muda, 24–25
Keramat, 13
Khutbah, 56
Kuala Lumpur, 5–6, 41–43, 123, 173n.18

Life in the Spirit Seminar, 76, 80–83
Ligor, 17
Lingua do Christam, 27
London Missionary Society, 29
Lutherans, 31, 32, 174n.22

Macao, 27
Madrasah, 25, 171n.16
Mahabharata, 18
Majapahit, 21
Majlis Ugama, 44
Malay: identity of, 4, 6, 11; legal definition of, 41; Nationalist Party, 37. See also Islam in Malaysia

Malayan Emergency, 185n.12
Malayan Union plan, 37, 40, 172n.3
Malaysian Hindu Sangam, 47, 97, 115, 126
Malaysian Hindu Youth Council, 182n.11
Maritime trade. See Trade
MATA (Supreme Religious Council), 37
May 13th riots, 59, 148, 149, 176n.38, 187n.24
MCA (Malaysian Chinese Association), 39, 134, 148–151; Chinese Unity Movement in, 148
Melaka, 18, 21–22; Portuguese and Dutch in, 26–27
Methodist, 31, 32, 65, 66, 88, 171n.18, 174n.22
MIC (Malaysian Indian Congress), 39
Ministry of Culture, Youth, and Sports, 182n.11
Missionaries, linguistic specialization of, 30
MPAJA (Malayan Peoples' Anti-Japanese Army), 35–36
Munisvaran, 92, 181n.4

Nadra Action Committee, 38
Naicker, E. V. Ramasamy, 96
Nakshabandiya tarekat, 23
National Council for Muslim Affairs, 44
National Cursillo Convention, 69, 179n.13
National Evangelical Council, 65
National Operations Council, 187n.24
National Unity Board, 162, 182n.11
New Economic Policy, 183n.20

Orang asli, 12, 168n.2, 171n.18

Padri movement, 170n.14
Paramesvara, 21–22
Paris Foreign Missions, Society of, 28–29
PAS (Pan-Islamic Party of Malaysia), 37, 55–58, 172n.5
Pastoral Renewal Conference, 73
Pentecostalism, 66–72. See also Charismatic Renewal
Perlak, 21
Petaling Jaya, 42, 173n.14
Presbyterians, 31, 32, 174n.22
PUTERA (Center of People's Power), 37

Index

Qing government, 125

Ramayana, 18
Religious dissent: control of, by Malaysian government, 58, 160–161, 164; by Kaum Muda, 25; in Sumatra, 24
Religious organizations, formal, 53–54, 164
Restricted Residence Enactment, 185n.14
Roberts, Oral, 69, 75
Roman Catholics, 26–29, 31, 63, 64, 66, 70–72, 75
Royal cults, 16

Sabil'ullah movement, 36
Sai Baba of Shirdi, 100
Sakti, 18, 110, 170n.10, 181n.5
Samudra (Pasai), 21, 22
Sanskritization, 16, 90, 94–96, 174n.24
Satya Sai Baba: background of, 99–101; disputes in movement, 102, 110–112; his impact on Malaysian Hinduism, 112–116; Malaysian devotees of, 102–110, 116–119
Second Vatican Council, 71–72
Secularization, 1–4, 154–155, 163–165
Sejarah Melayu, 18
Semangat, 12
Seven Praying Sisters, 128, 185n.11
Seventh Day Adventists, 31, 65, 174n.22
Shakarian, Demos, 69, 179n.11
Shamanism, 13, 150, 186n.17
Shari'ah, 23, 44, 57
Shaykh Mohamad Abduh, 25
Shenism, 121, 184n.2
Siddhi, 101, 108

Sikhism in Malaysia, 49
Sinru Temple, 125–126
Siva, 16, 17, 18, 93, 110
Societies Act, 112, 175n.29, 183n.19
Sri Maha Mariyamman Temple, 46–47, 93
Sri Tri Buana, 18
Srivijaya, 15, 17–19
State formation, 14–15, 90
Straits Settlements, 25, 30

Taipucam, 93, 181n.7, 183n.21
Tantrism, 18, 169nn.5,9, 170n.10
Taoism in Malaysia, 50. See also Chinese popular religion
Tarekat, 36, 37, 164
Tauliah, 56
Trade, 10–12, 14–16, 19–22, 24, 26

UMNO (United Malay National Organization), 37, 39, 55–57, 172n.4
Unfederated Malay States, 168n.1
Urbanization, impact on ethnicity, 5, 42, 115

Virgin Mary, Cult of, 72, 80, 87, 175n.28
Vishnu, 16, 17

Wahabi reform movement, 23–24, 170n.14
World Council of Churches, 64
World Council of Sri Satya Sai organizations, 104

Yap Ah Loy, 184n.4

About the Authors

Susan E. Ackerman received her Ph.D. in anthropology from the University of California, San Diego. She is presently on the faculty of Damansara Utama College, Petaling Jaya, where she teaches anthropology. She has done extensive research on women factory workers and on religious movements in Malaysia. Her previous publications on spirit possession and religious innovations have appeared in *American Ethnologist* and *Journal of Anthropological Research*.

Raymond L. M. Lee obtained his Ph.D. in sociology from the University of Massachusetts, Amherst. He is presently an associate professor of anthropology and sociology at the University of Malaya at Kuala Lumpur. He is the editor of *Ethnicity and Ethnic Relations in Malaysia*. His articles on Hinduism and Indian ethnicity in Malaysia have appeared in *Contributions to Indian Sociology* and *Modern Asian Studies*.

Production Notes

This book was designed by Roger Eggers. Composition and paging were done on the Quadex Composing System and typesetting on the Compugraphic 8400 by the design and production staff of University of Hawaii Press.

The text typeface is Sabon and the display typeface is Compugraphic Palatino.

Offset presswork and binding were done by Vail-Ballou Press, Inc. Text paper is Glatfelter Offset Vellum, basis 50.